READING FOR PROFIT

READING FOR PROFIT
How the Bottom Line Leaves Kids Behind

Edited by
BESS ALTWERGER

HEINEMANN
Portsmouth, NH

Heinemann
A division of Reed Elsevier Inc.
361 Hanover Street
Portsmouth, NH 03801–3912
www.heinemann.com

Offices and agents throughout the world

Library of Congress Cataloging-in-Publication Data
Reading for profit : how the bottom line leaves kids behind / edited by Bess Altwerger.
     p.   cm.
  Includes bibliographical references.
  ISBN 0-325-00792-6 (alk. paper)
  l. Business and education—United States.   2. Reading (Elementary)—United States.   3. English
language—Study and teaching (Elementary)—United States.   I. Altwerger, Bess.
  LC1085.2.R43   2005
  379.2'4'0973—dc22   2005003033

Acquiring Editor: Lois Bridges
Editor: Gloria Pipkin
Production editor: Sonja S. Chapman
Cover design: Jenny Jensen Greenleaf
Compositor: TechBooks
Manufacturing: Jamie Carter

Printed in the United States of America on acid-free paper
09 08 07 06 05 VP 1 2 3 4 5

This book is dedicated to the memory of my mother, Lillian Altwerger, whose loving kindness and tenderness have guided my personal life and inspired all my work on behalf of children.

Contents

Acknowledgments

As every academic woman knows, it is a constant challenge trying to manage family, home, and university responsibilities and still find time and heart to produce a meaningful publication. Without the inspirational, caring, and dedicated women I have known in my life, neither this publication nor any of my other academic achievements could have ever been accomplished. First, I am indebted to my beloved mentors Dorothy Menosky and Yetta Goodman, who gave me a sense of possibility that working-class women who stand for children, learning, and a more just society can find a satisfying life of intellectual activism in the academic world.

My dearest friends and companeras Barbara Flores and Carole Edelsky should share in whatever success I achieve in my career, for they have so influenced and challenged my work that I honestly can't distinguish between their thinking and my own. They have never failed to support me through all of the challenges in my professional and personal lives. My love and gratitude for them are boundless.

My Towson family has been the joy of my university life and revitalized my love of research and inquiry. Danling Fu, Patricia Wilson, Lijun Jin, Nancy Jordan, Nancy Wiltz, Barbara Laster, Poonam Arya, Nancy Shelton, and especially my good friend Prisca Martens have all contributed to the evolution of the thinking that underlies this book. We have a gift of collegiality and friendship that I cherish.

I owe much of my theoretical and pedagogical knowledge, as well as my political chutzpah, to my larger professional community—Gerry Coles, Dick Allington, Steve Krashen, Elaine Garan, and Susan Ohanian, to mention but a few. My CELT colleagues have been a constant source of intellectual inspiration throughout my professional life. I am immeasurably grateful for the model of academic collaboration and camaraderie these outstanding educators have provided. Dorothy Watson, Jerome Harste, Carolyn Burke, and so many others have taught me more than they will ever know.

Words cannot express my gratitude, respect, and affection for Kenneth S. Goodman. He is truly the education giant of our time, not only for his revolutionary advances in our understanding of reading but also for his unrelenting courage and commitment to stand for what's right for children and our world. Nothing I have accomplished, including this book, could have been possible without his kind, loving, and steady guidance throughout my career. It has been my great fortune to have learned beside him.

My colleagues in NCTE's Commission on Reading who helped with the initial plans for this book deserve a special note of recognition. I am particularly indebted to Margaret Moustafa, who invested time and energy in helping me develop an early version of the proposal and in editing chapter drafts.

I want to express my deep appreciation to my Heinemann colleague Lois Bridges, who saw the potential in this project, and to my wonderful editor, Gloria Pipkin. Gloria's support and guidance, superior editorial skills, and steadfast commitment to quality have been indispensable to the successful completion of this book. How fortunate I was to work with an outstanding editor who is also an inspirational educator in her own right. Even hurricanes can't stop this woman!

My family has been my deepest source of love and inspiration. I will be forever grateful to my wonderful parents for giving me the strength of character to continually develop and challenge myself while contributing to the success of those around me. I owe so much to my in-laws, Selma and Seymour Strauss, whose generosity, support, and love have been among my life's greatest gifts. I want to thank my "big" brother, Stan, who has stood by me since childhood, and my beloved friend Joanne Heisel, who has been every bit the devoted sister to me for more than thirty years, supporting me from both far and near. My wonderful and loving children, Erika and Asher, have been the impetus for my determination to work for a better world. They will carry my heart into the future.

And finally, I owe my greatest thanks to my husband and cothinker, Steve Strauss. We have shared every aspect of our personal and professional lives, learning and growing together for more than twenty-five years. He has continually challenged my thinking, contributed to my understanding, and broadened my perspective in both education and politics. Most importantly, he taught me, through his own example, how to live a rich and rewarding intellectual life without abandoning the struggle for justice and freedom.

—Bess Altwerger

1

Reading for Profit:
A Corporate Coup in Context

BESS ALTWERGER

Mom has a pot
Mom has a hot pot
Mom has a spot
Dad has a mop
Dad mops the spot.
——OPEN COURT DECODABLE BOOKS, LEVEL B, SET 1

(Following at least three read-alouds by students): *After they read,*
have the children tell in their own words what happened after Mom
dropped the pot. Encourage the children to create a new page using
the words in the story.
——OPEN COURT, TEACHER'S EDITION, LEVEL 1-A

In the 1980s and 1990s, when so many of our children were learning to read
through quality children's literature, we would hear the artful words of Eric
Carle, Mercer Mayer, Cynthia Rylant, and Bill Martin Jr. emanating from our
classrooms. We would hear teachers' own thoughtful words encouraging children to read, appreciate, and understand that literature. We would see the creative works of children displayed proudly along the school corridors, reflecting
their own language and imagination, sparked by those of these celebrated
authors. It would have been unthinkable then that in the dawn of the twenty-
first century, we would hear the lifeless words of the above "story" and teachers
manual echoing through the corridors of our elementary schools. Hadn't thirty
years of emergent literacy, miscue analysis, and comprehension research firmly

1

established, once and for all, the primacy of meaning and authentic text in early reading development? Hadn't we built a rock-hard foundation of theory-in-practice to guide us in facilitating students' use of multiple cuing systems and strategies amid a range of literary genres and social contexts?

And hadn't we invested years in our struggle against the behaviorist, reductionist practices of traditional literacy instruction to win the right to holistic, meaning-centered, critical, and democratic education for our children? After all, we had spent our precious free time in study groups with our colleagues, studied the newest professional literature, enrolled in university classes, and attended national conferences to become the knowledgeable, responsive educators our students and this nation deserve.

Thus, many of us have witnessed this cataclysmic change in reading education with both shock and awe—shock that we could have returned to a bygone pretheoretical era in reading instruction when children "read" meaningless texts and teachers taught letters and sounds with manual in hand; awe at the sources of power and influence that so swiftly and stealthily stole our nation's schools and classrooms from us, their rightful guardians: teachers, parents, and communities. We stand in near paralysis as our school systems continue to loot our reading programs and curricula by order of state and federal law and then punish and demean us when their own mandates don't meet their expectations for success. No wonder so many teachers are fleeing the profession, with frustrated hand-wringing and broken spirits.

And yet, the future of our nation's children and the right to a free, quality public education cannot be abandoned. We simply must shake ourselves from our despair or resignation and begin the journey toward acknowledgment, understanding, and, ultimately, action. Through a meticulous examination of the "black box" of this educational disaster, we must begin to understand the powerful, interrelated forces that together have succeeded in imposing a united, yet destructive educational agenda.

With this volume then, we are poised to begin our investigation into that black box and, fueled by answers, to once again take flight. The powerful research and analyses of our authors enable us to abandon our shoulder-shrugging appeal to the tired ol' swinging-pendulum metaphor to explain how and why we find ourselves "back to the future" in reading education. Each chapter shines a light from a different angle on the causes as well as the consequences of current policies and practices in reading instruction. Perhaps most importantly, we will better understand the world of economic power and influence that too often escapes the scrutiny of democratic processes and, if left uncontested, can erode other cherished public institutions and constitutionally protected rights.

A Corporate Coup in Context

Examining the social and historical context from which a problem arises is always critical to understanding and solving that problem. This is particularly important for our current investigation. Reading instruction, and education more generally, seems almost to have transformed overnight with the passage of the No Child Left Behind legislation signed by President George Bush in 2001. Suddenly, commercial reading programs are not just offered, but mandated by our school systems. Teachers are "trained" to follow the scripts and directions in the teachers manuals as if they are unskilled workers. States are refused federal dollars when they stray from officially prescribed components of reading instruction and assessment, and they must resort to hiring federally "approved" consultants, such as Louisa Moats, to right their paths. Even preservice and inservice reading education falls under federal control, with the same chosen few deciding which courses comply with narrowly defined specifications for "scientifically based" reading research and instruction and may therefore be counted toward teacher certification. Children are being left behind by the thousands as their reading scores on commercially published standardized tests don't reach the federally prescribed standard. And sadly, fine schools that have achieved recognition for excellence by their own state ("Bad School," 2004) are labeled failing and threatened with student transfers and closure for not achieving "adequate yearly progress" on standardized tests.

It may seem that this has all occurred overnight, but it has indeed been a long time comin'. Back in 1989, when teachers were busily planning holistic, creative, and critical literacy programs for their students, George H. W. Bush called for comprehensive school reform, and the National Business Roundtable responded. Composed of the CEOs of two hundred of the most powerful U.S. corporations, employing some thirty-four million people, the National Business Roundtable issued its Education Initiative, thereby making a ten-year commitment to "reform the entire system of public education" (Business Roundtable, 1995). Its goal was to ensure that U.S. corporations maintain future competitiveness in the global economy by producing students with the skills and competencies required of a "twenty-first century workforce" (Altwerger & Strauss, 2002).

Although the Business Roundtable did not elaborate on just what these twenty-first century skills might be, or suggest any particular pedagogical path for teaching them, it proclaimed its commitment to "helping educators and policy makers set tough standards, applicable to every student in every school, assessing student and school-system performance against those standards; and third, using that information to improve schools and create accountability, including rewards for success and consequences for failure"

(Augustine, 1997). As Strauss as well as Edelsky and Bomer further discuss in their chapters (see Chapters 4 and 2), the intrusion of the National Business Roundtable and its corporate ideology into public education is nothing short of a hostile takeover, transforming schools into training grounds for the production of workers with narrowly defined literacy skills. The standardization of reading instruction required to "train" future corporate workers would be easily attained through one of the CEOs of the Business Roundtable, Harold McGraw of McGraw-Hill Companies. That company's education division just happened to have long produced the McGraw-Hill basal reading program. In 1996, just after the media defamed whole language and literacy-based instruction as the cause of California's drop in ranking on the National Assessment of Educational Progress (NAEP), McGraw-Hill acquired SRA's phonics-based products, Open Court and SRA Reading Mastery (also known as Direct Instruction, or DI). Another product in McGraw-Hill's portfolio would fulfill the Business Roundtable's goal of accountability—the Comprehensive Test of Basic Skills (CTBS), one of the most widely adopted standardized reading tests in the country. McGraw-Hill was poised for windfall profits if just a few more pieces fell into place.

In 1997, the year after McGraw-Hill acquired SRA's phonics-based products, Douglas Carnine, long associated with SRA Reading Mastery, and Siegfried Englemann (one of the original authors of DISTAR, the predecessor of the current program) were directly involved in shaping the Reading Excellence Act. This landmark legislation specified what would qualify as valid (and fundable) reading research and prescribed reading instruction with a strong emphasis on phonics. Furthermore, because of the long association between the McGraw and Bush families (Metcalf, 2002) and between the company's entrepreneurial team of consultant-researchers and Reid Lyon, director of reading research at the National Institute of Child Health and Human Development (NICHD), McGraw-Hill could look forward to a future of pro-phonics "research" and legislation. Elaine Garan's hair-raising chapter in this volume (Chapter 3) provides more details of the scandalous ties between business, research, and government figures that ultimately led to the rigidly prescribed Reading First guidelines of NCLB, the legislation that turned the use of explicit, systematic phonics instruction into law. The year following passage of NCLB, the McGraw-Hill education division boasted bonanza profits to its shareholders from state adoptions of Open Court and SRA Reading Mastery. Currently, McGraw-Hill has surpassed its rivals (including Houghton Mifflin) as the largest publisher of K–12 instructional reading materials (see *www.mcgraw-hill.com*).

The unparalleled success of McGraw-Hill and the larger corporate community in controlling federal reading policy cannot, however, be totally explained by cronyism and back-scratching. Fertile ground had already been sown throughout the era of whole language and literature-based instruction by the religious and the far right; conservative think tanks and foundations; and some special educators and researchers aligned with the position of the fanatically phonics-oriented Orton Dyslexia Society (now the International Dyslexia Association).

The Religious and the Political Right

The Christian Coalition launched an extensive pro-phonics, anti–whole language campaign nationally, but particularly in conservative states such as Texas, publishing pamphlets and voters guides to influence state school board and legislative elections. Although its abhorrence of whole language had more to do with its desire to control reading material and its bias toward more traditional models of instruction (Weaver & Brinkley, 1998), mandating commercial phonics-based programs would be the answer to its prayers. With the help of many other ultraright organizations such as the Eagle Forum, headed by Phyllis Schlafly, the Christian Coalition's well-funded and coordinated campaign eventually resulted in the introduction of pro-phonics legislation throughout the country. In 1997 alone, legislative bills mandating phonics instruction were pending in states such as New York, West Virginia, South Carolina, Nebraska, Nevada, and Massachusetts. Thanks to the religious and the far right, the stage was set for the state Business Roundtables to reap the rewards of such legislation, clearing whole language and other meaning-centered, literature-based instructional models from the path of their own agenda. After all, such models of reading and reading instruction stood in direct opposition to the key goals in their education initiative, as Figure 1–1 illustrates.

With the media doing their job in presenting phonics and holistic reading instruction to the public as mutually exclusive paradigms and fierce opponents in the reading wars, the mandate of phonics instruction was

BRT Education Initiative	Whole Language/Literacy-Based Models
standardized curriculum	collaborative, responsive curriculum
accountability and testing	authentic, classroom-based assessment
twenty-first-century information technology skills	reflective, critical reader response
standards applied uniformly to students	teaching for individual strengths and needs

Figure 1–1. *BRT Education Initiative—Whole Language*

framed as certain death for whole language and literature-based instruction. Both the National BRT and the religious and the conservative right would joyfully attend that funeral for somewhat different, yet mutually compatible reasons. And the profiteers of phonics-based commercial programs, hungry after the dry spell of whole language, would engage in a feeding frenzy.

Think Tanks and Foundations

Supporting the goals of both the religious right and the BRT throughout the last decade were the powerful and influential conservative think tanks and foundations who have lent a firm hand in pushing for pro-phonics policies (Goodman, Shannon, Goodman, & Rapoport, 2004). Numerous reports, white papers, and pamphlets extolling the virtues of phonics and maligning whole language and its advocates (such as "See Dick Flunk," Palmaffy, 1997) were produced variously by the National Right to Read Foundation (formerly the Reading Reform Foundation), the Heritage Foundation, the Hoover Institution, and the American Enterprise Institute. The Packard Foundation went so far as to provide huge grants to purchase Open Court for entire school districts across the state of California. Bob Sweet, a cofounder of the National Right to Read Foundation and a prominent figure in the pro-phonics world, has long been influential in federal policy, serving as director of the National Institute of Education under President Reagan and as a member of the team that designed the Reading Excellence Act under the auspices of the House Committee on Education and the Workforce.

Celebrated conservatives such as Diane Ravitch, Chester Finn, E.D. Hirsch, and even Lynne Cheney have been, or still are, affiliated with the Hoover Institution, authoring numerous publications that support the aims of the religious and/or the political right and the BRT (see *www-hoover.stanford.edu/koret/members.html*). Hoover's Koret Task Force on K–12 Education published "Privatization: A Solution for School Inequities?" written by visiting fellow John Chubb (2001), who also happens to be chief education officer for the Edison Schools (a private school management company). Another Hoover Institution Press publication, a book titled *Education and Capitalism: How Overcoming Our Fear of Markets and Economics Can Improve America's Schools* (Walberg & Bast, 2003), leaves no doubt of the institute's goal of corporatized education for "government" schools. The influence of the Koret Task Force members cannot be underestimated, given the high positions many have held within the federal education establishment: Chester Finn was assistant secretary for research and improvement and counselor to the secretary of the U.S. Department of Education; Caroline Hoxby, editor and author of pro–school choice publications, was nominated by President Bush to serve on the National Board of Education Sciences; Diane Ravitch served as assistant secretary of education and counselor to then Secretary of Education Lamar Alexander (see *www-hoover.stanford.edu/koret/members.html*).

Science in the Corporate Interest

These mutually supportive forces merged elegantly into a cohesive education policy that would lead to the widespread mandate of commercial phonics programs. And yet, scientific validation was still a necessary ingredient in the campaign to win over public confidence. Where would that science come from? Throughout the eighties and nineties, most educators were advocates of at least some principles and practices of holistic, meaning-centered instruction. But a subgroup of educators and researchers, predominantly within the areas of special education and dyslexia, remained steadfastly supportive of explicit, systematic phonics instruction. The International Dyslexia Association (IDA) has long been the professional organization representing this group, promoting the Orton-Gillingham program and other phonics materials for teaching reading to dyslexic readers. Interestingly, many of the most influential figures in current reading policy are strongly associated with the IDA, including Reid Lyon and many recipients of NICHD reading research grants. Since at least 1998 (and probably earlier), the roster of NICHD researchers and associates presenting sessions and keynote addresses at IDA conferences has included Reid Lyon, Barbara Foorman, Joseph Torgesen, Sally Shaywitz, Louisa Moats (also on the IDA board), and Catherine Snow (lead author of the highly influential 1998 government-commissioned report *Preventing Reading Difficulties in Young Children*).

What does this mean? It means that there is a single theoretically based research agenda representing the "science" used to validate federal policies on reading. The fact that this phonics fringe group of researchers (virtually unknown by the larger educational community prior to Reid Lyon's appointment to the NICHD) comprises the scientific community driving reading policy makes the objectivity of this science highly suspect. Their research starts and ends with the premise that phonemic awareness and phonics are the foundational components of reading. It underlies the highly hyped brain imaging research conducted by Sally Shaywitz and others (Strauss, 2004; Coles, 2003). And it was affirmed by the National Reading Panel, despite its meager research findings, in its report (National Reading Panel, 2000)—the very report that formed the "scientific" basis of NCLB's Reading First. Despite the numerous publications questioning the validity of the NRP report (Garan, 2001; Yatvin, 2002; Krashen, 2001; Allington, 2002), the NRP's findings continue to be used as justification for widespread mandating of commercial systematic phonics programs. More recent research evidence, in fact, has revealed the weaknesses of Open Court and SRA Reading Mastery in developing comprehension strategies or producing any advantage in phonic analysis (in or out of context) as compared with literature-based programs (Altwerger et al., 2004; Wilson, Martens, Arya, & Altwerger, 2004). Chapter 13, by Wilson, Wiltz, and Lang, and Chapter 10, by Arya, Laster, and Jin, in this volume provide details of the findings for these two programs and should not be overlooked. With further independent research, the weak foundation of science underlying federal reading policy will surely begin to crumble.

A Look Inside the Black Box

As many of us know, a complex phenomenon can be understood only in its full context. Reading for profit and corporate control of reading instruction is one such phenomenon that needs to be understood within its social, political, and historical contexts. As I have demonstrated, a whole set of conditions had to be in place over a long period of time in order for corporate America to kidnap reading instruction and public education right from under our noses. But as we regain our composure, we must be ready to resist with knowledge and vision. And that is why I believe we need this book at this time.

The chapters within this volume will provide classroom teachers and the larger educational community with the economic and political analyses, scientific research, stories of damage, and visions of hope that are needed to successfully reclaim our classrooms. The chapters in Part 1 deconstruct the corporate goals and ideology driving the "reform" of public school reading programs. The corporate connections and conflicts of interest that permeate the scientific research community are also dramatically revealed. Through a focus on the state of Pennsylvania, Shannon and Edmondson help us begin to understand the political and economic realities of corporate-driven federal policy in Chapter 5. Part 2 provides readers with several excellent studies, both quantitative and qualitative in design, that draw a very different picture of the effects of commercial phonics programs and materials on children's reading development. Within this section you'll also find some startling answers to questions concerning the impact of mandated programs on classroom teachers and what children might be learning, besides the long vowel sounds, in the pages of these programs. Part 3 gives us stories of despair, but also of resistance and hope, as we consider the question of whether reading programs should be designed for profit or for children.

The black box is open—take a look!

References

Allington, R. L. (Ed.). (2002). *Big brother and the national reading curriculum: How ideology trumped evidence.* Portsmouth, NH: Heinemann.

Altwerger, B., Arya, P., Laster, B., Jin, L., Martens, P., Renman, N., Wilson, G.P., & Wiltz, N. (2004, January) When research and mandates collide: The challenges and dilemmas of teacher education in the era of NCLB. *English Education*, 36, 2.

Altwerger, B., & Strauss, S. (2002). The business behind testing. *Language Arts*, 79(3), 256–262.

Augustine, N. (1997, July). *The business leader's guide to setting academic standards.* The Business Roundtable. Available: *www.brtable.org*

Bad School, or Not? Conflicting Ratings Baffle the Parents. (2004, September 5). *New York Times*, sect. 1, p. 1, col. 1.

Brinkley, E. (1998). What's religion got to do with attacks on whole language? In K. S. Goodman (Ed.), *In defense of good teaching: What teachers need to know about the "reading wars."* York, ME: Stenhouse.

Business Roundtable. (1995). *Continuing the commitment: Essential components of a successful educational system.* Available: *www.brtable.org*

Chubb, J. (2001). *Privatization: A solution for school inequities?* Hoover Institution. Available: *www-hoover.stanford.edu/pubaffairs/we/current/chubb_0801.html*

Coles, G. (2003). *Reading the naked truth: Literacy, legislation, and lies.* Portsmouth, NH: Heinemann.

Garan, E. M. (2001). What does the report of the National Reading Panel really tell us about teaching phonics? *Language Arts*, 79(1), 61–70.

Goodman, K., Shannon, P., Goodman, Y., & Rapoport, R. (2004). *Saving our schools.* Berkeley, CA: RDRs.

Koret Task Force on K–12 Education: Members. (n.d.) Hoover Institution. Available: *www-hoover.stanford.edu/koret/members.html*

Krashen, S. (2001, October). More smoke and mirrors: A critique of the National Reading Panel (NRP) report on "fluency." *Phi Delta Kappan*, 83(2), 119–123.

Metcalf, S. (2002, January 28). Reading between the lines. *The Nation.* 18–22.

National Reading Panel. (2000). *Teaching children to read: An evidence-based assessment of the scientific research literature on reading and its implications for reading instruction.* Washington, DC: National Institute of Child Health and Human Development.

Palmaffy, T. (1997, November–December). See Dick flunk. *Policy Review.* Heritage Foundation. Available: *www.policyreview.org/nov.97.html*

Strauss, S. (2005). *The linguistics, neurology and politics of phonics.* Mahwah, NJ: Erlbaum.

Walberg, H., & Bast, J. (2003). *Education and capitalism: How overcoming our fear of markets and economics can improve America's schools.* Stanford, CA: Hoover Institution.

Weaver, C., & Brinkley, E. (1998). Phonics, whole language and the religious and political right. In K. S. Goodman (Ed.), *In defense of good teaching: What teachers need to know about the "reading wars."* York, ME: Stenhouse.

Wilson, G. P., Martens, P., Arya, P., & Altwerger, B. (2004) Readers, instruction, and the NRP. *Phi Delta Kappan, 86*(3), 242–246.

Yatvin, J. (2002, January). Babes in the woods: The wanderings of the National Reading Panel. *Phi Delta Kappan, 83*(5), 364–369.

2

Heads They Win; Tails We Lose

CAROLE EDELSKY

Arizona State University

RANDY BOMER

University of Texas–Austin

"Heads they win; tails we lose." That may overstate the case a bit in summing up what happens as a result of for-profit reading curricula. While there are huge losses for us, it's not a complete rout. There's also one tiny potential loss for them. But let's save hope for the end of our discussion and first consider the blunt realities of the bind we find ourselves in. First, who are *they* and who are *we.* They are the corporate conglomerates and their corporate subsidiaries that publish the programs described in this volume as well as the predecessors to those programs that now seem benign—the old standby basals. They are also the multinational conglomerates that don't publish reading series but whose interests are identical to those that do; they are the few corporations that own all the major media and thus "mediate" common sense about reading and education (McChesney, 1999); they are the lobbyists for the corporations and the government officials who made deals with legislators to vote for the law known as No Child Left Behind; they are the corporations whose CEOs sit around the Business Roundtable and whose enormous power has earned them increasing success in implementing their agenda to steal the public's education (Draffan, 2000; Goodman, Shannon, Goodman, & Rapoport, 2004).

We are the vast majority of students, parents, teachers, teacher educators, and just plain folks who need adequate food, housing, and medical care, safe living and learning and working conditions, time for satisfying relationships with family and friends, freedom for creating and imagining, an education that makes us critically literate, and real outlets to act as democratic citizens. We're the ones who lose big in the imposition of for-profit reading curricula. As readers will no doubt surmise from other chapters in this volume, the latest for-profit reading packages are dangerous for

11

learners, dangerous for teachers, and dangerous for a society claiming to be a democracy.

Let's take learners first. For-profit reading curricula have students spending huge chunks of the school day doing reading exercises, learning "reading instruc- tion"— literacy practices that are useful only in school. By eating up the school day, these instructional packages deprive learners of time they might have spent reading for pleasure, for shutting out the world, for getting to the bottom of something, for proving a point—in short, learning the literacy practices associ- ated with communicative purposes (McNeil, 2000; Meyer, 2002).

As authors in this volume have implied, for-profit reading curricula also damage teachers. They take away the professional rights teachers have earned through study and experience—rights to use their own judgment about how to teach different kids to read. Teachers become clerks, delivering someone else's ideas about how and what to teach. More than that, these corporate sales forces push not just programs that presumably teach students but also pro- grams that are supposed to teach teachers—in some districts, they're called "support," in others, they pass for "professional development" (Goodman, 2000). In a rapid and significant change for this industry, textbook publishers, taking a page from the books of software companies, increase profits by providing support for a fee. That means money that might have been used for real professional development, deepening teachers' understanding and prompting them to question their own practices, gets used instead for training them how to use a product. It's a perfect example of deprofessionalization; the for-profit program takes away teachers' autonomous judgment over all that's involved in teaching and substitutes training in efficient "delivery" of a pack- age (Apple, 1986). The damage to teachers is passed on to teacher educators as districts (and teachers too) who hitch their stars to one of these programs can now blame education professors for not preparing new teachers to teach (i.e., manage or deliver) the one program the district just bought.

From the accounts in this book, it's also clear that for-profit reading programs harm society as a whole. For one thing, they harm through omis- sion. Minority kids may see their faces in these packages, but they don't see their cultural perspectives. The reading selections and the right answers to the comprehension questions that go along with the texts have to tell some story; they have to take some perspective. But you can be sure that even if the story is about a kid who lives in a housing project, the spin of the story and the right answers to the questions won't reflect the worldviews of the streets and the projects—or the values and viewpoints of any other minor- ity culture. The language acts—answering questions asked by a book that obviously knows the answer; the brevity and certainty of the expected answers—also ignore the instability, complexity, indeterminacy, and every-day language norms common among ordinary people of most cultures (Heath, 1988; Hill & Larsen, 2000). Nonmainstream students don't get a chance to have their culturally specific background knowledge and ways of knowing validated in the reading curriculum while mainstream kids do. That makes the mainstream kids look smarter when, actually, they've just been handed one more huge head start (Gee, 1990). The bias in the programs thus reinforces structured societal inequities and makes them harder to untangle. The harm to society also comes from barriers erected by these for-profit programs. They block out curricula that might contribute to transforming the social world rather than perpetuating it—curricula that would get kids to question what's taken for granted, that would help kids do systematic social critique, that could lead to thoughtful action to challenge injustices. Instead, at their best, these programs provide a few critical think-ing activities, shams that prevent the curricular foregrounding of principled inquiry. (It is more than a little interesting that, just as literacy educators have in large numbers begun to view their work as focusing on social jus-tice, corporate interests, government bodies, and the standards and testing movement have combined in the most coercive coalition in educational history.)

Moreover, the programs indoctrinate—subtly of course. With their emphasis on low-level, single, right answers, they promote a mentality that looks for simple—and simpleminded—solutions to complex real-world problems. More directly, through the stories, the comprehension questions, the right answers to those questions, and the explicit leveling of materials and therefore students' abilities, they promote individualism, competition, and other features of a market mentality beloved by corporate conglomer-ates and accepted as commonsensical by a public whose wisdom has been manufactured by the corporate media (Rushkoff, 1999). Of course, it's no wonder the for-profit reading packages promote a market ideology. They are concrete manifestations of a piece of the corporate agenda for education (Engel, 2000). That agenda includes standardizing or rationalizing education (Shannon, 1989; Goodman et al. 2004), making it predictable and efficient (which are basic business values) through standards, mechanistic curricular packages, and high-stakes testing, which in turn makes it easier to reduce labor costs by hiring nonprofessional teachers who get trained in those cur-ricular packages. By focusing on "outcomes" rather than "inputs," big business can act as if it is doing something about education—cheaply (Spring, 1998). A streamlined system, deprofessionalized teachers, the employment of all educators under a few corporate bosses—these streams flow neatly into the corporate sector's main agenda for education: the conversion of publicly controlled schools into a publicly funded but privatized system (Berlet & Lyons, 1995; Strauss, 1999; Altwerger & Strauss, 2002).

Earlier basals were also a reflection of a corporate agenda (Shannon, 1989), but because those had some—you should excuse the expression—competition from other pedagogies and ideologies, they didn't take over to the same extent as this more recent generation of instructional materials. Until recently, that corporate agenda wasn't well defined and explicit. Now the context has changed. The corporate takeover of all aspects of life all over the world has accelerated and intensified to such an extent that all manner of what used to be intangibles—like learning—are being standardized, globalized, and commodified. The overall corporate net, with for-profit reading curricula being just one sticky string, is being drawn tighter than ever before. You don't have to go to the Business Roundtable's website (*www.businessroundtable.org*) and read its business leaders' stated desires for what direction education should take in order to see ties between a corporate agenda and corporate-produced curricula (though seeing those blatant statements on the website and knowing they are being increasingly enacted into policy and law ought to clarify much about our current situation).

You can see the ties in Reid Lyon's bullying of New York City schools until they accepted a "scientifically proven" curriculum by Voyager Expanded Learning, a company whose executive staff is headed by Bush appointees and fund-raisers (Gotbaum, 2003). You can also see the ties in Hewlett Packard's bribing of financially strapped districts with grants if they adopted Open Court as their language arts program (Saunders, 1999). You can see it in GATX Corporation's—whose major assets include locomotives and commercial aircraft—pushing the Waterford Early Reading Program in Chicago and elsewhere (Catalyst, 2004). The corporate agenda isn't seen only in the outright bribes and the research commissioned by conservative business think tanks like the Heritage Foundation, the Bradley Foundation, and the Hudson Institute to prove something about reading that then becomes the basis for instructional packages produced by other corporations and mandated for millions of kids (see, for example, Rothstein, 2001). Underlying corporate values and perspectives are also taught through those packages. Some corporate messages are outrageously unsubtle, such as Proctor and Gamble's promotion of specific policies like the benefits of clear-cutting forests, a position directly tied to its environmentally harmful, profit-making activities (Beder, 1994). Most of the time, however, for-profit reading packages teach slightly more invisible, generalized pro-market ideas. For example, they teach market ethics (probably an oxymoron) and values like getting ahead through competition and having one's productivity measured quantitatively by someone else (MacEwan, 2000). As Pat Shannon (1986) showed years ago, the stories promote individualism rather than concern for the common good or the community's needs.

The corporate agenda includes standards with not just strings attached, but chains—standards locked into high-stakes testing and of course reading series that look suspiciously like test-preparation curricula as well as special materials for test preparation. The same corporations that sell the reading series not only sell what used to be offered free (e.g., consulting services to help teachers use the materials—only now they're an enforcement system to ensure teachers are sticking to the packaged program) but also sell the high-stakes tests and sometimes the test-prep packages. McGraw-Hill Companies educational division, for example, produces Open Court, Reading Mastery, and SRA along with its test-prep series Scoring High. This division showed a respectable increase in revenue for the first quarter in 2000, but its CTB/McGraw-Hill testing business had, to quote its own report, an "outstanding quarter," contributing to an overall 100 percent increase in earnings from the previous year. (See this quarterly report at *http://investor.mcgraw-hill.com/ireye/ir_site.zhtml?ticker=MHP&script=410&layout= -6&item_id=86974.*) The years since 2001 have seen a steady increase in profits for shareholders. Harold McGraw III, CEO of McGraw-Hill and a member of George W. Bush's transition team, reported in April of 2004 that the reading and testing markets were responsible for the company's recent improved performance, and he attributed the growth directly to the No Child Left Behind Act. Furthermore, the company is seeing whole new markets emerge in pre-K reading as a result of Early Reading First and is thrilled to see a burgeoning market in remedial products for grades 4–6 (see *http://investor.mcgraw-hill.com/ireye/ir_site.zhtml?ticker=MHP&script=410&layout= -6&item_id=519491*). Now, through its business and finance subsidiary, Standard and Poor's, McGraw-Hill is also offering school evaluation, analysis, and strategizing, and in fact, the company is involved in an extensive collaboration with the U.S. Department of Education. The project, known as the School Information Partnership (*www.schoolresults.org*) reports the test scores of schools across the country—tests made by McGraw-Hill, which are connected to textbook-based curricula provided by McGraw-Hill. Really, how far is McGraw-Hill from owning the schools?

As we critique for-profit reading curricula, we have to look seriously at statements made by Business Roundtable members and by conservative foundations like the Heritage Foundation and the Bradley Foundation. Reading pedagogy is merely a vehicle for them. So are standards and high-stakes testing. True, some corporations profit financially from those enterprises, but the corporate push for phonics, measurable reading skills, and high-stakes testing of those skills is just a means to a much more desirable end. That's the golden ring: a privatized education system as part of a total victory for market ideology (Engel, 2000; Goodman, 1998; Goodman et al., 2004). In that ideology, kids are investments—future workers (entry level if they're poor and minority, professional if they're white and suburban). In that ideology, education is for increasing productivity—test scores in school, worker output later on. And productivity is, in part, an excuse for tracking, with test score productivity a major means of justifying for students their own ranked future (Kozol & Raney, 1998; MacEwan, 2000).

In the long run, while for-profit materials may have just the ideological effect the Business Roundtable intends, it will be impossible for them to have the proclaimed educational effect of making all kids succeed at school reading. That's because the corporatism that puts these materials into so many schools has also defined success as scoring at or above grade-level on a standardized test. Now grade level is a normalized level. That means that over time, half will fall below that statistically designed grade-level norm. In the short run, however, the for-profit packages can appear to succeed by raising scores, not just because of all the test prepping and the support and enforcement packages schools are buying but also because teachers are "cheating" to appease their own professional consciences. As Denise Ross (2000) described in an email, teachers are supplementing the for-profit programs with better practice in order "to be able to sleep at night." So in the short run, a sudden infusion of resources and extra time along with caring teachers subverting them with richer instruction may make the "research-based" programs look effective. But over time, that bell curve attached to mandated high-stakes tests, which are connected to these for-profit reading packages, will toll for them too. Someone must fail. And then, as Tom Lehrer sang, "Aha, the fun begins." There will have to be someone to blame. As Ken Goodman (2000) wrote in an email, it can't be the materials because those are based on "proven" scientific research. It will have to be the teachers, the kids, poor parenting, bad culture, and—the best scapegoat of all because it's the one headed for extinction by the market ideologues—the institution of public education (Goodman et al., 2004).

There are some real ironies in all this. On the one hand, market ideology is antibureaucratic, favoring autonomous individuals working to maximize their self-interest (Engel, 2000). And yet the corporate agenda for education, including a corporate reading curriculum, demands bureaucratically defined productivity and a bureaucracy for measuring productivity. Another irony: corporatism advocates for local control and a generally free market and argues for vouchers as a way to exercise individual choice, yet a hallmark in the latest educational horror show is blanket standards for all and mandated literacy curriculum for all, which includes legislative outlawing of certain pedagogies. These advocates of small and humble government have even redefined educational research in order to position the outlaw pedagogies as unscientific (Coles, 2003; Garan, 2004; Smith, 2003).

The irony that intrigues us most is this one: educational progressives, who tend to analyze society through the lens of a political economy in the interests of the vulnerable, want education to be about developing individuals to their fullest, including their fullest capacities for critical literacy and active citizenship. The market ideology–influenced mainstream, however, espousing hyperindividualism and nationalist patriotism, wants education to be about producing people who'll fit into the economy—economic units, cogs in a global economy (Apple, 2000; Spring, 1998).

Now we could take an ironic stance toward these ironies—bemusedly, postmodernistically distancing ourselves. But, modernistically speaking, that's a mistake. These ironies need spotlighting. They don't see the light of day or have a chance to enter the public conversation because the media who mediate our understandings don't want them to. No surprise—the corporate bias of the corporate media works. That's not a conspiracy; it's merely a media culture emanating from who owns what. Despite the huge number of TV channels, radio stations, magazines, film companies, newspapers, book publishers, and even Internet sites, major media speak with almost one voice. That's because fewer than ten conglomerates own them all (Nichols & McChesney, 2000). The position on pedagogy that promotes the ultimate educational agenda of the CEO and major stockholders of Time Warner is the position that will be favored on CNN, in *Time* magazine, in Little, Brown editorial choices, and by Warner Brothers, Cinemax, the *Atlantic*, Time Warner Cable, and fifty-plus other media (We Interrupt This Message, 2000).

Of course, we're oversimplifying, leaving out the op-ed columns that oppose Time Warner's positions and the actual if narrow range of permissible perspectives. But we're not oversimplifying by much. In August and September of 2000, only one story—despite considerable scholarly analysis to the contrary—appeared in print and television news throughout the United States about the meaning of the rise in Latino kids' test scores after California ended bilingual education (Crawford, 1998; Crawford, 2000; Moustafa, 2000). And a couple of years ago, despite considerable counterargument, media all over North America told only one story about the research basis for phonics (Goodman, 1998). That media story was part of the phony, manufactured grassroots campaign calling for adoption of programs analyzed in this volume. Brian Cambourne (2000) calls such "grassroots" efforts Astro-turf campaigns—all artificial, no grass, no roots.

We noted at the start that, even though the corporate reading machine and its market ideology win all around, there's one tiny potential benefit for us, one slim chance of potential loss for them. The blatant ties among politicians mandating reading curricula; corporations profiting from the whole package of readers, exercise books, training for teachers, testing, and test-prep materials; conservative think tanks and conservative-led legislatures commissioning "research" (Taylor, 1998); and researchers working for publishers whose products are supported by that research (Coles, 2000), as well as the fact that the Widmeyer Baker Group, a public relations corporation that handled publicity for the National Reading Panel report (and wrote its summary) also counts McGraw-Hill and the Business Roundtable among its clients (Mendéz, 2004; Metcalf, 2004), are so outrageous that they provide us with material for organizing teachers, students, and parents to protest the travesty. While we're being taken, at least we don't have to keep on taking it. They may have turned the screws so tightly that they're actually provoking us to organize against them (Horvitz & Postal, 2001). And you can never tell what might happen when people begin to act like organized, public, critical citizens.

References

Altwerger, B., & Strauss, S. (2002). The business behind testing. *Language Arts,* *79*(3), 256–262.

Apple, M. (1986). *Teachers and texts.* Boston: Routledge & Kegan Paul.

Apple, M. W. (2000). *Official knowledge: Democratic education in a conservative age.* New York: Routledge.

Beder, S. (1994). *Global spin: The corporate assault on environmentalism.* Melbourne, Australia: Scribe.

Berlet, C., & Lyons, M. N. (Eds.). (1995). *Eyes right! Challenging the right wing backlash.* Boston: South End.

Business Roundtable. (n.d.). Business Roundtable home page. Available: *www.brtable.org*

Cambourne, B. (2000). Politics, literacy education, and democracy. Presentation to Center for the Expansion of Learning and Thinking; Whole Language Umbrella Conference, Nashville, TN.

Catalyst (2004). Grants. Available: *http://www.catalyst-chicago.org/09-04/ 0904grantsprint.htm*

Coles, G. (2000). *Misreading reading: The bad science that hurts children.* Portsmouth, NH: Heinemann.

Coles, G. (2003). *Reading the naked truth: Literacy, legislation, and lies.* Portsmouth, NH: Heinemann.

Crawford, J. (1998). *The bilingual education story: Why can't the news media get it right?* Presentation to the National Association of Hispanic Journalists, Miami. Available: *http://ourworld.compuserve.com/homepages/jwcrawford/*

Crawford, J. (2000). Bilingual education: Strike two. *Rethinking Schools, 15* (2). Available: *http://www.rethinkingschools.org/archives/15_02/Az152.shtml*

Draffan, G. (2000). *The corporate consensus: A guide to the institutions of global power.* Blue Mountains Biodiversity Project. Available: *www.endgame.org/corpcon1.html*

Engel, M. (2000). *The struggle for control of public education: Market ideology vs. democratic ideals.* Philadelphia: Temple University Press.

Garan, E. (2004). *In defense of our children: When politics, profit, and education collide.* Portsmouth, NH: Heinemann.

Gee, J. (1990). *Social linguistics and literacies.* London: Falmer.

Goodman, K. S. (1998). Who's afraid of whole language? Politics, paradigms, pedagogy, and the press. In K. S. Goodman (Ed.), *In defense of good teaching: What teachers need to know about the "reading wars."* (pp. 3–38) York, ME: Stenhouse.

Goodman, K. (2000, May 26). Re: [LiteracyForAll] to supplement or not to supplment [*sic*] Open Court [Listserve message].

Goodman, K., Shannon, P., Goodman, Y., and Rapoport, R. (2004). *Saving our schools.* Berkeley, CA: RDR.

Gotbaum, B. (2003). New York City public advocate letter to Chancellor Joel Klein. Available: *www.pubadvocate.nyc.gov/press/050603.shtml*

Heath, S. B. (1988). Questioning at home and at school: A comparative study. In G. Spindler (Ed.), *Doing the ethnography of schooling* (pp. 102–131). Prospect Heights, IL: Waveland.

Hill, C., & Larsen, E. (2000). *Children and reading tests.* Stamford, CT: Ablex.

Horvitz, L., & Postal, L. (2001, January 30). Foes give school tests poor marks. *Orlando Sentinel.* pg. A1.

Kozol, J., & Raney, M. (1998). Interview with Jonathan Kozol. *Technos Quarterly, 7*(3).

MacEwan, A. (2000). Why business likes more testing. In K. Swope & B. Miner (Eds.), *Failing our kids: Why the testing craze won't fix education* (pp. 128–129). Milwaukee: Rethinking Schools.

McChesney, R. W. (1999). *Rich media, poor democracy: Communication politics in dubious times.* Urbana: University of Illinois Press.

McNeil, L. M. (2000). *Contradictions of school reform: Educational costs of standardized testing.* New York: Routledge.

Mendéz, T. (2004, January 29). Reading choices narrow for schools with federal aid. *The Christian Science Monitor.* Available: *www.csmonitor.com/2004/0129/p12s02-legn.html*

Metcalf, S. (2004). Reading between the lines. *The Nation, 274*(3), 18–22.

Meyer, R. (2002). *Phonics exposed: Understanding and resisting systematic, direct, intense phonics instruction.* Mahwah, NJ: Lawrence Erlbaum.

Moustafa, M. (2000, August 27). Media campaign against bilingual ed [Listserve message].

Nichols, J., & McChesney, R. W. (2000). *It's the media, stupid.* New York: Seven Stories.

Ross, D. (2000, May 26). To supplement or not to supplment [*sic*] Open Court [Listserve message].

Rothstein, R. (2001, January 3). Poverty and achievement, and great misconceptions. *The New York Times,* p. A3.

Rushkoff, D. (1999). *Coercion: Why we listen to what "they" say.* New York: Riverhead.

Saunders, D. J. (1999, June 29). Eureka! School reform that works. *San Francisco Chronicle,* p. A21.

Shannon, P. (1986). Hidden within the pages: A study of social perspective in young children's favorite books. *The Reading Teacher, 39,* 656–663.

Shannon, P. (1989). *Broken promises: Reading instruction in twentieth century America.* Granby, MA: Bergin & Garvey.

Smith, F. (2003). *Unspeakable acts, unnatural practices: Flaws and fallacies in scientific reading instruction.* Portsmouth, NH: Heinemann.

Spring, J. (1998). *Conflicts of interests: The politics of American education* (3rd ed.). Boston: McGraw-Hill.

Strauss, S. L. (1999, January). Phonics, whole language, and H.R. 2614: The big business agenda for reading and education. *Z Magazine.* Available: *www.zmag.org/ZMag/articles/jan99strauss.htm*

Taylor, D. (1998). *Beginning to read and the spin doctors of science: The political campaign to change America's mind about how children learn to read.* Urbana, IL: National Council of Teachers of English.

We Interrupt This Message. (2000). *Analysis of public policy messages in news coverage of education 1998–1999.* Available: *www.arc.org/gripp/researchPublications/publications/witm_education.pdf*

3

Scientific Flimflam: A Who's Who of Entrepreneurial Research

ELAINE M. GARAN

California State University, Fresno

What need is there for a criterion of responsibility? I believe that the horrifying deterioration in the ethical conduct of people today stems primarily from the mechanized dehumanization of our lives—a disastrous byproduct of the development of the scientific and technical mentality . . . Man grows cold faster than the planet he inhabits.
—ALBERT EINSTEIN, LETTER TO DR. OTTO JULIUSBURGER,
APRIL 11, 1946

I begin this discussion in an environment in which we are bombarded with rhetoric extolling the glories of scientific research as a cure for reading difficulties. Science has now supposedly proven that rather than be treated as a complex, interactive process, reading instruction should be a commercially franchised recipe based on phonics and phonemes, with worksheets that can be packaged, processed, and sold to teachers who don't need to know anything more than how to read a script. Since "scientific" research now signals a radical shift in the definitions of teaching and learning, it is essential that as consumers we explore the soundness of that research and the objectivity of the researchers—and that we demand accountability for any nonscientific breaches in the process.

The Silver Bullet: Phonics Instruction and the Report of the National Reading Panel

President Bush's reading czar, Reid Lyon, has publicly declared that research has now discovered that phonics instruction is the silver bullet for eliminating reading problems. The big gun shooting that scientific silver bullet is the 2000 report of the National Reading Panel (NRP).[1] It is this report that sits at the heart of No Child Left Behind (NCLB), the sweeping legislation signed into law by George W. Bush that is redefining what it means to be a teacher.

I have critiqued this report in considerable detail in articles and books.[2] See also the excellent work of Gerry Coles,[3] Stephen Krashen,[4] and Richard Allington.[5] In a nutshell, evidence-based critiques of the NRP report show that there is a discrepancy between the actual data and the claims made in the official NRP summary that synthesized the findings (published by the NICHD in 2000). In other words, the claims don't match the data. It is the misrepresentations rather than the facts that are controlling education under the guise of science.

Before we can move on to the conflicts of interest that saturate the science of NCLB, we need to ground ourselves in a brief overview of the documented contradictions between the NRP's claims and the facts, because it is those misrepresentations on which NCLB is based. Those misrepresentations control what we teach, when and how we teach, and what materials we can bring into our own classrooms. What follows, then, is a brief overview of the errors in the report that have in fact framed policy in the form of NCLB and Reading First grants:

- Contrary to the claim that phonics instruction benefits all children in kindergarten through sixth grade, there is no evidence that phonics instruction significantly benefits the comprehension of connected text or the conventional spelling of children at any grade level.[6]
- The findings of the NRP report cannot be applied to second language learners or gifted students at any grade level, nor can the findings apply to normally progressing students in kindergarten, second, third, fourth, fifth, or sixth grade.

That said, we are faced with a mystery. Obviously, one of the basic tenets of any ethical research is that it not only is open to scrutiny but welcomes such scrutiny. How then have the scientifically committed panelists reacted to the critiques documenting their errors, not just in procedures but in the reporting and, therefore, the use of the NRP results? To date five NRP panel members or contributors have acknowledged that the reported findings in the small summary booklet do not match the data.[7] Given those admissions, why then does the NRP website tout the botched summary booklet as being an "ideal resource," and why do panel members and researchers continue to circle the wagons and defend the report? Why haven't the acknowledged errors been corrected and why haven't federal and state mandates, including Reading First requirements, changed accordingly? In order to answer these questions, it is our responsibility to examine the objectivity of those who are the major players in the educational research arena.

The Objectivity of the NRP Scientists: Following the Money

We need to establish at the outset that it's hard to distinguish between personal and professional motives in anyone's actions. For that reason, in legal proceedings, judges and lawyers are ethically bound to remove or recuse themselves from participation in matters in which they have a vested personal or financial interest to preclude even the *appearance* of impropriety.

Unfortunately, we see many links between the falsely reported findings of the NRP report, "scientific" researchers, their lucrative involvement in their own commercial reading program enterprises, and the administration of President Bush. It is important to trace these financial conflicts of interest that saturate educational research as it translates into educational mandates. Such scrutiny can serve as a cautionary tale for the future lest we be duped again. But more importantly, even a new president in 2008 and possible policy change will not effect an immediate turnaround in schools. We are stuck with expensive commercial reading programs such as Open Court because they are alleged to be based on science. Therefore, a hard look at the conflicts of interest behind the research can help us put these programs and practices in perspective and help free caring teachers so they can do what's best for kids instead of what's best for commercial publishers and the researchers who profit at our expense.

The links among researchers, politics, and big money are so incestuous that it would be impossible to create a flowchart. To make it a little easier to follow, I'll **boldface** the major researchers and their financial conflicts of interest. Of course, we need to remember that the profits these scientists stand to make on their research may not have influenced the misreported, misapplied NRP findings.

Here now are a few of the major players:

Barbara Foorman/Open Court: Applicants for Reading First grants are "encouraged" to include scientifically proven core reading programs such as Open Court. Recall that Bush's reading czar, Reid Lyon, has publicly praised Open Court as being scientifically proven. Given this context, it is essential to examine the NRP's findings for Open Court and the connections of the NRP to the Open Court research. Barbara Foorman was the author of the only study in the NRP report that looked at Open Court Reading.[8] The Foorman, Francis, Fletcher, Schatschneider, and Mehta study (1998) compared first-and second-grade students taught with Open Court with children taught by whole language.[9] The results were as follows:

- In first grade, the outcomes for isolated skills such as decoding phonetically regular words were moderate to high. For comprehension and spelling in first grade, the outcomes were small. This statistically weak result for comprehension of students in Open Court dropped precipitously by second grade.
- The findings for second grade showed a drop in every single area. Most notably, the findings for comprehension and spelling dropped from a small (albeit statistically significant) positive effect size to a negative one:– .19.

In spite of the drop in every skill from first to second grade and in spite of the huge negative outcomes in comprehension and spelling, Open Court Reading is touted as being scientifically proven and is the favored core program for Reading First grants.

Joanne Yatvin, the only panel member who spoke out against the report, states that the written record of emails among panel members shows that Foorman was the sole reviewer for the phonics section. Thus, we see a conflict already. Foorman reviewed her own studies and also acted as an adviser to the reporting of the findings, which we recall were inaccurately reported. This in and of itself is a conflict. However, let's look beyond the fact that Foorman was in a position to "objectively" review her own work. Let's look at how she could potentially benefit financially from the falsely reported findings in the summary booklet and from the policy stressing phonics and phonemic awareness.

Foorman has her own commercial phonemic awareness program—*Phonemic Awareness for Young Children: A Classroom Curriculum*—that she coauthored with another NRP contributor and educational entrepreneur, **Marilyn Adams**. Adams just happens to be an author of McGraw-Hill's Open Court Reading and is also the author of another government-sponsored report, *Beginning to Read*.[10] Therefore, Adams, like Foorman, has a lot of research clout and, just coincidentally, a lot to gain from selling phonics and phonemic awareness.

As a matter of fact, the Open Court series boasts that Adams is "cited in the 2000 Politics of Education Yearbook as one of the *five most influential people in the national reading policy arena*" (italics mine). And so we have an indisputable link between yet another major public policy maker and her own for-profit use of research paid for with our tax dollars. Of course, this doesn't mean that self-interest motivated Adams and Foorman in their research or in their influence in framing public policy. The fact that they stand to profit from the misrepresented findings may be just a coincidence. Let's be clear about that.

The coauthors of Foorman and Adams' profitable commercial program are **Ingvar Lundberg** and **Terri Beeler**. Three of their studies are included in the phonemic awareness section of the NRP report, and their coauthor, Foorman, was the "technical advisor" for one of the sections. Barbara Foorman was a researcher in four of the thirty-eight studies in the phonics section. In summary,

1. Both Foorman and Adams have a commercial interest in the promotion of phonics and phonemic awareness as well as influence over public education policy.

2. Foorman was a technical adviser and reviewer of not only her own studies but those conducted by the coauthors of her and Adams' commercial phonemic awareness curriculum.

3. The misreported findings in the summary make false claims in favor of the impact of phonics on learning to read and apply them to all children in grades K–6.

You can buy the phonemic awareness program profiting these NRP panel contributors on Amazon. Just look for *Phonemic Awareness in Young Children: A Classroom Curriculum*.[11] You can buy Open Court Reading from McGraw-Hill Publishing. You can get the NRP report that your tax dollars subsidized for "free."

Louisa Moats: Louisa Moats is the project director of a large National Institute of Child Health and Human Development (NICHD) research grant. The NICHD is the government agency that sponsored the NRP report. Moats is also the research and professional development director for her own entrepreneurial pursuit, a commercial program called *Language!* that pushes decodable "Cat spat at rat" programs on middle and high school students. The company that distributes *Language!* in California is **Sopris West and Glencoe/ McGraw-Hill**.[12] Consider that the professional training for teachers for *Language!* begins with a clip from the NRP video that was directed by Widmeyer-Baker, McGraw-Hill's public relations agency, the same agency that helped write the NRP summary.[13] Recall that our tax dollars paid for this video. The video clip states, "Now we know through science how kids learn to read," and extols the use of phonics and decodable text such as that used in *Language!* This in spite of the fact that the NRP did not even include research on kids above sixth grade *or* on decodable text *and* in spite of the fact that above first grade, phonics did not help kids' reading growth. Furthermore, at this writing, the only research for the *Language!* program was done by Jane Fell Greene . . . the creator of *Language!*[14] On its website *(http://www.language -usa.net/research.html)*, you will see that *Language!* is not only "research based" but is "Commended for Excellence" and "Adopted by the State of California" in 1999–2005. And so this program is approved for middle and high school students, based on one study—done by its creator—published in a journal on dyslexia. It doesn't take a rocket scientist to see serious problems with this whole scenario.

In addition to a large early literacy grant from the NICHD, Moats is also receiving NICHD-SBIR (Small Business Innovation Research) grant money to develop interactive CD-ROMs for Sopris West's LETRS [Language Essentials for Teachers of Reading and Spelling] program, another entrepreneurial professional development enterprise.[15] Consider that our tax dollars are subsidizing the CD-ROMs for LETRS. Don't we see a clear case of public moneys supporting the researchers who sell their own commercial programs for profit? Again, the fact that so many researchers stand to profit from their own research doesn't mean that they were influenced by their potential to profit from their efforts.

Linnea Ehri: Ehri was the chair of the Alphabetics Committee of the NRP. She was also a paid research consultant to Houghton Mifflin's reading series, and her name is included in that series as a consultant. Ehri's contributions preceded the NRP report, and in all fairness, she may have been paid one set fee with no ongoing royalties. However, Houghton Mifflin uses Ehri's role as its consultant *and* her connection to the NRP in its sales presentations. In California, state law requires that for grades K–6, schools have a choice of five reading series.[16] In spite of this law, California teachers have had only two choices: Houghton Mifflin and McGraw-Hill's Open Court. Both of these series could boast authors and/or consultants who participated in the NRP report.

The press release heralding the completion of the NRP report by its chair, Donald Langenberg, clearly states that the panel *reviewed* studies in order to draw its conclusions.[17] In her role as chair of the Alphabetics Committee, Ehri, like Foorman, was in a position to review her own studies since her work was among the research on which the NRP findings are based. One of the tenets of peer-reviewed research is that it is blind. That is, authors' names are removed from studies before review in order to diffuse any possible prejudicial treatment in the reviews. It is reasonable to assume that Ehri and Foorman recognized their own work, and therefore, by the scholarly standards of the profession, the NRP's report can hardly be called an independent, peer-reviewed scholarly effort.

McGraw-Hill Publishing: After the first inauguration of George W. Bush, one of the first visitors to the White House was none other than Harold McGraw III, chairman and chief executive of the nation's largest K–12 publisher. Such a visit was not surprising since McGraw was on the board of directors of the **Barbara Bush Foundation**.[18] And so we see a publishing mogul with input into education policy that has continued over a number of years. In 1990, Harold McGraw Jr.'s "support of literacy," which just may have profited his own company, earned him the nation's highest literacy award, presented by President George H. W. Bush in 1990.

Harold McGraw Jr. gave one million dollars to the Hechinger Institute on Education and the Media at Columbia University to sponsor an annual (free) seminar for new education reporters. [19] Such "educational" initiatives may help explain the pro-phonics/back-to-basics slant that permeates the media and "informs" the public. Now, as a reminder, lest you lose track of all the McGraw-Hill–Bush public policy connections, NRP contributor and McGraw-Hill's Open Court author **Marilyn Adams** is linked to both NRP research and public education policy; Adams coauthored a phonemic awareness curriculum with **Barbara Foorman,** who was also a contributor to the NRP report.

Rod Paige was superintendent for the Houston Independent School District until 2001. As such, he solicited input from **business leaders** for strengthening school support services and programs. Paige launched a system of charter schools and had broad authority in decisions regarding staffing, textbooks, and materials as well as increased testing. Shortly after the Houston schools implemented **McGraw-Hill's Open Court program,** Paige was awarded the **Harold W. McGraw Jr. Educator of the Year Award** for his "service."[20] This award included a large cash bonus. Rod Paige is now a strong proponent for the scientific research sponsored by the NICHD, which, as we have seen, is replete with entrepreneurial researchers such as Open Court author **Marilyn Adams** and one of the coauthors of her commercial phonemic awareness program, **Barbara Foorman.**

As Secretary of Education, Paige claimed that "there is not an 'approved list' of programs and materials to be used in connection with Reading First."[21] He said this in spite of his selection of Open Court for the Houston schools. Nevertheless, both he *and* George W. Bush have made what sounds very much like a public endorsement of the **Voyager Learning program.** In fact, you can find these on the Voyager website. It's part of Voyager's sales brochure. Here's what they said:

Rod Paige: "In the Houston Independent School District, we are determined to teach all our children to read, and we expect the Voyager Universal Literacy System to be a major factor in our quest for 100% literacy."

Governor George W. Bush (who is now our president): "The Voyager Expanded Learning program is making a big difference in people's lives. The philosophy behind this program is one that says we're going to teach every child to soar." [22]

It is easy to see how school districts could be led to believe that there *are* approved programs and that McGraw-Hill and Voyager are the publishers of those core reading and supplemental programs. We have actions telling us certain programs and publishers are approved. And we have the words of our president and our secretary of education.

Perhaps just coincidentally of course, **Voyager's founder, Randy Best,** and Voyager investors made "generous contributions" to the campaign of then Governor George W. Bush, according to the *Dallas Morning News*.[23] And **Bush's former Texas Education Commissioner, Jim Nelson,** took a job at Voyager. But the fact that Voyager made campaign contributions to Governor Bush *just* when the company was bidding to run after-school programs in Texas may have no connection at all to Bush's endorsement of Voyager, or Rod Paige's either. It might all be just more of the coincidences that characterize the relationship between the money, the researchers, the politicians, and the programs that are declared to be "objective and scientific."[24]

Joseph Torgesen is yet another government-subsidized researcher who has links to the programs he's objectively studying. He is one of the researchers of Voyager and is also on its Design Team and also just happens to be a big player and governmental research grant recipient in Florida, the state governed by **Jeb Bush, George W. Bush's** brother.

There are more connections. Other **Voyager Design Team** members are **McGraw-Hill** authors **Edward J. Kame'enui** and **Deborah C. Simmons,** who also wrote the **reading language arts framework for California**.[25] They constructed the rubric schools must use to comply with scientific standards although the language arts framework *preceded* the NRP report. Guess whose bottom-up sequence and methodology the framework of these McGraw-Hill authors matches? Might this link explain why California schools could choose from only two approved programs instead of the five the law promises them?

Yet another political-financial link worth considering is the president's brother **Neil Bush,** who has his own educational software enterprise called **Ignite**.[26] So here we have the brother of the self-proclaimed education president selling education programs.

Too Many Colors

For one of my presentations, I made an overhead transparency of some of the vested financial interests of the scientific researchers and their connections to government policy. I tried color-coding to make the links easier to follow. When I came to Edward Kame'enui, I ran out of colors. He has financial links at so many levels, I can't list them all here. He and **Douglas Carnine,** another research mogul out of the **University of Oregon,** are both **McGraw-Hill** authors. Kame'enui has financial interests in educational testing. He is one of the creators of DIBELS (Dynamic Indicators of Basic Early Literacy Skills), a test for oral reading fluency that is one of the government-favored assessments. The DIBELS home page (*http://dibels.uoregon.edu*) indicates that much of the research support for DIBELS was done by members of the **Voyager Design Team,** including **Torgesen** (again), **Roland Good III,** and, of course, **Kame'enui.**[27] Furthermore, DIBELS is distributed by Sopris West and, in California, by McGraw-Hill. In Maryland and no doubt elsewhere, the state Reading First application was accepted only after DIBELS was included for assessment and Louisa Moats of Sopris West was included for professional development.

Incidentally, Kame'enui and Simmons also serve as advisers for Reading First grants and helped write the "scientific" criteria for grant acceptance, including the core programs to be used, the supplemental programs, the teacher training, and the assessments. So we have Kame'enui reaping the rewards of his research at every level of our government's "reform." The bottom line is that we have a handful of researchers with financial links to their own research. They

do the research

that supports their programs

that supports their own professional development enterprises

that matches the assessments they designed

that supports their own learning programs

that align with government mandates

that are based on their own scientific research.

And so on and so on and so on.

You'll also notice that government leaders such as Rod Paige do a lot of speaking at meetings sponsored by corporations. Of course, this all may be for the public good rather than the good of the corporations, and the government-research-corporate links may be only coincidental. But it's something to think about and there are indeed a lot of links, aren't there?

In summary, we have education policy that is ostensibly based on scientific research. That research is verifiably misreported based on the data and as confirmed by five of the fourteen NRP members or contributors.[28] There are links within links among the researchers and the programs their research supposedly supports. Those programs are being foisted on us in the name of science. As responsible teachers—to say nothing of consumers—we need to galvanize our resources and take back our profession. We have the tools, we have the facts, and we have the intelligence and commitment.

Notes

1. National Reading Panel. (2000). *The report of the National Reading Panel: Teaching children to read: An evidence-based assessment of the scientific research literature on reading and its implications for reading instruction.* Washington, DC: National Institute of Child Health and Human Development. This report is available for free at *www.nationalreadingpanel.org.*

2. Garan, E. (2004). *In defense of our children: When profit, politics, and education collide.* Portsmouth, NH: Heinemann. See also Garan, E. (2002). *Resisting reading mandates: How to triumph with the truth.* Portsmouth, NH: Heinemann.

3. Coles, G. (2003). *Reading the naked truth: Literacy, legislation, and lies.* Portsmouth, NH: Heinemann.

4. Krashen, S. (2001, October). More smoke and mirrors: A critique of the National Reading Panel report on fluency. *Phi Delta Kappan,* pp. 119–123; Krashen, S. (2002). The NRP comparison of whole language and phonics: Ignoring the crucial variables. *Talking Points, 13.* 13(2): 22–28.

5. Allington, R. (2002). *Big brother and the national reading curriculum: How ideology trumped evidence.* Portsmouth, NH: Heinemann.

6. For kindergarten and first-grade children, comprehension was assessed using "extremely short (usually one sentence) 'passages'" (Report of the Subgroups, pp. 2–115). For students above first grade, the NRP report states, "Phonics instruction appears to contribute only weakly, if at all, in helping [the students assessed in the studies] apply these decoding skills to read text and spell words" (Report of the Subgroups, pp. 2–108).

7. The articles in which the NRP panel members or contributors acknowledge the disconnect between the official summary and the data in the report itself are as follows: panel member Linnea Ehri and NRP contributor Steven Stahl, (2001, September). Beyond the smoke and mirrors: Putting out the fire. *Phi Delta Kappan,* pp. 17–20; panel member Timothy Shanahan, (2001). Response to Elaine Garan: Teaching should be informed by research, not authoritative opinion. *Language Arts, 79,* 71–72; panel member Joanne Yatvin, (2002, January). Babes in the woods: The wanderings of the National Reading Panel. *Phi Delta Kappan,* pp. 364–369; panel contributor Barbara R. Foorman and Jack M. Fletcher, (2003, May). Backtalk: Correcting errors. *Phi Delta Kappan,* p. 719. *Note:* On the title page, the NRP report lists those who made contributions to the report and thanks them for their help. However, the report does not describe the roles of the contributors or the extent of their contributions. I have identified panel members and distinguished them from those the report identifies as contributors.

8. Study 11 in Appendix G of the Subgroup Report on Phonics in the National Reading Panel. (2000). *The report of the National Reading Panel: Teaching children to*

read: An evidence-based assessment of the scientific research literature on reading and its implications for reading instruction. Washington, DC: National Institute of Child Health and Human Development.

9. Foorman, B., Francis, D., Fletcher, J., Schatschneider, C., & Mehta, P. (1998). The role of instruction in learning to read: Preventing reading failure in at-risk children. *Journal of Educational Psychology, 90,* 37–55.

10. Adams, M. J. (1990). *Beginning to read: Thinking and learning about print.* Cambridge, MA: MIT Press.

11. Adams, M. J., Foorman, B., Lundberg, I., & Beeler, T. (1997). *Phonemic awareness in young children: A classroom curriculum.* New York: Paul H. Brookes.

12. See *www.sopriswest.com.*

13. Boucher, D. (2003, June). Email. Fresno, California, teacher Derek Boucher attended *Language!* training for six hours a day for an entire week. He took notes.

14. Greene, J. F. (1996). *Language!* Effects of an individualized structured language curriculum for middle and high school students." *Annals of Dyslexia 46,* 51–76.

15. Moats, L. LETRS: Like anatomy for the physician. *LETRS: Language Essentials for Teachers of Reading and Spelling, 1* (3), 1–3. *Note:* I retrieved this newsletter by typing in "Moats" and "NICHD" on Google.

16. See *www.cde.ca.gov/ci/cr/cf/ rla 2002.pub.asp*

17. Press release. (2000, April 13). Available at *www.nationalreadingpanel.org*

18. Press release. (2001, January 23). Washington, DC: Business Wire.

19. *Hechinger News.* Hechinger Institute on Education and the Media, Teachers College, Columbia University. Winter/spring 1999–2000.

20. This information is available at *www.mcgraw-hill.com/community/mcgraw-prize/2000/ winners.html* web page. He was introduced as the recipient of this honor at his keynote address to the International Reading Association in May 2001.

21. Paige, Rod. 2002. Letter to the Honorable Pat Schroeder. 5 April. Accessed at *www.gov/policy/elsec/guid/letter/026901-html?exp=0*

22. The endorsements are available on the Voyager web page and are part of the product's advertising brochure. See *www.voyagerlearning.com/literacy/research/design.jsp*

23. In *City Limits Weekly.* Accessed at *www.citylimits.org/content/articles/weeklyview. cfm?articlenumber=8207*

24. Hawke, C. (2002, August 12). All but one company left behind. *City limits weekly, 343.* Available: *www.citylimits.org/content/articles/weeklyview.cfm?articlenumber=820*

25. The Voyager Design Team and the research supporting it are listed at *www.voyager learning.com.* The research supporting DIBELS, conducted by the Voyager Design Team as well as those with interests in the program, includes the following: Buck, J., Torgesen, J. (2003); Good, R. H., Kaminski, R. A., Smith, S., Simmons, D. S., Kame'enui, E. J., & Wallin, J. (in press); Good, R. H., Simmons, D. S., Kame'enui, E. J., Kaminski, R. A., & Wallin, J. (2002).

26. Neil Bush debuts Ignite Learning.(2001, November). *News Connection. Note:* The Ignite! Learning website (*www.ignitelearning.com*) has a series of news releases touting Neil Bush's promotion of his educational endeavor. I typed in "Neil Bush" and "Ignite! Learning" on Google and obtained a great deal of information on the president's brother and his entrepreneurial pursuits.

27. This information is available on both the Voyager and the DIBELS websites.

28. The articles in which the NRP panel members or contributors acknowledge the disconnect between the official summary and the data in the report itself are as follows: panel member Linnea Ehri and NRP contributor Steven Stahl, (2001, September). Beyond the smoke and mirrors: Putting out the fire. *Phi Delta Kappan,* pp. 17–20; panel member Timothy Shanahan, (2001). Response to Elaine Garan: Teaching should be informed by research, not authoritative opinion. *Language Arts, 79,* 71–72; panel member Joanne Yatvin, (2002, January). Babes in the woods: The wanderings of the National Reading Panel. *Phi Delta Kappan,* pp. 364–369; panel contributor Barbara R. Foorman and Jack M. Fletcher, (2003, May). Backtalk: Correcting errors. *Phi Delta Kappan,* p. 719. *Note:* On the title page, the NRP report lists those who made contributions to the report and thanks them for their help. However, the report does not describe the roles of the contributors or the extent of their contributions. I have identified panel members and distinguished them from those the report identifies as contributors.

4

Operation No Child Left Behind

STEVEN L. STRAUSS

Division of Clinical Neurophysiology
Franklin Square Hospital, Baltimore

What's Behind No Child Left Behind?

As school systems increasingly succumb to the use of mandated commercial reading programs and to the correlative use of high-stakes testing to measure how well teachers are getting their children to learn the required material, a host of associated changes are visibly on the rise in the lives of teachers and students. Punitive accountability measures, based on the test scores, are leading to the retention of children by the tens of thousands. It has been suggested that heightened pressure from the new testing climate is responsible for the rising incidence of child and adolescent depression and other mental disorders (Mitka, 2001). Increasingly, scripted lesson plans complement the high-stakes tests in an effort to guarantee adherence to the mandated programs. Still, more and more schools are being labeled as failing, the optimistic proclamations of Secretary of Education Rod Paige and his boss in the White House notwithstanding, leaving teachers, parents, and students with uncertainty about what to do next.

With such devastating changes unfolding daily, it is tempting to point to No Child Left Behind (NCLB) as the culprit, because it is the legal basis for the new mandated curriculum and therefore for the associated untoward consequences. It might even be argued, convincingly, that a successful struggle to overturn NCLB could right the ship of public education. But if we do not understand where NCLB itself came from, the driving force behind its genesis may simply rise up again and assert itself in another form.

Some argue that, as a piece of conservative legislation, NCLB can be defeated by rallying more progressive forces that should at least recognize its

33

harmful effects. But this approach would quickly reveal that NCLB was supported by liberals and conservatives alike, from both leading parties. Democratic Senator Edward Kennedy spoke out publicly on the importance of phonics, and conservative President Bush signed it into law. What this shows is that NCLB reflects what the two parties have in common—where they agree, not where they differ.

Where they agree is in the protection and preservation of the economic system that defines the framework within which we all live our lives. Both parties agree that the economic health of the nation depends on the rights of giant corporations to pursue their profit-making ambitions, both domestically and overseas. Perhaps the Democrats go on record as supporting a kinder and gentler corporate-controlled economic system, and the Republicans go on record as advocating a loosening of environmental and other constraints on corporations' rights to do business. But where they overlap is the key fact in how U.S. politics really works.

And they overlapped on NCLB. Therefore, if we are truly to understand NCLB, we must go beyond this or that detail on where the two parties differ and recognize NCLB as reflecting something *systemic*. Then we might discover that mandated reading programs themselves reflect a political policy in the interest of the overall system and of corporate America's control over it.

By facing head-on the fully bipartisan support of NCLB, we are actually in a better position to address the question What lies behind No Child Left Behind? We will not be fooled into thinking that it is a plot of the more conservative wing of Congress or an oversight on the part of the more liberal wing. Incorrectly identifying friend and foe can lead only to missed opportunities in the fight against NCLB and even to the fight itself earning the label of failure.

Let's consider the various possibilities of what lies behind No Child Left Behind. Perhaps NCLB is the long-anticipated attempt by opponents of democratic classrooms to once and for all rid schools of the pernicious, liberating effects of progressive education, including whole language and bilingual education. Perhaps it is fundamentally an attack on poor and minority communities by extirpating them from their neighborhood schools. Perhaps it is an attempt to do away with public education by means of a calculated series of incremental privatizations. Or perhaps it is a plan to stuff even more money down the capacious pockets of the likes of McGraw-Hill and Houghton Mifflin, manufacturers of the mandated reading programs themselves.

In fact, most, if not all of these, have been suggested as ultimate explanations of NCLB. A magnificent recent anthology titled *Saving Our Schools* (Goodman, Shannon, Goodman, & Rapoport, 2004), which should be on the shelves and in the hands of all those concerned about saving public education, asserts that the driving aim of NCLB is the destruction of public schooling. But the problem that exists in singling out one or another of NCLB's unfortunate manifestations is that it begs an explanation of the other unfortunate manifestations. Still, no comprehensive treatment has yet been formulated.

For example, those who have quite accurately pointed to the harm being done to public education by NCLB, and who have also suggested that destroying public education is its real goal, cannot easily explain why this entails intensive phonics in the classroom, whether mandated or otherwise. It is not enough to say, for example, that phonics lends itself more readily to scripted lesson plans than any other instructional method and that this explains why it is a pillar of NCLB. At best, such an assertion entails only a more docile and disciplined teaching staff and student population, but not the destruction of public schooling. Phonics was alive and well in the pre–whole language era and was a very popular instructional approach to reading whose only serious competition at the time was sight word reading. On its own, though, it posed no serious threat to public education during that period.

To truly understand NCLB, we must delve below the surface of all of its most obvious manifestations and try to understand what ties them together. In doing so, we can discover, I believe, that the driving force is even more nefarious than any one of the possibilities already mentioned. It is an attempt by the most powerful and privileged sector of the economy—corporate America—to take over and manipulate the public education system for its own long-term goals, namely, protecting and safeguarding its economic privileges and profits well into the future. Contrary to what some have suggested, this means the retention, at least for the time being, of some version of public education.

NCLB: A Workforce Development Bill to Secure Corporate Profits

To understand what lies behind NCLB, it will be useful to begin with an analysis of one of its most striking contradictions. Unraveling this contradiction lays bare the leading players in the drama.

To the surprise of very few, No Child Left Behind is inflicting countless casualties in the wake of its assault on young people. Under the banner of raising academic standards, the NCLB bulldozer is winding its way through the schools and communities of America, armed with high-stakes testing and punitive accountability. These patently cruel and antichild weapons are leading, quite predictably, to the retention of large numbers of students and to great schools being labeled as failing, that is to say, to many children being left behind.

Despite its claims, therefore, failure is built into the very structure of NCLB. And it is not only high-stakes testing and punitive accountability that exemplify this. Certain groups with a vested interest in student failure have been strengthened by the law. Military recruiters, for example, are keeping a close eye on the test scores. Because NCLB gives the Pentagon the right to access directories of students' names, addresses, and telephone numbers, it can now circle overhead, like a vulture, waiting to pick off children who fall victim to the grim new realities. How fortunate a prize this is for the Pentagon, since colleges and universities have historically been the military's main competition for the recruitment of warm bodies, making it difficult to meet quotas, as the Pentagon itself acknowledges (Flowers, 2002). To the extent that students are discouraged from pursuing a bachelor's degree or higher because of their test scores, they will become the targets of recruitment pitches to choose the other fork in NCLB's road—serving in uniform in this era of endless, unwinnable war. What better way, then, to have its competitive edge improved against institutions of higher learning, when the need arises, than to leave children behind by means of arbitrarily drawn scores on ill-conceived tests?

There is, therefore, a fundamental contradiction between the federal government's word and its deed, between the fantasy world evoked by the disingenuous moniker of its education bill, in which blissful children frolic in the land of letters and sounds, and the real world of social embarrassment, rising levels of childhood depression, teacher burnout, and children being left more behind than ever. According to the National Association of School Psychologists, this real world of schooling in the United States now includes children who fear being retained—that is, left behind—more than they fear the death of a parent, a reversal from just a few years ago (Anderson, Whipple, & Jimerson, 2002).

How do we make sense of the contradiction between NCLB's promise of improving educational achievement for all and the reality of increasing school failure for some coupled with Pyrrhic success for others? Crucially, we must appreciate that despite its official title as the revised Elementary and Secondary Education Act, NCLB is *not* primarily about education, that is to say, about education in the child-friendly sense of the term.

Indeed, given what decades of research have taught us about child development and schooling, especially the negative effects of punitive classrooms and grade retention, a socially enlightened education bill would never be as cruel and frightening to young children as No Child Left Behind is. Rather, it would promote caring and loving learning environments in which students feel safe asking their own questions and exploring their own interests. It would seek to develop well-rounded, thoughtful young people who care about philosophy and the arts, literature and human culture, and music and the human spirit, the real standards of any educational curriculum and the best benchmarks against which to measure society's level of enlightenment. It would promote learning as its own motivator rather than strike the whip of retention, social embarrassment, and funding cuts. And if democracy were taken seriously, it would cultivate the capacity for self-confident critical thinking rather than internalization of an external authoritarian code of right and wrong.

To be sure, nothing less than this is standard fare at expensive, secular, private schools. Such schools, which serve the children of the corporate class that is actually leading the pep rallies for NCLB, operate outside the law and are exempt from its testing and accountability requirements. In fact, taking into account not only who is covered by NCLB but also who is *not* covered by the law can shed much light on its real motives.

If NCLB were truly as scientific and research based as its proponents declare, if it were truly as "trustworthy" (Lyon, 2001, para. 15) and efficacious as its architects have asserted, and if it were truly part of the arsenal of weapons mobilized to fight a "significant public health problem" (Lyon, 1998, para. 36), one would expect not only that the exempted schools would have been included under and subject to the law, like everybody else, but also that these very same schools would be clamoring on their own to partake of its fruits. Certainly, the privileged children who attend them are not exempt from other scientifically proven methods, such as getting vaccinated to prevent polio. Nor are such schools averse to using other scientifically supported educational methods, especially small class sizes.

Yet it would be naïve to imagine that a privileged class would jeopardize its privileged status by advocating policy that would raise the educational level of public schools to that of its own schools. And indeed, we can expect No Child Left Behind to do nothing of the sort. NCLB applies to working-class children, not to the children of society's elite, and its essence is to provide these working-class children with working-class skills. But whereas the skills themselves may be new and changing, using them in a working capacity to generate profits for the corporate boss is not.

The Congressional Twenty-first Century Workforce Commission released a document in the year 2000 (*A Nation of Opportunity: Building America's Twenty-first Century Workforce*) in which it identified those skills the next generation of U.S. workers would need in order to maintain the viability of corporate America vis-à-vis its overseas competitors. Its chief conclusion was that the new U.S. worker needs to be an information technology (IT) worker, "an individual who is responsible for designing, building and/or maintaining an information

technology infrastructure that businesses and consumers use" (p. 15). It identified "skills clusters" of an IT worker, all revolving around a purported "21st Century Literacy." This new type of literacy was "defined by the Commission as the
ability to read, write, and compute with competence, think analytically, adapt to
change, work in teams, and use technology" (p. 22).

By virtue of becoming twenty-first century literate, the new worker
would be able to "read and compute at a level adequate to . . . compete in the
IT labor market" (p. 23). But the Twenty-first Century Workforce Commission lamented that "far too many high school graduates, entrants into post-
secondary education, and American adults in the labor force" currently
lacked the requisite skills.

To bridge the gap between the current level of twenty-first century illit-
eracy and the desired level of twenty-first century literacy, the commission recommended that "community leaders concerned about meeting tomorrow's
workforce needs should insist that community and school-based early reading instruction programs implement practices that are supported by the most
authoritative research on reading. The research, most recently summarized by
the National Reading Panel (NRP), clearly indicates what elements must be in
place for a child to become a successful reader" (p. 67).

In other words, the Twenty-first Century Workforce Commission established a connection between the systematic, intensive phonics instruction
proposed by the NRP and corporate America's new literacy requirements for
its labor force. It defined these literacy requirements in very narrow terms,
joining together in adjacent clauses the notions of *reading* and *computing* and
using technology. This is reading, therefore, as a *working-class skill*. Real reading, done freely and volitionally for the pursuit and development of one's own
interests, whether that means information processing or becoming immersed
in surrealist fiction or modern poetry, is to remain the private school curricular privilege of the already privileged.

No Child Left Behind is therefore not only an anti-education law but a
class-based anti-education law. What it refers to as a literacy crisis is nothing
more than the notion that working-class students lack a skill corporate
America wants them to have when they become its workers in the future,
namely, the ability to read for technical information. The system that NCLB
sets up leaves real choice about quality education only to those who can
afford it, whereas for working-class families there is but an illusion of choice,
and this only when their neighborhood schools are labeled as failing. In that
circumstance, parents of children who attend such schools can now "choose"
to send their children across town, outside the home community. But class
sizes at the receiving schools will rise above the already high levels, lowering
their quality of education even further. And the increasing diversity of the

receiving schools will now put them at higher risk for being labeled as failing (Novak & Fuller, 2004).

No Child Left Behind is anti-education most dramatically insofar as it damages the crucial caring relationship that needs to exist between teachers and students, a key element in quality learning. NCLB drives a wedge between teachers and students, setting them up as mutual adversaries in a struggle to survive punitive accountability threats rather than nurturing collaboration and cooperation for facing the problems and challenges of young people's development.

If NCLB is about education at all, it is about education narrowly conceived, as vocational training for the "twenty-first century knowledge worker," as corporate America likes to characterize its future employee. Even more, it is vocational training itself narrowly conceived, in which those labor skills that maximally elevate corporate America's profit margins, and keep it competitive with overseas corporations, constitute the new curricular standards. The core skill of the new curriculum is a very narrow type of reading and literacy, one that emphasizes the encoding and decoding of the language of software and hardware and various wares in between.

Indeed, it is more accurate to regard NCLB as a *workforce development bill* than an education bill. Recall that, in coordination with recommendations from the National Institute of Child Health and Human Development (NICHD), No Child Left Behind was hammered out by the House Committee on Education and the Workforce. And in corporate America's behind-the-scenes agitation for the bill, a coalition of its leading CEOs, known as the Business Roundtable, probably the staunchest proponent of NCLB, referred to the kinds of public schools it now wants, and which NCLB is supposed to help manufacture, as "workforce development systems," whose mission is to "serve its principal customers, focus on total quality and contribute to U.S. international competitiveness" (Business Roundtable, 1993, para. 1).

In other words, No Child Left Behind only parades as an education bill because it seeks to expropriate public schools as the sites where the training of corporate America's new twenty-first century labor force will take place. An education bill that opposes quality education and that mandates reading instruction that actually prohibits and discourages real reading in favor of information processing is more than enough evidence that we are truly experiencing a "pedagogy of the absurd" (Goodman, 2004, p. 39).

The "Battle for the Classrooms"

Corporate America, through its Business Roundtable, has made it clear that it needs a new workforce development system to produce a new type of domestic workforce, one with world-class skills in digital technology, in order to maintain its hegemonic lead in the global economy. It fears loss of this lead to competitors from corporate Europe and corporate Asia and has therefore declared that it "wants Americans [to] expect students to master the difficult substance in core academic subjects that is routinely expected of the most advanced Asian and European countries" (Business Roundtable, 1995, p. 7). By "advanced," of course, it means economically and technologically advanced, not socially or humanistically advanced.

For purposes of public consumption, corporate America has launched its agenda, with obliging support from its bipartisan clients in Washington, under the pretext of a literacy crisis. But this is a crisis of corporate America's own making, not of those who are the objects and victims of NCLB. The supposed literacy crisis is nothing more than corporate America's own fear of falling from first place in the global economy. It has projected this fear onto the real world by declaring that "countries that do not lead will be more than economically disadvantaged; they will be economically irrelevant" (Augustine, 1997, para. 3). The fall to economic irrelevance can be averted only if the domestic workforce knows how to read the instruction manuals of the new technology, since "in the integrated global economy, workforce quality drives national competitiveness" (Business Roundtable, 1993, para. 2).

NCLB is therefore the domestic reflection of profit-driven corporate globalization. Each is a long-term policy, concerned not with immediate, short-term money making, but with setting in place the preconditions for continued profit turning over the foreseeable future. Corporate globalization is a strategy to prepare the international playing field for penetration by U.S. corporate capital. NCLB is a strategy to produce a workforce that can take advantage of the new openings, in the interest of corporate America.

With each serving the interests of corporate America, the one foreign and the other domestic, globalization and NCLB share crucial characteristics. Corporate globalization views the democratic rights of local populations as obstacles to its goals. These include trade union rights and the rights derived from public ownership of energy supplies, water, health care, and even education. NCLB views the democratic rights of teachers as obstacles to its goals. Chiefly, this includes the right to use professional judgment in deciding on curriculum and methods of assessment. Each understands the crucial role of militarism in the pursuit of its goals, with corporate globalization materially defending itself by yearly increasing the number of U.S. military bases being built overseas and NCLB enabling Pentagon recruiters to defuse public anger by offering an alternative career to the many children whose futures will otherwise be cut short as a result of NCLB's socially backward and punitive approach to schooling.

Corporate America understands the globalization-NCLB connection only too well. One of its leading spokespersons, Norman Augustine, the former CEO of Lockheed Martin, former chair of the Education Task Force of the Business Roundtable, and education adviser to President Bush II, has formulated it succinctly. Says Augustine (1997, para. 6), "More and more we see that competition in the international marketplace is in reality a battle for the classrooms."

The battle for the classroom, like all other battles driven by the profit motive, is really a battle for control of territory and natural resources. In the present case, the territory is the classroom and the natural resources are those of the classroom itself. The two fundamental resources of the classroom, from corporate America's point of view, are the raw material of fresh, malleable brains, called students, and the machines used to mold these brains, called teachers. In the factory that we call the public school, the job of the teachers is to turn the students' brains into razor-sharp readers and writers of digital language (Altwerger & Strauss, 2002). Again, according to Augustine,

> To those of us in business, it is obvious that large segments of our educational system are failing today. We are the ones, after all, who get the first real-world view of the young people emerging from the American educational "pipeline." Unfortunately, many of them arrive at our doors unable to write a proper paragraph, fill out simple forms, read instructional manuals, do essential mathematical calculations, understand basic scientific concepts, or work as a team. . . . Perhaps these examples would be less disconcerting if our economy were still based on an early industrial model where hard work, a strong back and common sense could secure a decent job for even an illiterate person. But today's global, information-based economy is defined more and more by constantly evolving technology involving, for example, fiber optics, robotics, bioengineering, advanced telecommunications, microelectronics and artificial intelligence. (1997, para. 3)

In every battle there is an enemy. The enemies in the battle for the classroom are the students, parents, and teachers themselves, for they have no interest whatsoever in a system that retains students in grade on the basis of an arbitrary, unscientific number from a test score; that destroys communities (especially poor and minority ones) by closing down neighborhood schools; that downplays the arts, music, and physical education; that turns teachers into mere test preparers; and that contains a back door into union busting by privatizing schools that fail. There is bound to be resistance from those most affected by the new law. But corporate America has announced its high-stakes aims in this battle and its readiness to take on any resistance. According to the Business Roundtable, its aim is "not simply to improve individual schools but to reform the entire system of public education" (Business Roundtable, 1995, para. 1). And not to be defeated in its global and domestic designs, the Business Roundtable is already tracking opposition to its scheme of high-stakes testing and discussing ways to counter it (see its report titled *Assessing and Addressing the "Testing Backlash,"* Business Roundtable, 2001).

Like in all battles, there will be high levels of collateral damage. Students' mental health is one of these, with increasing depression, anxiety, and family dysfunction being reported by the American Academy of Child and Adolescent Psychiatry, as well as an astonishingly pathologic fear of grade retention, both cited earlier.

The driving force behind this radical transformation of schooling is the maintenance of corporate profitability into the future, and reading is the pivotal labor skill around which the new curriculum is to be built. But, again, this is a narrow form of reading. Corporate America does not need Shakespearean scholars. It needs information manipulators.

The government, through the resources and willing collusion of scientists from the National Institute of Child Health and Human Development, created the necessary pseudoscience to justify to the public an approach to reading instruction that, it believed, would solve corporate America's literacy needs. Direct, systematic, intensive phonics, we were all told, will finally teach our kids how to read. But the real agenda, mostly hidden from the public, was revealed in NICHD director Duane Alexander's speech to Congress, when he presented the final report of the National Reading Panel (NRP). Said Alexander (2000, para. 7), "The significance of these findings for the future literacy of this nation and for the economic prosperity and global competitiveness of our people is enormous."

Alexander's remarks were carefully directed to both the public and corporate America. Equivalently, the NICHD had to sell its intensive phonics snake oil not just to ordinary working people, which it has tried to do with its NRP report and with embedded reporters in the media, but to the Business Roundtable as well. Corporate America had to be convinced of the merits of intensive phonics in serving its own perceived needs. It had to believe that intensive phonics would truly be able to manufacture a workforce with the narrow type of literacy skills it felt it would need to keep its profits high for years to come and keep at bay the threats from the corporate classes of other nations.

Corporate America is interested in reading only as information processing and in education only as training the workforce it wants the public to believe it needs. It wants its new workers to be able to create and troubleshoot new software and hardware. The appeal of phonics and phonics-based programs to corporate America is that they represent the most elemental form of information processing as applied to print. Children are first taught to process letters as sounds, then concatenated sounds as words, and so on, until, eventually, the entire focus of reading is on the information encoded on the page by the author and its decoding by the reader. Intensive phonics in the elementary school is really Introduction to Information Processing 101.

From the standpoint of a scientific understanding of reading, corporate America has been sold a bill of goods by the NICHD, and it will be interesting to see how it responds if the scientifically vapid intensive phonics program fails to deliver. But to prove itself worthy, the NICHD and its supporters will have to continue to betray the institute's own mission to promote and safeguard child health and human development, by advocating, in a completely unscientific fashion, increasingly intense pressure on the schools to prove that children are learning how to be world-class information processors.

There are a number of options available to the NICHD to fulfill its own prophecy of educational success, all in keeping with its new antiscience tradition. It can advocate a redrawing of test score cutoffs, a wholly arbitrary and unscientific extrapolation of its current arbitrary and unscientific advocacy of high-stakes testing and accountability (Lyon, 2001). It can remain silent when school administrators deny biologically needed naptime to kindergartners in order to allow the little ones more time to prepare for the big test (Associated Press, 2003). In the same vein, it can remain silent when mentally and physically stimulating after-school "frills," such as team sports and band practice, find themselves on the budget chopping block in order to save school districts money they are required to spend on phonics and phonemic awareness. And, when all else fails, and since its "research-based" curriculum is so foolproof that it has dictatorially placed itself in the position of approving and disapproving classroom materials, the NICHD can continue its policy of scapegoating teachers for any persistent problems (Lyon, 2000).

That the NICHD enterprise is an exercise in pseudoscience is hinted at in the acknowledgment by NICHD researchers themselves that "anyone who only reads the summary report (of the NRP) is likely to be misinformed" (Foorman, Francis, & Fletcher, 2003, p. 720). This remark appeared only after NRP personalities could no longer ignore repeated challenges to the embarrassing discrepancies between the full NRP report and the short summary report (Garan, 2002; Strauss, 2003). Yet nothing has changed as a result of this confession. If the manufacturer of my automobile acknowledged that a driver who read its temperature gauge would likely be misinformed, I would expect an immediate recall of the product.

The pseudoscience is more clearly discerned in the observation that the NRP never in fact studied reading. Rather, it arrogantly granted itself the right to assume as correct one particular model of reading and reading research from among a number of competing models. The model it assumed was one that views reading an alphabetic script as requiring an initial conversion of print to sound, via rules of letter-sound decoding, followed by a conversion of sound to meaning. No matter that forty years of research have exposed the serious weaknesses of this model. Following the selection of its favorite model of reading, the NRP then looked at an instructional method consistent with that model, namely, intensive systematic phonics, in order to assess its effect on students' decoding abilities. It claimed to have scientifically determined that intensive instruction in decoding improves decoding—not too surprising.

In approaching the problem this way, the NICHD "first denigrated, then ignored, the preponderance of research" (Cunningham, 2001, p. 327) in the field of reading. Without consensus from the leading thinkers, researchers, and practitioners in the field of reading, it claimed in elitist fashion that decoding was "nonnegotiable" (Lyon, 1997, para. 11). But even granting this premise, the NRP never showed that intensive phonics instruction is the *only* method for improving decoding skills, nor that non-skills-based approaches to reading instruction, such as meaning-centered approaches that use authentic texts, do not *also* improve decoding skills. This glaring omission notwithstanding, it then participated in promulgating the completely unscientific conclusion that only certain approved phonics-based materials can be used in classrooms receiving Reading First funding.

A Declaration of War on the Classroom

This story is by now a familiar one. An odious policy agenda that would certainly be opposed by the public needs a crisis to win it an audience and evidence to win it acceptance. Both are manufactured. When caught, its manufacturers acknowledge the evidence to be misinforming, though the alleged crisis persists, and we are told that we are still better off for having pursued the misinformed policy. Thus, there is no apology to those hurt by the misinformation, no backpedaling from the policy that was based on the misinformation, no about-face. Even the loyal opposition limits its criticism to saying it would have done the same job, only better, and with more brute force and more money. But the initial, necessary step in achieving the long-range goal has been accomplished. The armed agents of the government have invaded the desired territory and hold it in occupation.

No Child Left Behind is tantamount to a declaration of war by the government on the classrooms of the United States of America. Corporate America identified the battle, and NCLB is its legal cover. The weapons of the battle, which include the threat of funding loss unless an approved intensive phonics program is used, are ultimately designed to create a new twenty-first century workforce, one that is fluent in the new literacy's highest literary genre—the instruction manual.

As with any militaristic occupation, parasitic profiteering is the order of the day. But it would be a mistake to conclude that this profiteering is the fundamental driving force behind the adventure. Commercial manufacturers of classroom reading materials, such as McGraw-Hill and Houghton Mifflin, are just the Halliburtons and Bechtels of Operation No Child Left Behind. The deeper agenda, as we have seen, goes far beyond these war profiteers.

Likewise, it is an error, I believe, to regard No Child Left Behind as a government weapon designed primarily to do away with public education, as many outstanding critics of the bill have claimed (Goodman et al., 2004). Aspects of public education, such as the still not deceased element of local control, the still not extinct morsel of unscripted teacher professionalism in deciding on particulars of classroom organization, and the still not busted requirement that school districts bargain collectively with teachers unions, represent obstacles to corporate America's plans to turn classrooms into economic boot camps for its global war for profits. As obstacles, they need to be cleared away.

More specifically, child-centered whole language and teachers unions must be eliminated because they both keep control of classroom decision making in the hands of the citizens of the classroom itself—the teachers, parents, and students—and not in the hands of outside forces that seek to shape schools to serve their own narrow and selfish needs. But corporate America will not stop there. Unless a digitalized workforce is achieved, it still has not won its battle for the classroom.

On the other hand, public schools offer something to corporate America that it would not as easily have if schools were no longer public. Public schools are funded by taxes on the local community, and they are subject to laws that dispense public funds. Therefore, by keeping schools public, at least in a formal sense, corporate America can let federal law coerce local communities into adopting its agenda and paying for it with their own money at the same time.

For the time being, therefore, it is only the fact that schools are public that makes them subject to No Child Left Behind. Private schools are exempt from its draconian measures, a not very surprising state of affairs, since the children of corporate executives certainly do not aspire to become corporate America's knowledge workers. Therefore, it can be anticipated that, as long as decisions are made by the federal government in support of its corporate patrons, schools will remain public for the foreseeable future.

There is therefore an important distinction to be drawn between private schools and privatized schools. The former are exempt from NCLB. The latter will be created by NCLB and subject to its provisions. Privatized schools are public schools that use public revenues to pay the salaries of the private companies that run them, a situation in which workers pay their bosses without even having hired them. Unless the American Federation of Teachers and the National Education Association put up a fight, these companies will be free to hire and fire outside the unions and to set curriculum and class scheduling without democratic input from those most affected. The talented and gifted teachers of America will either burn out and leave, to be replaced by a new generation of docile test coaches, or lead the necessary fight to defend children and quality public education.

Ending the Occupation

Teachers, parents, and students either will be pacified by the occupying power or will resist it. If the former, the casualties will be enormous. These will include a well-rounded curriculum, creative and caring teaching, real reading, and students' mental health. Democracy will suffer to the extent that the protection of corporate profit takes precedence over uninhibited scientific inquiry and over input from all affected parties—teachers, parents, students—on the design and implementation of curriculum.

To the extent that curriculum is constrained in the interest of corporate profit, it must be forced on those who do not share corporate America's reason for living. This coercion takes the form of high-stakes testing and accountability. According to Ed Rust Jr., another education task force director of the Business Roundtable and education adviser to President Bush II, "schools [must] adopt higher standards, use high-quality assessments aligned to these standards, hold schools accountable for results, and provide supports to help students and teachers reach the standards" (2001, para. 6). But it is precisely around these coercive means that an opening exists to build an effective opposition to the plan.

High-stakes testing is a tool of corporate America. It is frightening to children and deprofessionalizing to teachers, especially when the latter see how it transforms their profession into mere test preparation. The public wants to support teachers and will do so to the extent that teachers support its children in meaningful and humanistic ways. This can lead naturally to a strong united front of teachers, parents, and students, together demanding an immediate end to high-stakes testing.

There are now dozens of statewide coalitions against high-stakes testing. They represent a powerful starting point for resistance. With patience and democratic participation, it can become a large popular movement, much like the antiglobalization movement, its twin, with the power to mobilize hundreds of thousands of parents in defense of their children and teachers in defense of quality education. Opponents of No Child Left Behind can then truly become a force to reckon with, exposing its contradictions and working towards its repeal.

Corporate America, and its government clients, will have no cogent argument to counter parents' desires to protect their children's educational experiences and mental health or teachers' desires to protect their profession in order to better serve the children of their communities. It will not be enough for corporate America to say that profits are more important than anything else under the pretext that without profits none of us would have a job. The existence of the teaching profession itself is proof enough that quality jobs can exist precisely because there is a need for them and that they can exist outside the confines of private corporations. Furthermore, corporate America's appeal to a manufactured literacy crisis, even if initially believed by the public, cannot convince the average parent that his or her child needs to be a sacrificial lamb to solve this crisis, without first exploring all the available alternatives. But in exploring the alternatives, the phoniness of the crisis will be increasingly revealed.

The choice is between resignation and resistance. When it comes to defending children, democracy, and even reading, against child abuse, undemocratic government occupation of the classroom in support of corporate profit, and playing games with letters and sounds, the choice is quite clear.

References

Alexander, D. (2000, April 13). *Testimony: Hearings on the National Reading Panel report before the Subcommittee on Labor, Health and Human Services, and Education of the Senate Appropriations Committee.* Available: *www.nichd.nih.gov*

Altwerger, B., & Strauss, S. L. (2002). The business behind testing. *Language Arts 79,* 256–263.

Anderson, G. E., Whipple, A. D., & Jimerson, S. R. (2002, October). Grade retention: Achievement and mental health outcomes. *National Association of School Psychologists.* Available: *www.nasponline.org*

Associated Press. Schools drop naptime for testing prep. (2003, October 2). Gadsden, Alabama.

Augustine, N. R. (1997). A business leader's guide to setting academic standards. *Business Roundtable.* Available: *www.brtable.org*

Business Roundtable. (1993, August 1). *Workforce training and development for U.S. competitiveness.* Available: *www.brtable.org*

Business Roundtable. (1995, January 1). *Continuing the commitment: Essential components of a successful education system.* Available: *www.brtable.org*

Business Roundtable. (2001, spring). *Assessing and addressing the "testing backlash": Practical advice and current public opinion research for business coalitions and standards advocates.* Available: *www.brtable.org*

Cunningham, J. W. (2001). The National Reading Panel report. *Reading Research Quarterly, 36,* 326–335.

Flowers, S. (Senior Supervising Producer). (2002, November 18). *The Tavis Smiley Show* (Analysis: Civil liberties of high school students in regard to military recruitment). National Public Radio. Available: *www.npr.org*

Foorman, B. R., Francis, D. J., and Fletcher, J. M. (2003). Correcting errors. *Phi Delta Kappan, 84,* 719–720.

Garan, E. (2002). *Resisting reading mandates: How to triumph with the truth.* Portsmouth, NH: Heinemann.

Goodman, K. (2004). NCLB's pedagogy of the absurd. In K. Goodman, P. Shannon, Y. Goodman, & R. Rapoport, *Saving our schools: The case for public education: Saying no to No Child Left Behind* (pp. 39–48). Berkeley, CA: RDR.

Goodman, K., Shannon, P., Goodman, Y., & Rapoport, R. (2004). *Saving our schools: The case for public education: Saying no to No Child Left Behind.* Berkeley, CA: RDR.

Lyon, G. R. (1997, July 10). Testimony before the Committee on Education and the Workforce, U.S. House of Representatives. Available: *http:// edworkforce.house.gov*

Lyon, G. R. (1998, April 28). *Overview of reading and literacy initiatives.* Testimony before the Committee on Labor and Human Resources, U.S. Senate. Available: *www.readbygrade3.com*

Lyon, G. R. (2000, May 4). *Education research and evaluation and student achievement: Quality counts.* Testimony before the Committee on Education and the Workforce, U.S. House of Representatives. Available: *www.nichd.nih.gov*

Lyon, G. R. (2001, March 8). *Measuring success: Using assessments and accountability to raise student achievement.* Testimony before the Subcommittee on Education Reform, Committee on Education and the Workforce, U.S. House of Representatives. Available: *http://edworkforce.house.gov*

Mitka, M. (2001, May 23–30). Some physicians protest "high-stakes" tests. *Journal of the American Medical Association (JAMA), 285,* p. 2569.

Novack, J. R., & Fuller, B. (2004). Penalizing diverse schools: Similar test scores, but different students, bring federal sanctions. In K. Goodman, P. Shannon, Y. Goodman, & R. Rapoport, *Saving our schools: The case for*

public education: Saying no to No Child Left Behind (pp. 218–222).
Berkeley, CA: RDR.
Rust, Ed, Jr. (2001, March 8). Statement before the Subcommittee on Educa-
tion Reform, Committee on Education and the Workforce, U.S. House
of Representatives, Hearing on Business Views of Assessments and
Accountability in Education. Washington, DC. Available: *http://edwork
force.house.gov*
Strauss, S. L. (2003). Challenging the NICHD reading research agenda. *Phi
Delta Kappan, 84,* 38–42.
Twenty-first Century Workforce Commission. (2000, June). A nation of oppor-
tunity: Building America's twenty-first century workforce. Washington,
DC: National Alliance of Business and U.S. Department of Labor.

5

Follow the Money: Reading First Grants in Pennsylvania

PATRICK SHANNON AND JACQUELINE EDMONDSON
Pennsylvania State University

In this chapter, we situate the Reading First initiative of the No Child Left Behind policy as part of a larger movement to privatize public education by pushing public school to compete in an economic market system in which private corporations can make profits. In a reverse Robin Hood effect, Reading First robs from the poor to give to the rich, by making school the conduit through which federal funds targeted for improved reading instruction are channeled to businesses. We begin following this money by telling the story of one school district's attempt to participate in No Child Left Behind.

"They're setting us up. That's just what they're doing. They're setting us up." These were the first words out of Shelley Warner's mouth when she stopped by our offices one cold January day to discuss her experiences with applying for Pennsylvania's Reading First grant. Nationally, Reading First is part of the Bush administration's federal initiative No Child Left Behind, the most recent reauthorization of the Elementary and Secondary Education Act. The Pennsylvania Department of Education applied for Reading First money through this federal program. Once funding was awarded to it, the state identified districts that were eligible to apply based upon a combination of high poverty rates and low test scores. Shelley is the reading coordinator for one of those districts.

The Pennsylvania version of Reading First shares the federal intention to transform reading instruction in American classrooms from an "art into a science" (Neuman, as quoted in Schemo, 2002). Accordingly, the application for Pennsylvania's Reading First funding included the following explanation of the program:

The Reading First program focuses on putting proven methods of early reading instruction in classrooms. Through Reading First, school districts will receive support to apply scientifically based reading research—the proven instructional assessment tools consistent with this research—to ensure that all children learn to read well by the end of third grade. (p. 3)

The state lists the components of an effective reading program as phonemic awareness, phonics, vocabulary development, reading fluency, and reading comprehension—all of which are consistent with the National Reading Panel's report (2001), upon which the Reading First initiative is based. To be accepted for PA Reading First funding, school districts must account for these components across the primary grades or propose a plan that will bring their programs into compliance.

As the reading coordinator, Shelley was given the responsibility to complete her district's application for this grant. Five of the nine elementary schools in her district qualified for Reading First money based on the combination of high poverty rates and low scores on the Pennsylvania State System of Assessment (PSSA) reading test. As Shelley spoke more about her experiences with the PA Reading First initiative, it became obvious that there was substance to her claim that her district was being set up. Shelley completed and submitted her district's application in September 2002. She proposed that the government support the research-based language arts work already in place in her school by funding professional advisers to identify existing gaps in their current approach and to hire literacy coaches who could help support teachers' classroom instruction. Shelley was optimistic about the chances of her proposal because her district was concluding a state-funded five-year project to improve reading instruction based on the Ohio State Literacy Framework (see Literacy Collaborative® at Ohio State University, 2002). By emphasizing reading aloud, shared reading and writing, guided reading and writing, and independent reading and writing, the teachers in her district had helped students raise their test scores considerably on the PSSA tests. The latest third-grade scores were two points below the state average.

Just before Thanksgiving, however, the state rejected Shelley's application and the district's reading program, requesting that representatives from the district be sent to a technical support meeting in Harrisburg in early December. At that meeting, an assigned adviser would help the district rewrite its application in order to make sure that state officials would approve it. Until that meeting, Shelley would not be privy to reviewers' comments concerning the original application in order to prepare for the meeting. Because of the importance of the funding, the school district sent Shelley, three elementary school principals, and several teachers to Harrisburg. Upon their arrival, they learned that their assigned technical support adviser would not be available that day. In fact, he did not meet with them until the third day of the three-day event, and then he stated that lack of time prevented him from helping them with revisions to their grant. When Shelley and her colleagues left that meeting, they were unsure of what their next steps might be because their adviser had told them to review carefully the original application instructions for Reading First in Pennsylvania and to rewrite the grant by strictly adhering to those guidelines, which required (1) ninety minutes of uninterrupted reading instruction for all K–3 students; (2) purchase of instructional materials based on scientifically based research; (3) a plan for professional development of teachers based on the instructional program adopted; and (4) evaluation of student achievement through valid, reliable, replicable assessment tools. Shelley thought that her original application had met those guidelines with the Ohio State framework substituting for the instructional materials. However, her official Reading First technical support adviser explained to her that the Ohio State Literacy Framework was based on Reading Recovery theory and practice, which is not scientifically based. According to the adviser, the grant money was intended for the purchase of a federally approved reading program, like Open Court. Shelley explained:

> [Pennsylvania] wrote our [state's] proposal to the federal government that said that schools would adopt core-reading programs, and their translation of that is a book in a box. You'll buy the box of books. Not only will you buy the box of books, you will implement the box of books across the board. . . . [Pennsylvania officials] did not want to know about how things were going [for us]. They did not really want to know. They didn't have to know. . . Pennsylvania has basically put a straightjacket on their districts. (personal communication, January 17, 2003)

In effect, the state told Shelley that her district's reading program was too artistic, too labor intensive to be scientific. If the district desired Reading First funding, it must substitute technology for people—a scientific core reading program for the human expertise and presence that her district proposed. As Shelley explained, the state seemed uninterested in districts' accomplishments or plans for their local community. Rather, the state and its federal sponsors sought a universal solution, which denied the importance of the local. In the end, the federal money intended to help students learn to read would land in the coffers of educational publishers.

We have learned that Shelley's situation is not unique. For example, the *New York Times* recently described National Institute for Child Health and Human Development director of research on learning and behavior G. Reid

Lyon's disapproval of a phonics program that New York City school officials intend to adopt in order to qualify for New York State Reading First funding. Lyon argued that the program, Month-by-Month Phonics, had no scientific evidence to prove its effectiveness, even though the author of the program reports that it is research based. New York City schools stand to lose seventy million dollars if they do not cancel their order for Month-by-Month Phonics (Goodnough, 2003). Perhaps many school districts across the United States find themselves in similar situations as they attempt to improve reading instruction for their students by participating in the Reading First initiative of the No Child Left Behind policy. A very few eligible districts have decided to ignore the possibilities of new federal funding for reading instruction. Most, however, act like Shelley's district, working earnestly to secure the much needed funding in order to keep their financially strapped districts afloat while they work to find local solutions to the challenges of reading instruction.

Of course, financial incentives have been the lever to secure compliance with federal mandates for nearly fifty years. Although the federal government has no constitutional authority to determine the curricula in local schools, every presidential administration since Johnson has used financial incentives in order to induce compliance with federal laws and policies. In this way, the mechanisms of the Reading First initiative are nothing new. The George W. Bush administration does appear, however, to be meaner and more aggressive in its application of this financial carrot-and-stick approach, by restricting who can speak with authority about reading education to a small group of insiders and insisting that this authority determine what happens in every primary-grade classroom. Consider that Shelley's district made great progress in its local reading program through the federal and state Reading Excellence and America Reads funding. Now, continuation of that progress is in jeopardy because the district is denied a voice in defining what will happen during reading instruction in its schools. It appears that New York City will suffer the same fate. Why would Shelley's district or New York City schools choose to contradict their own better judgment in order to adopt a core reading program that they do not want or value? In order to address that question, we return to the story of Shelley's district to find that in fact, the decision may not be based on free choice at all.

Shelley's School District

Shelley's school district serves approximately five thousand students and covers an area equivalent to the size of Rhode Island. The district spans mountainous areas with many large land tracts designated as state game preserves. The poverty rate averages 40 percent across the district, with some schools serving communities in which as many as 82.7 percent of the children come from low-income families. Some children in the poorer regions of the district live in mountain hunting camps, often with dirt floors, no running water, and no telephone. These situations pose unique challenges for teachers. As the government mandates have increased for all students to meet the same standards and to score high on standardized reading tests, both teachers and students have experienced stronger pressures to cover more information in shorter periods of time than their peers in more affluent school districts. In part, this is what Shelley meant when she explained that the state and federal governments were setting up her district for failure.

Gainful employment is hard to find in many of the towns in the Shelley's district. Over the past fifty years, the economy in the district has come to a screeching halt. Logging, coal, and brickmaking industries that originally attracted immigrants to the region are now largely nonexistent, and the railroad that ushered in economic prosperity in the early part of the twentieth century left during the 1950s. In more recent years, the closing of a paper mill and an aircraft plant ended the region's employment in manufacturing and forced many small subcontractors out of business in its wake. Today, children attending district schools and growing up in this vastly beautiful part of Pennsylvania have no recollection of economically better times, and many parts of their towns now resemble war zones, with crumbling buildings and empty businesses. Burned-out shells of buildings have become a common sight because old electrical wiring and disrepair contribute to a large number of fires, and there are no public funds to remove the remains. The U.S. economy and the state and federal governments that regulate it have not been kind to Shelley's district or the community it serves.

Not only are jobs difficult to come by, but the local tax base to support local government and schools is low. Homes in some parts of the school district sell for as little as $4,000–$5,000, making real estate taxes minimal at best. There are no large entertainment venues to generate amusement taxes, and the amount of local money derived from state occupational and occupational privilege taxes throughout the region has decreased steadily over the past decade. These points are important to note because Pennsylvania's system for funding schools relies primarily on local sources, including real estate taxes (86 percent), earned income and net profit taxes (9 percent), and other taxes (5 percent). On average, Pennsylvania's public school districts receive 57 percent of their revenues from local taxes and 38 percent from the state. Because there is a vastly unequal tax base across Pennsylvania, in the

2000–2001[1] school year, some districts allocated as much as $11,855 per student while others could afford only as little as $3,675 per student. Shelley's school district falls a little below the middle of this continuum, spending approximately $5,404 per student. While at first glance this figure may seem to be a reasonable amount, closer examination of the district's revenue sources shows that only 43 percent of its general fund is from local sources. The remaining 57 percent of the district's budget depends on revenues from outside sources—the state and federal governments or private contracts. In order to economize, the district has consolidated many small community schools, trading the expense of busing for the savings on the maintenance on aging buildings and duplication of staff support.

Similar conditions haunt many rural communities throughout the United States (Beeson & Strange, 2000; Elder & Conger, 2000). Small rural communities are deteriorating because the businesses and farms that once sustained them are no longer considered viable in a market economy that does not value their existence. Despite the rhetoric that small business and family farms are the backbone of our democracy, small rural communities are often considered to be a drain on the economy, requiring expensive public programs to support their infrastructures and to maintain their schools and other social services. Unprotected economic vulnerability in a hostile economy and political climate forces these communities to compete against each other for their survival. Consider communities' eagerness to provide businesses large tax breaks to locate in their regions and their efforts to attract state and federal prisons in this light. Such competitions to attract capital from outside sources encourage communities to operate according to business principles in which the rationality of the bottom line is considered the primary means to protect the social welfare of both individuals and society as a whole. This has been the driving force in the U.S. economy for 250 years, and during the last 30 years it has become the primary force in all public and private matters.

Privatization of Shelley's District: A Lesson in Economic Policy

Before Margaret Thatcher, Ronald Reagan, or Alan Greenspan, before we heard of monetarism or supply-side economics, neoliberalism, or the Washington consensus, Milton Friedman rearticulated the central tenet of classical capitalist economics: free market rationality would fulfill all human needs, and eventually wants, if left alone to follow its nature. In fact, Friedman argued,

[1] This is the most recent data available.

whenever the government tried to address social problems, it proved futile at best and injurious to the very people it intended to help at worst. The grand plans of liberals, he argued, would certainly build government bureaucracy, but they would just as certainly make mistakes because of their scope and the complexity of our lives. With the ascendance of the International Monetary Fund, the Trilateral Commission, Reagan, George H. W. Bush, Clinton, and now George W. Bush, each part of the social welfare state created in the 1930s and the 1960s has been curtailed or eliminated, and many of the constraints on business created at the turn of the twentieth century, the 1930s, and the 1960s have now been cut back or repealed. In combination, these trends have enabled the nature of capitalism to force more people and more institutions into the marketplace regardless of their social circumstances, and all aspects of our lives have become open for business. The only remaining public programs are social security and public schooling. Until the latest round of securities fraud and corporate crime, social security was headed toward the privatization of Wall Street.

We see evidence of the movement to privatize public schools in the No Child Left Behind policy as it plays out in Shelley's district. Because the district's budget has been squeezed dry and it needs Title I federal dollars to keep its per pupil funding near the state average, the district is under pressure to demonstrate adequate yearly progress on test scores. For Pennsylvania, this means that schools cannot have more than 35 percent of their student scores at or below the basic level in math or more than 45 percent at or below that level in reading on the PSSA exams. If each school in a district does not meet or make progress toward those selected targets, then the state places sanctions on the failing schools and district until they right themselves. Sanctioned schools enter a "school improvement" sequence. During the first phase, district officials must alert parents that their children's school is failing and inform them that parents can choose to send their children to any public school within their district at the district's expense. If no adequate improvement on test scores is noted after one year, state sanctions require the addition of private tutoring or other supplemental services (paid for by the district) to school choice. If again test scores do not improve dramatically, the state intervenes in the administration and curriculum of the school and district, which might include adopting a new curriculum, hiring new administration, or replacing staff. If this too fails to raise test scores accordingly, then the state restructures the district. In Pennsylvania, restructuring has meant the subcontracting of some or all school duties to private corporations (see Shannon, 2002, for a brief account of Edison Schools Corporation in Philadelphia schools). According to No Child Left Behind policy, every student must be above the basic level by 2013 or restructuring is in order.

The absurdity of these sanctions is not lost on Shelley. Notification of school failure (that the school is "in need of improvement") is a rhetorical act that undercuts the school's authority within a community. Once labeled and without necessary support in classrooms, schools will find it difficult to accelerate the progress of children from homes that the economy has long ago left behind. The costs for busing students across her district and providing private tutoring would cut deeply into an already inadequate budget. Even if the district could afford the transportation costs, school buildings are already filled to capacity. Shelley explained, "Where are we supposed to put them? Our schools are full. And we've sold a bunch. They've sold all the extra ones they have. They consolidated to try to save money because we're so strapped." State advice and policies have also proved costly in the past. A charter school, full-day kindergarten, and private tutoring for special needs students (who must travel great distances to meet with tutors) without increased funding have substantially weakened the budget, making the district less likely to reach the arbitrary goals of No Child Left Behind and more vulnerable to the marketplace for increased funding in the Reading First initiative. The economy has made sure that there can be little increase in local contribution.

Therefore, if Shelley is not successful in securing the Reading First funds by accepting the forced purchase of a core reading program, her district is likely to enter the school improvement privatization spiral. This is not an expression of the freedom to choose in which, as Milton Friedman suggested, the free market will provide for all of us. Freedom is the right to participate in the development of alternative solutions and then to select from among them the one that is most likely to work toward the consequences we value. Shelley's district did not and could not participate in the identification of alternatives because the governmental apparatus that is supposed to help them will not allow it, and the district cannot afford to refuse state and federal funding and still keep its schools open. The district, like so many across the country, is trapped.

What's Going on Here?

Shelley and we know that the outcomes in reading instruction in public schools are not perfect, much as we'd like them to be. Too many students do not learn to use print literacy to meet the textual demands on their lives or to make better sense of themselves, others, or the social structures that surround them. Too many of these students are poor, minorities, or second language learners. We agree with the federal government that no child should be left behind at, in, or from school. All parties accept reading as a first priority of elementary schooling. Yet we disagree about what to do in order to improve the chances that all children will learn to use reading well. Shelley believes in freedom. That is, she seeks a community-based mechanism that can address community problems. She has been working toward this goal for at least five years. In consultation with teachers, parents, and community members, her district decided to develop the teaching knowledge and capacities of classroom teachers in order to meet the challenge of teaching the children in their communities to read. The district recognized that it needed financial help from the state and outside expertise to accomplish its goals. It expected and still hopes that the government will reward its initiative and continuing success. And the district can supply scientific evidence that it is succeeding.

We value Shelley's approach to the problem, but we think that the approach must be embedded in a larger social program to be effective. As we have tried to explain, Shelley was correct in her initial statement, "They are setting us up." The federal and state governments have positioned her district as a consumer of official scientific solutions that ignore local concerns and needs, solutions that should blame themselves when they do not help the community or its citizens. The teachers and students in Shelley's district do not start with the same chances of success as their more affluent counterparts across that state and the nation. Yet they are required to accomplish the same goals as all others during the same time period with fewer resources. This seems unfair to us, and we seek justice in and outside of reading programs. To begin, we call for a renaming of the problem. As we see it, the problem is not that students are failing schools or that schools are failing students. Rather, the state and federal governments are failing to protect rural and urban communities from an economy that will not keep their well-being clearly in mind. As a consequence of that failure, too many students and schools are not able to work productively. There are too many families living in poverty, too many without adequate health and dental care, too many hungry, too many without adequate housing. We believe that an adequate policy to leave no child behind would address these fundamental issues.

To begin to help students learn, the government must admit its responsibility for a heartless economy and begin to fight poverty much more aggressively. We recognize that our solution will not be the free choice of the Bush administration, nor was it Clinton's. There is no scientific evidence that guaranteed income, health care, nutrition, and housing will raise test scores. But there is no scientific evidence that high academic standards, high-stakes testing, forced core reading programs, or state takeovers will raise test scores or teach students to use reading wisely (Levin, 1998). All of these are political and moral decisions based on our answers to the question How do we wish to live together? We choose to live in a democracy in which freedom is defined as the opportunity to frame the choices of our future as well as to make those choices. In such a democracy with attention to human needs, Shelley's district would be free to choose whether or not to follow federal government initiatives in reading.

The federal government's only solution at this point is the marketplace because the liberal solution of public schooling is too expensive, too independent, and too community based to benefit the economy. By cutting public schools' economic security and forcing them to compete for necessary funding and by setting test scores as the official goal of all schooling, the government creates many new markets and transforms school personnel from educators to consumers. For example, in order to compete for Reading First funding, districts seek expert advice on how to increase the chances of success. Across the country, businesses like Voyager Expanded Learning incorporate to meet that market. Once districts are funded, educational publishing corporations compete as core reading programs. They employ consultants in order to increase their chances of remaining or being added to the official list. State tests to measure continuous progress open another market for Microsoft, Scantron, and others to fill. State takeovers make room for Edison Schools, and the list goes on. According to market logic, the effective products and services will drive the ineffective products and services from the market because all consumers will act rationally in their own interests. But what are the real interests of Shelley's district? Certainly the market has already cast its judgment on the adults in that community. What scientific or any other type of evidence do we have that the market will be kinder to their children?

No Child Left Behind and Reading First policies should not surprise those who live in Shelley's district. Longtime residents in towns throughout the region are well aware that the government will not advocate for them. Instead, the government has allowed businesses to move in and out of the community, and it has continued to support exploitative policies that endorse a view that bigger is better. The result is a vicious cycle that depletes the tax base from rural communities, where services like public education and health care are dwindling or no longer available, in turn making it difficult if not impossible to draw more residents and new businesses to the community. Instead, the government continues to subsidize corporations under the pretense that competition is healthy and should be rewarded, further endorsing an erroneous view that large-scale efficiency will bolster the American economy and eventually benefit all Americans. More than nine million rural Americans now live in poverty, and countless more feel the effects of rural decline.

What Can We Do?

School districts without sufficient budgets to keep schools open and operating have no free choice to refuse Reading First money and the mandated reading curricula that follow. Shelley and we recognize this. Although we have not looked closely enough to identify them for ourselves, we are certain that teachers and supervisors will find spaces within the programs to subvert some of the negative effects that come from unfair competitions and pointless objectives. For the moment, teachers and students in districts like Shelley's and New York City Schools must find ways to persevere. We recommend two actions that might make that moment as short as possible.

First, we suggest a campaign to make the citizens in their communities aware of the vital importance of public schools and the movement to make them private spaces for profit. This is a literacy campaign to help citizens read beyond the rhetoric of choice, high standards, and science to see the antidemocratic objectives of federal and state educational policies based on classical economic principles of free markets. When they look closely, adults recognize that these markets are not free (as some businesses and industries get government protection and others do not) and that they are not kind (as very few adults seem secure in their jobs). Biased, cruel markets cannot be what adults want for their children. Perhaps with protection for their children, they can remember what government protections might mean for adults as well.

With this new knowledge or even with the sentiment that No Child Left Behind and Reading First do not have children's interests at heart, citizens and teachers can work in a political campaign to reverse the direction of educational policy. This means making an effort to question politicians about their understandings of reading and its role in a democratic society. As Thomas Jefferson acknowledged in 1786, "If a nation expects to be ignorant and free, in a state of civilization, it expects what never was and will never be" (as quoted in Ford 1893). If this is still true today, and we believe that it is, reading education must be an important criterion on which we base our votes for anyone from school board officials to presidents and all the levels of government in between. If they cannot see the damage that unrestricted markets can and will do in schools, then vote the bastards out.

And that's just what happened. The November 2002 state election brought a new governor and political party to the administrative branch of the Pennsylvania state government. Governor Rendell replaced the administrators of the department of education (the old ones went to Washington, DC), who in turn replaced those in charge of the Reading First initiative in our state. These new officials seemed to recognize that Shelley's district's use of the Ohio State Literacy Framework is producing positive instructional results and rewarded their efforts with funding to continue and extend their efforts. This was Shelley's interpretation of her conversation with the new Reading First state coordinator, Corinne Eisenhart, who informed Shelley that her district was awarded $425,600 for each of six years in order to implement its original plan to improve reading instruction. Because nothing else changed in the relationship between the district and the state, it seems reasonable to conclude that the change in governing party is the reason for the new funding.

Since the grant requirement that reading programs had to be scientifically based did not change, the new Pennsylvania Reading First administration must deem the Ohio State Literacy Framework to be sufficiently scientific to warrant funding. Accordingly, it must have a broader or different definition of science than the previous administration. And here is where the politics become most apparent. There is more than one reasonable definition of science in both the so-called hard and soft academic disciplines, and education is not immune to the debate about the definition of science. In reading education, the gauntlet was tossed down during a federally sponsored public meeting for the National Reading Panel when Ed Kame'enui stated that the basic task of the NRP was to determine the single definition of science for reading education in the United States. Since that time, the NRP and the officials at the National Institute for Child Health and Human Development have tried to enforce one definition. Despite their best efforts, multiple definitions continue to circulate.

Although the new Pennsylvania Reading First administration seems more trusting and open and somewhat less wed to the immediacy of the marketplace, it still set up Shelley's rural district by not recognizing its unique problems of struggling with poor funding, job flight, and diminishing prospects. The area just lost its largest manufacturing plant and one thousand jobs. Yet the state still expects the district to meet the same standards during the same time frame as suburban districts that face none of these challenges. Moreover, the state has not revised the costly steps of NCLB school improvement. In short, the district is still underfunded and susceptible to market forces.

This, of course, is the reality of any changes in school reform. They will not automatically ameliorate the social conditions that led to the problems of schooling in the first place. But there are rumblings about No Child Left Behind and Reading First policies in many states, and they may be the start of a fundamental shift in citizens' support for current governmental policies on other issues as well. On April 27, 2004, on the floor of the U.S. Senate, Democratic Leader Tom Daschle called for Congress to follow the money that was promised in the original No Child Left Behind law but not delivered to public schools. He noted that twenty-three states have lodged formal complaints against the law and that Republican-controlled legislatures in Utah and Virginia debated whether or not to comply with the law. These are important first steps.

References

Beeson, E., & Strange, M. (2000). Why rural matters: The need for every state to take action on rural education. Report prepared for the Rural School and Community Trust.

Elder, G., & Conger, R. (2000). *Children of the land: Adversity and success in rural America.* Chicago: University of Chicago Press.

Goodnough, A. (2003). Bush adviser casts doubt on the benefits of phonics program. *New York Times.*

Jefferson, T. (1893). A bill for the more general diffusion of knowledge. In. P. Ford, ed. *The Writings of Thomas Jefferson.* New York: Putnam.

Levin, H. (1998). Educational performance standards and the economy. *Educational Researcher, 27*(4), 4–10.

Literacy Collaborative® at Ohio State University. (2002). Primary literacy framework. Available: *http://www.lcosu.org/geninfo/fwprimary.htm*

National Reading Panel. (2001). Summary. *http://www.nichd.nib.gov. publications/nrp/intro/htm*

Schemo, D. (2002, January 9). Education bill urges new emphasis on phonics as method for teaching reading. *New York Times,* p. A16.

Shannon, P. (2002). Philadelphia freedom. *The Reading Teacher 56*(1), 48–50.

6

Scripted Reading Instruction: Help or Hindrance?

ROBERT LAND AND MARGARET MOUSTAFA

California State University, Los Angeles

With the governor of California by his side, the superintendent of instruction of the Los Angeles Unified School District, our country's second largest school district, released the district's 2002 test scores, grades 2–11, on the ninth edition of the Stanford Achievement Test, or SAT 9 (pronounced as the verb *sat*). *Los Angeles Times* writers Helfand, Moore, and Hayasaki (2002) began their front-page report with "Los Angeles elementary schools have raised their standardized test scores for the fourth straight year—the strongest evidence yet that the district's reading and math reforms are working . . ."

Appearing not to notice the contradictions in what they were saying, Helfand and his colleagues reported, "Elementary students posted the highest scores and showed the most growth in math," but then attributed the growth in test scores to Open Court, "a heavily scripted, step-by-step" reading instructional program. They went on to report that Open Court, the program they credited for having "raised [the district's] standardized test scores the fourth straight year," was not used in almost all of the districts' second-grade classrooms until the last two of the four years, nor in almost all of the districts' third-, fourth-, and fifth-grade classrooms until the last of the four years.

Helfand and his colleagues are not alone in crediting Open Court for raising scores. A California Department of Education administrator told the professors of education at a meeting hosted by the Center for the Improvement of Reading Instruction in Ontario, California, in January 2002, that "Open Court raises scores." An administrator for Sacramento City Unified School District told educators at the May 2002 International Reading Association Convention in San Francisco that since her district had begun using Open Court, the students' SAT 9 test scores had been rising.

Vickie Boyd (2001) interviewed administrators and classroom teachers in four central California school districts on their views of scripted instructional programs. She found administrators saw scripted programs as a remedy for teacher deficits while classroom teachers were concerned about scripted programs not addressing students' varying instructional needs, limiting or eliminating large areas of the school curriculum, and discouraging teachers from continuing in the profession. However, both administrators and classroom teachers saw scripted programs as advantageous for new and substitute teachers and having positive effects on SAT 9 test scores.

In this chapter, we examine the propositions that (1) scripted reading instructional programs raise reading scores on high-stakes tests, and (2) scripted reading instructional programs compensate for a lack of teacher professional preparation. The two scripted reading programs we studied were Open Court, published by McGraw-Hill, and Success for All, published by the Success for All Foundation. The high-stakes test we compared them with was the SAT 9. We begin by defining scripted reading instruction and then, to provide context for our study, describe the recent history of high-stakes testing and scripted reading instruction in California and two school districts in California, Sacramento City Unified School District (Sacramento City) and Los Angeles Unified School District (LAUSD). We then draw from Robert Linn's research on high-stakes testing and report on our own study on the effectiveness of scripted reading instruction as measured by high-stakes testing.

Scripted Reading Instruction

Scripted and unscripted instructional programs are distinguished by the amount of professional judgment teachers are allowed to exercise in teaching. Traditionally scripted programs provide teachers with a script for what they are to say *verbatim* during instruction. Unscripted programs describe activities, provide examples, and expect teachers to use their professional knowledge of their particular students to choose activities that would be most helpful to them.

While it is generally agreed that Success for All is a scripted program, some object to Open Court being called a scripted program. They point to the teacher's manual in Open Court as proof that Open Court is *not* a scripted program.

We agree that the teacher's manuals of the 1995, 2000, and 2002 editions of Open Court look like those of unscripted programs. However, in every districtwide adoption of Open Court we know of in California, the state in which our study took place, teachers are required to complete every activity described in the teachers manual with the entire class and to do it at a prescribed pace (i.e., so many lessons within so many days), whether it is appropriate for the particular students in their classes or not. In the greater Los Angeles area, we have observed teachers of the same grade in different school districts teaching the same lesson from Open Court within the same week.

Deborah Anderluh (1998) of the *Sacramento Bee* in Sacramento, California, wrote that Open Court "lasts two to three hours a day, with half that time spent in whole group instruction. The detailed scripting, combined with the oversight of roving coaches, means that from school to school, teachers are presenting basically the same lesson at a given grade level in a given week."

Michael Bazeley (2000) of the *San Jose Mercury News* in San Jose, California, said, "As one of the most strictly orchestrated programs on the market, *Open Court* is helping bury a notion central to public education for decades—that the classroom revolves around the teacher as a trained professional in control of what happens and when. With *Open Court*, teachers are told what to do from the minute class starts."

Hence, as currently being implemented in California, we see the 1995, 2000, and 2002 editions of Open Court as a new form of scripted instruction, not one where the teacher's words are scripted verbatim, but one in which *what, when,* and *how* teachers teach is controlled by people outside the classroom, not amenable to classroom teachers' judgment based on their knowledge of their students.

High-Stakes Testing in California

In 1997 the governor of California signed into law Senate Bill 376 which required all public school districts in California to use a single standardized test, designated by the California Board of Education, to test each student in grades 2 through 11. The board chose the SAT 9, a norm-referenced test. In norm-referenced tests, questions are designed so that 75 percent of the test takers will score at or above 25 percent, 50 percent will score at or above 50 percent, and 25 percent will score at or above 75 percent. A score of 50 percent is average.

In the spring of 1998, California began the first of five consecutive years of statewide testing in grades 2 through 11, using SAT 9 and publishing the state's and each district's and school's reading, language arts, and math scores on the California Department of Education's website, *www.cde.ca.gov*. Coupled with the testing were a series of laws passed under the next governor, Assembly Bill 1626 (1998), Senate Bill IX (1999), and Assembly Bill X 12 (1999), which rewarded students, teachers, and school staffs with cash bonuses in schools that met target scores on the SAT 9 and threatened students with retention in grade, teachers with loss of jobs, and school districts with loss of autonomy if they did not meet target scores.

Scripted Reading Instruction in California and Two School Districts

California is a "textbook adoption" state, not a "local control" state. In local control states, each school district makes its own decisions about which textbooks to purchase. In textbook adoption states, the state decides which textbooks can be bought with state money.

In California, eighteen months before the adoption year in each curricular area, the state tells textbook publishers the criteria it will use to decide whether it will adopt given textbooks during the next adoption cycle in that curricular area. Then, during the adoption year, a committee reviews texts submitted for adoption and recommends to the California Board of Education that texts be state adopted or not. California school districts, then, can use state textbook money to purchase state-adopted texts. Districts wishing to purchase texts that are not state adopted need to find alternative funding sources for such purchases, a formidable challenge for California's cash-strapped schools.

In 1996, the reading/language arts teacher specialists on California's Instructional Resources Evaluation panel, the panel that reviews texts for inclusion on the state's list of adopted texts, recommended that Open Court's 1995 edition, *Collection for Young Scholars, not* be placed on California's textbook adoption list (Holland, 1996). Nevertheless, in December of the same year the California Board of Education added Open Court to the list.

In 1997 the Board of Education of Sacramento City Unified School District adopted Open Court for fifty-five of its sixty elementary schools, K–6, and accepted a grant from the Packard Foundation for Open Court coaches (Saunders, 1999). The remaining five schools used Success for All. Thus, from the 1997–98 school year until the present, Sacramento City has used only scripted reading programs in its K–6 elementary schools.

In June of 1999, a year after the second statewide administration of the SAT 9, Debra Saunders of the *San Francisco Chronicle* wrote that since signing on with Open Court and receiving a grant from the Packard Foundation for teaching coaches, "[SAT 9 reading] scores for the Sacramento City Unified School District rose from the 35th percentile nationally in reading for first-graders [in 1997, before Open Court was used] to the 54th percentile [in 1998, the first year Open Court was used] to the 62nd percentile [in 1999, the second year Open Court was used]." The following August, the *LA Times* ran a similar article on its Sunday front page lauding Sacramento City's rising test scores due to its use of Open Court (Helfand, 1999).

In September of 1999 the Los Angeles Unified School District Board of Education "adopted a comprehensive District Reading Plan, 1999–2003, for elementary schools scoring below the 50th percentile on spring 1999 Grades 2 and 3 SAT 9 reading tests" (Schroeder, 1999). The district required schools with average scores below the fiftieth percentile in reading to choose one of three scripted reading programs, Open Court, Reading Mastery, or Success for All, by November 24, 1999 (Schroeder, 1999). Most elementary schools in LAUSD had average scores below the fiftieth percentile in reading on the SAT 9 in 1999.

In January of 2000 the *Los Angeles Times* reported that "92% of the district's low-performing campuses—372 elementary schools—recently picked Open Court when given three options" (Helfand, 2000a), thus creating the largest reading textbook adoption ever recorded (McGraw-Hill, 2000, p. 11). The change was phased in over a two-year period. Kindergarten through second-grade classrooms began using Open Court at the beginning of the 2000–2001 school year, and third- through fifth-grade classrooms began using it at the beginning of the 2001–2002 school year (Helfand, 2000b).

Rising Test Scores

Figure 6–1 shows the percent of "all students" (i.e., native and nonnative speakers of English, newcomers and longtime residents alike) who scored at or above the fiftieth national percentile rank on the SAT 9 in reading for LAUSD from 1998 to 2002. Figure 6–2 shows the percent of "English only and fluent English proficient students" (i.e., native speakers of English and nonnative speakers of English who have become as proficient as their English-only peers in spoken and written English) who scored at or above the fiftieth

SPRING	GRADE			
	2nd	3rd	4th	5th
2002	44	33	35	31
2001	37	31	29	29
2000	32	25	26	26
1999	24	21	22	24
1998	26	21	21	23

Source: California Department of Education (*www.cde.ca.gov*)

Figure 6–1. *Los Angeles Unified School District, All Students, 1998–2002. Percent Scoring at or Above the Fiftieth National Percentile Rank on SAT 9 in Reading.*

SPRING	GRADE			
	2nd	3rd	4th	5th
2002	60	53	51	47
2001	55	50	46	44
2000	50	45	44	42
1999	42	40	40	39

Source: California Department of Education (*www.cde.ca.gov*)
* District scores were not disaggregated by this category in 1998.

Figure 6–2. *Los Angeles Unified School District, English Only and Fluent English Proficient Students, 1999–2002*. *Percent Scoring at or Above the Fiftieth National Percentile Rank on SAT 9 in Reading.*

national percentile rank on the SAT 9 in reading for LAUSD from 1999 to 2002. (The state did not publish the 1998 district scores of "English only and fluent English proficient students.")

While the press cited the percent of "all students" who scored at or above the fiftieth percentile on the SAT 9, for purposes of judging student progress, the percent of "English only and fluent English proficient students" is a more valid statistic. There are several reasons for this. Although it takes five to seven years for nonnative speakers of English to achieve in English at levels equivalent to native speakers (Collier, 1989), the scores of nonnative speakers of English still learning English included in the "all students" category are not disaggregated by the number of years the children have been in U.S. schools, rendering these scores meaningless. Moreover, the percent of children still learning English in a given district varies from district to district and from year to year. Hence, the impact of these students' scores on the percent scoring at or above the fiftieth percentile would vary accordingly. Finally, the SAT 9 was normed on a population of students where only 1.8 percent of the students were still learning English.

As can be seen in Figure 6–2, LAUSD's SAT 9 reading scores rose from 1999 to 2002. What would explain this? Clearly it cannot be attributed to Open Court for all four years as Open Court was used in only 49 of 426 elementary LAUSD schools until July 2000 (Helfand, 2000b; Helfand et al., 2002). It was not implemented nearly districtwide in second grade until the 2000–01 school year, and it was not implemented nearly districtwide in grades 3–5 until the 2001–02 school year. In LAUSD's own study of its first year of almost districtwide implementation of Open Court in second grade, Oliver (2002) described the 37 Open Court schools in the study as high-implementing and low-implementing Open Court schools. She found *lower* normal curve equivalent (NCE) gains (a measure of how individual students have done from one grade to the next) on the reading comprehension subtest on SAT 9 in the high-implementing Open Court schools than in the low-implementing Open Court schools (p. 79, Table 41). She also found that none of the Open Court schools in the study that were experienced with Open Court were high-implementing Open Court schools (p. 81, Table 44).

A better explanation for LAUSD's rising SAT 9 reading test scores from 1998 to 2002 can be found in how the test is administered and how the scores are interpreted. Robert Linn (2000) reviewed the last fifty years of high-stakes/accountability testing. He found gains in scores each successive year a given test was used for accountability purposes. He provides an example of a district's third-grade math test scores rising from a grade equivalent of 3.7 the first year, to 4.0 the second year, to 4.1 the third year, to 4.3 the fourth year it was given but returning to 3.7 when an alternate version of the test was also given the fourth year.

Linn (2000) explains rising test scores over successive years as a consequence of using the same test questions with the same norms for high-stakes purposes year after year. To this, we add that, unlike the Scholastic Aptitude Test that older students take for admission to college, for which the people who administer and proctor the exam have no vested interest in the test results, the people who administer and proctor the SAT 9 in elementary schools are the teachers of the students taking the test. In California, laws that reward and sanction teachers based on the test scores of their students compel teachers to have an interest in high-stakes test outcomes. In the course of administering and proctoring the SAT 9, teachers see the questions. By the second year the test is administered, they see the same questions repeated. Once teachers see the questions, they cannot help but consciously or unconsciously teach to the test in subsequent years.

Whether one interprets SAT 9 scores as rising from year to year or not depends on how one compares scores. Figures 6–3 and 6–4 show the percent of students scoring at or above the fiftieth national percentile rank on the SAT 9 in reading for California from 1998 through 2002. Figure 6–3 shows the percent of "all students" scoring at or above the fiftieth percentile on the SAT 9 and Figure 6–4 shows the percent of "English only and fluent English proficient students." If we read Figure 6–3 from bottom to top, comparing percentiles within the same grade (e.g., from second grade in 1998 to second grade in 2002), we see an increase each year in the percent scoring at or above the fiftieth percentile. From 1998 to 2002 there was a thirteen-point increase in second grade, a nine-point increase in third grade, a nine-point increase in fourth grade, and a five-point increase in fifth grade.

	GRADE			
SPRING	2nd	3rd	4th	5th
2002	53	47	49	46
2001	51	46	47	45
2000	49	44	45	44
1999	44	41	41	42
1998	40	38	40	41
Source: California Department of Education (*www.cde.ca.gov*)				

Figure 6–3. *State of California, All Students, 1998–2002. Percent Scoring at or Above the Fiftieth National Percentile Rank on SAT 9 in Reading.*

However, if we read Figure 6–3 diagonally upward, following the children from second to fifth grade, the increase in the percent of children scoring at or above the fiftieth percentile is much smaller. Of the children who were in second grade in 1998, there was only a five-point increase from second to fifth grade. Similarly, of the children who were in second grade in 1999, there was only a two-percentile point increase from second to fifth grade.

When we look at the percent of English-only and fluent English-proficient students scoring at or above the fiftieth percentile in Figure 6–4, we see the same pattern of greater gains in same-grade comparisons over successive years than when we follow the children through the grades. For example, between 1998 and 2002 there was a seventeen-point increase in the percent of children scoring at or above the fiftieth percentile in second grade. Yet of the children who were in second grade in 1998, there was only a nine-point increase from second to fifth grade. Of the children who were in second grade in 1999, there was only a two-point increase from second to fifth grade.

	GRADE			
SPRING	2nd	3rd	4th	5th
2002	65	61	61	58
2001	63	59	59	57
2000	61	57	57	55
1999	56	53	53	53
1998	48	47	49	50
Source: California Department of Education (*www.cde.ca.gov*)				

Figure 6–4. *State of California, English Only and Fluent English Proficient Students, 1998–2002. Percent Scoring at or Above the Fiftieth National Percentile Rank on SAT 9 in Reading.*

Figures 6–1 and 6–2 show the same pattern of higher test scores in same-grade comparisons than in successive-grade comparisons in LAUSD as at the state level. Additionally, LAUSD's scores may have been positively impacted by its retention policy. In her study of fifty sample LAUSD schools, Oliver (2002) found higher average normal curve equivalent (NCE) gains as measured by the SAT 9 among the schools in her study when the scores of retained students were included than when they were excluded. Altogether, LAUSD's SAT 9 rising scores speak more to teachers getting better at teaching to the test—and retained children getting better at taking the test—than to children progressing at accelerated rates.

Linn (2000) suggests there are several reasons that high-stakes/account-ability testing appeals to policy makers: (1) tests are relatively inexpensive compared to changes such as class size reduction or hiring and training teacher aides, (2) testing can be externally mandated and hence is easier to implement than changes within the classroom, (3) testing can be rapidly implemented within the term of office of elected officials, and (4) results are visible; they can be reported to the press. Elaborating on the fourth reason, Linn says:

> Based on past experience, policymakers can reasonably expect an increase in scores in the first few years of a program . . . with or without real improvement in the broader achievement constructs that tests and assessments are intended to measure. The resulting overly rosy picture that is painted by short-term gains observed in most new testing programs gives the impression of improvement right on schedule for the next election. (p. 4)

The insistence of one California governor on high-stakes testing and the presence of his successor at the event to announce LAUSD's rising test scores are consistent with Linn's observation that high-stakes tests are politically motivated.

Scripted Reading Instruction and Reading Scores on High-Stakes Tests

Given this background, let us now look at our first research question: Do scripted reading instructional programs raise reading scores on high-stakes tests? Since Sacramento City used scripted reading programs in all of its elementary schools (Open Court in fifty-five schools and Success for All in the remaining five schools) each of the years the SAT 9 was given statewide, it serves as a good district to use in investigating if scripted reading instructional programs raise reading scores on high-stakes tests. Figures 6–5 and 6–6 show the percent of children scoring at or above the fiftieth percentile on the

SPRING	GRADE				
	1st	2nd	3rd	4th	5th
2002		55	40	44	41
2001		56	42	43	40
2000		53	40	39	38
1999	62	51	37	36	37
1998	54	35	29	33	33

Sources: First grade, Saunders (1999)

Second through fifth grades, California Department of Education (*www.cde.ca.gov*)

Figure 6–5. *Sacramento City Unified School District, All Students, 1998–2002. Percent Scoring at or Above the Fiftieth National Percentile Rank on SAT 9 in Reading.*

SAT 9 in reading in Sacramento City from 1998 through 2002. Figure 6–5 shows the percent of "all students" scoring at or above the fiftieth percentile while Figure 6–6 shows the percent for "English only and fluent English proficient students."

Once again we see a difference in year-to-year scores depending on whether we compare same grades over successive years or follow the children through the grades. If we read Figure 6–5 from bottom to top, comparing scores within the same grade, we see a dramatic increase in the percent of children scoring at or above the fiftieth percentile. Between 1998 and 2002 there was a twenty-percentile point increase in children scoring at or above the fiftieth percentile in second grade. Similarly, between 1998 and 2002 there was an eleven-point increase in third grade, an eleven-point increase in fourth grade, and an eight-point increase in fifth grade.

SPRING	GRADE			
	2nd	3rd	4th	5th
2002	58	48	53	51
2001	61	52	54	50
2000	61	51	49	49
1999	59	48	46	47

Source: California Department of Education (*www.cde.ca.gov*)
* District scores were not disaggregated by this category in 1998.

Figure 6–6. *Sacramento City Unified School District, English Only and Fluent English Proficient Students, 1999–2002*. *Percent Scoring at or Above the Fiftieth National Percentile Rank on SAT 9 in Reading.*

However, if we read Figure 6–5 diagonally upward, following the children through the grades, we see the percent of children scoring at or above the fiftieth percentile *declining*. The children who were in second grade in spring 1999 were in first grade in 1997–98, the first year scripted reading programs were used districtwide in Sacramento City. While 51 percent of these children scored at or above the fiftieth percentile in second grade, only 41 percent of them scored at or above the fiftieth percentile by fifth grade. While 53 percent of the children who were in second grade in 2000 scored at or above the fiftieth percentile in second grade, only 44 percent of them scored at or above the fiftieth percentile by fourth grade. While 56 percent of the children who were in second grade in 2001 scored at or above the fiftieth percentile in second grade, only 40 percent of them scored at or above the fiftieth percentile the next year.

The same declining pattern can be seen in Figure 6–6 if we follow the English-only and fluent English-proficient students through the grades, beginning with the children who were in second grade in 1998–99, or first grade in 1997–98, the first year scripted reading programs were used districtwide. This declining pattern in Sacramento City is consistent with the pattern we found in other school districts using Open Court (Moustafa & Land, 2002; Moustafa, 2002).

Scripted Reading Instruction, Teacher Preparation, and Scores on High-Stakes Tests

Now let us look at our second research question: Do scripted reading instructional programs compensate for a lack of teacher professional preparation? To answer this question, we turned to the Los Angeles Unified School District, where there was variability from 1998 to 2002 in schools as to whether schools used scripted reading instruction or not and as to how many teachers were credentialed or not.

Method

We compared the percent of English-only and fluent English-proficient students, grades 2 through 5, scoring at or above the fiftieth percentile on the SAT 9 in LAUSD schools using *scripted* reading instructional programs with the percent of English-only and fluent English-proficient students scoring at or above the fiftieth percentile on the SAT 9 in LAUSD schools using *unscripted* programs without decodable texts. The study was limited to schools with 50 percent or more of the children on free and reduced-price meals.

The scripted reading instructional programs in our study were Open Court and Success for All. The *unscripted* reading instructional programs without decodable texts were Invitations to Literacy (published by Houghton Mifflin), Literacy Places (published by Scholastic), and Signatures (published by Harcourt Brace). We excluded one *unscripted* reading instructional program, Spotlight on Literacy (published by McGraw-Hill), because it had decodable texts. Decodable texts are texts based on letter-sound correspondences that have been taught. Consequently, they have distorted language and are more difficult for children to read than texts with familiar, natural language (Bridge, Winograd, and Haley, 1982).

Schools that used a program in combination with a program not in the study, or used both scripted and unscripted programs, were excluded from the study. Schools and/or grades where programs were not used in a particular year (e.g., the spring 2001 second-grade scores of schools that switched from an unscripted to a scripted program in fall 2000) were excluded.

The first year we examined was 1999 because that was the first year the state disaggregated scores at the school level by whether the students were English proficient or still learning English. The last year we looked at was 2001 as that was the last year before Open Court was used almost districtwide in grades 3–5. Overall, the analyses included data from 98,345 student scores at 183 schools and 1,899 grades.

Schools in the study ranged in the level of credentialed teachers from 46 percent to 87 percent in 1999. Schools were divided into two groups: those with lower levels (71 percent or fewer) of credentialed teachers and those with higher levels (72 percent or more) of credentialed teachers.

Findings

We found that the percent of students scoring at or above the fiftieth percentile on the SAT 9 test of reading achievement was significantly lower in schools with scripted programs than in schools with unscripted programs ($p < .0001$). As shown in Figure 6–7, we found the percent of students scoring at or above the fiftieth percentile rose each year of the study regardless of the type of reading instructional program. Within this rising pattern, the percent of students scoring at or above the fiftieth percentile was (1) lower in schools with lower levels of credentialed teachers than in schools with higher levels of credentialed teachers, (2) lower in schools with scripted programs than in schools with unscripted programs, and (3) lowest in schools with low levels of credentialed teachers and scripted programs.

	71% or Fewer Teachers Credentialed		72% or More Teachers Credentialed	
SPRING	Scripted Programs	Unscripted Programs	Scripted Programs	Unscripted Programs
2001	31	38	44	44
2000	27	35	37	40
1999	22	30	31	35
Overall scripted programs mean = 31.2, unscripted programs mean = 36.8 $F (1/1870df) = 31.8$, $p < .0001$				

Figure 6–7. *Los Angeles Unified School District, English Only and Fluent English Proficient Students, 1999–2001. Percent Scoring at or Above the Fiftieth National Percentile Rank on SAT 9 in Reading by Year, Level of Teachers Credentialed, and Program Type.*

Discussion

The finding that the percent of students scoring at or above the fiftieth percentile was significantly lower in schools with scripted programs than in schools with unscripted programs is consistent with the fact that students vary in their instructional needs and scripted programs don't allow teachers to use professional judgment to adjust instruction to the needs of the children in their classrooms. Scripted programs may also discourage inexperienced teachers from learning how to address students' various instructional needs, discourage experienced teachers from mentoring inexperienced teachers, and discourage teachers from remaining in the profession.

The finding that the percent of students scoring at or above the fiftieth percentile in reading achievement was lowest in schools with both lower levels of credentialed teachers and scripted reading programs suggests that schools confronted with both lower levels of credentialed teachers and high-stakes testing will do better in high-stakes testing if they use unscripted programs.

Finally, the consistent finding across districts that children achieve less with scripted reading instructional programs than with unscripted reading instructional programs suggests that policy makers and educational administrators should not require teachers, whether they are credentialed or not, to use such programs. Scripted reading instructional programs are a hindrance, not a help.

References

Anderluh, D. (1998, February 1). Building with words: City schools hope phonics boosts reading. *Sacramento Bee.*

76 · READING FOR PROFIT

Bazeley, M. (2000, May 29). Method seems to lift scores. *San Jose Mercury News.*

Boyd, V. V. (2001). A Case Study of the Perceived Impact of Commercially Prepared and Increasingly Scripted Learning Programs in Elementary Schools (K–6th grades). Doctoral dissertation, University of LaVerne, LaVerne, CA.

Bridge, C., Winograd, P., & Haley, D. (1982). Using predictable materials vs. preprimers to teach beginning sight words. *The Reading Teacher 36*(9), 884–891.

Collier, V. P. (1989). How long? A synthesis of research on academic achievement in second language. *TESOL Quarterly 23*(3), 509–531.

Helfand, D. (1999, August 22). Sacramento gets high marks in school reform. *Los Angeles Times*, Orange County Edition, pp. A1, A38–39.

Helfand, D. (2000a, January 10). Decades later, frustrated father is phonics guru. *Los Angeles Times*, Orange County Edition, pp. A-1 & A-16.

Helfand, D. (2000b, July 30). Reading taught the scripted way. *Los Angeles Times*, Orange County Edition, p. B2.

Helfand, D., Moore, S., & Hayasaki, E. (2002, August 21). L.A. Unified hails reforms as test scores rise for fourth year. *Los Angeles Times.*

Holland, B. (1996). No more Wright Group or Rigby?? An open letter sent by the 1996 president of the California Reading Association's Inland Empire Reading Council to California Reading Association Council members and concerned educators.

Linn, R. (2000). Assessments and accountability. *Educational Researcher*, pp. 4–16.

McGraw-Hill. (2000). *This is the company . . . : Annual report 2000.* New York: McGraw-Hill.

Moustafa, M. (2002). Claims of "marked jumps" in children's literacy skills in *Open Court* schools not confirmed by children's *SAT 9* scores. Available: *http://instructional1.calstatela.edu/mmousta*

Moustafa, M., & Land, R. (2002). The reading achievement of economically-disadvantaged children in urban schools using *Open Court* vs. comparably disadvantaged children in urban schools using unscripted reading programs. In *2002 Yearbook of the Urban Learning, Teaching, and Research Special Interest Group of the American Educational Research Association* Ed. F. Uy (pp. 44–53). Available: *http://instructional1.calstatela.edu/mmousta*

Oliver, D. (2002). *K–3 district reading plan evaluation, year one: 2000–2001.* Program Evaluation and Research Branch, Los Angeles Unified School District. (Planning, Assessment, and Research Division Publication No. 114)

Saunders, D. (1999, June 29). Eureka! School reform that works. *San Francisco Chronicle.*

Schroeder, C. (1999, October 15). Guidelines for the purchase of grades K–1 reading series/Program (Memorandum No. M-139, LAUSD internal document).

7

The Influence of Decodable Texts on Readers' Strategies

PRISCA MARTENS AND YETTA GOODMAN

Debates among researchers and educators over how to teach reading have continued for decades with no end in sight. The issues include the nature of the reading process itself, the naturalness of the process of learning to read, and how much explicit skills instruction students need. The focus of most of the debate, however, continues to be the role of phonics in reading. While no one disputes that the relationship between letters and sounds is a necessary cue readers draw on to read, researchers do disagree on how separable a role it plays and how it should be taught.

Currently, the No Child Left Behind Act (NCLB) (2001) legislates a single narrow view of reading, based largely on the National Reading Panel (NRP) report (2000), which is equated with scientifically based reading research. The seriousness of this result is heightened since in order to receive federal funding through NCLB, states and school districts must show that their reading programs are grounded in "scientifically-based research" in which students are systematically and explicitly taught phonemic awareness, phonics, fluency, vocabulary, and comprehension.

As in other times of reading reform, decodable texts have again resurfaced as a cure for perceived reading difficulties (Hiebert, 1999) and a means of meeting the "systematic and explicit instruction" demands of NCLB. Descendants of the linguistic readers of the 1970s, decodable texts are constructed to provide children with controlled practice in reading words with letter-sound correspondences that the children have been taught prior to their reading, plus a limited number of sight words that have also been systematically taught. Though Grossen (1997) supported the use of these texts in the teaching of beginning reading in her synthesis of thirty years of research for the National Institute of

Child Health and Human Development, Allington (2002) has found that "no scientific evidence yet supports the use of decodable texts" (p. 195). He states, "No research studies were identified that systematically manipulated the proportion of words in texts considered 'decodable' to assess the efficacy of texts comprised of 'some,' 'many,' 'mostly,' or 'exclusively' words that could be pronounced based on the lessons previously taught" (p. 203).

Even the NRP report (2000) states, "Surprisingly, very little research has attempted to determine whether the use of decodable books in systematic phonics programs has any influence on the progress that some or all children make in learning to read" (pp. 2-137). As Allington (2002) points out, "So, in this era of 'evidence-based' decisions and reading programs based in 'rigorous scientific research,' textbook publishers are promoting reading curriculum materials that have no basis in science. None" (p. 196).

In spite of this lack of scientific evidence, decodable texts are a key component of the programs meeting NCLB criteria that are being widely adopted across the United States, including Open Court Reading (SRA/McGraw-Hill, 2000). SRA/McGraw-Hill claims that Open Court Reading 2002 is "the only reading program that provides: an educational philosophy based on scientific research . . . , a well-defined plan of systematic, [and] explicit instruction for teaching the strategies and skills necessary for reading" (SRA/McGraw-Hill, n.d.).

So what are decodable texts? What does a young child's reading of a decodable text look and sound like? How do decodable texts influence the strategies the reader uses? How does this same reader look and sound reading a predictable text? In this chapter we address these questions.

What Are Decodable Texts?

Decodable texts are based on the word recognition theory of reading, namely, that reading is a process of decoding letters into sounds to create words. Proficiency in identifying words fluently and effortlessly is believed to be central to reading (Mason, Stahl, Au, & Herman 2003). In learning to read, children are said to move from recognizing words as wholes to using more and more phonics cues until they recognize words automatically. When word recognition has reached this fluent, transparent stage, readers focus their attention on comprehension (Ehri, 1995). While word recognition isn't necessarily equated with reading, good word recognition skills are believed essential for good comprehension. As Stanovich and Stanovich (1995) claim, "The word recognition skills of the good reader are so rapid, automatic, and efficient that the skilled reader need not rely on contextual information. In fact, it is poor readers who guess from context—out of necessity because their decoding skills are so weak" (p. 92).

In order to become good readers, beginning readers are encouraged to use orthographic information to identify words and not rely on context (Juel, 1995).

In order to recognize words automatically and fluently in the word recognition view, readers need instruction in phonics and opportunities to practice using their phonics knowledge to decode connected text. Decodable texts fill this need by supporting word identification, facilitating the application of phonics skills during reading, and eliminating distractions so readers' attention is directed to letters and sounds (Adams, 1990; Mesmer, 2001a). "Readers in the full-alphabetic phase associate letters with sounds in a more efficient manner of word recognition. They fully apply their knowledge of all these associations, especially vowels, to read words. This more systematic approach allows full-alphabetic readers to read unfamiliar words and to move on to the more mature orthographic phase of word recognition" (Mesmer, 1999, p. 133).

Two features distinguish decodable texts from other texts: (1) a clustering of words with a high degree of phonic regularity in the text (Hiebert, 1998; Mesmer, 2001b), and (2) a match between the letter-sound relationship in the text and those that have been taught (Allington & Woodside-Jiron, 1998a; Mesmer, 2001b). The policy standard set for decodable texts in Texas and California is that 80 percent to 90 percent of the words in a text must be decodable based on the letter-sound relationships that have been taught (Allington, 2002). Allington points out, however, that this standard is not based on scientific research but on ideology and political mandates since there is no research on the amount or range of text that should be decodable to support children in becoming readers. When no percentage of decodable words is provided, a close examination of the relationship between the instructional sequence of phonic elements and the words in the text provides an indication of whether the text is decodable (Stein, Johnson, & Gutlohn, 1999). A word deemed to be not decodable one week may be considered decodable the next week if the rules needed to decode it have been explicitly taught (Hoffman, Sailors, & Patterson, 2002).

Although, as Allington (2002) points out, there is no research on "the relative efficacy of variations in 'decodable texts' in helping most students develop specific reading skills" (p. 212), there is some research related to decodable texts. In analyzing the research around decodable texts, Mesmer (2001a, 2001b) found that the differences between decodable texts and other texts have remained relatively stable for thirty years and that little research has examined the influence of decodable texts on readers and the strategies they use. The few studies grounded in a word recognition view of reading that have been done focus primarily on readers' word recognition strategies. Mesmer (1999) worked with Cametra, a struggling second-grade reader, who "often substituted words that were semantically and syntactically correct but that did not match the letters and sounds in words" (p. 132). Mesmer noted that after six months of reading decodable texts, Cametra was more consistently integrating her alphabetic knowledge with syntactic and semantic information and also increased her rate of self-correction, suggesting to Mesmer that "Cametra may have been more confident in the system she now used to recognize words" (p. 139). Mesmer (2001b) also worked with two groups of first graders who received the same phonics instruction, followed by one group reading decodable texts and the other nondecodable texts, to learn the readers' application of phonics knowledge as measured by the graphic similarity between their errors and the text words. She concluded that readers apply their letter-sound knowledge in reading decodable texts and possibly to other texts as well.

Hoffman, Roser, Salas, Patterson, and Pennington (2000) examined students' accuracy, rate, and fluency (measured on a five-point scale ranging from halting, choppy, or word-by-word reading to fluent, expressive, interpretive reading) in reading different types of leveled texts and found that texts labeled decodable correlated positively and significantly with accuracy but negatively and significantly with fluency. They concluded that decodability may have facilitated the students' word analysis and recognition but also may have slowed down the readers. Juel and Roper-Schneider (1985) compared the readings of two groups of first graders at three points during the year. Both groups received the same phonics instruction, but one group read a basal considered decodable and the other a basal with high-frequency words. Based on the children's ability to read core vocabulary from their own basal on lists and in context, a pseudoword reading test, and their reading of core vocabulary from the other basal series, Juel and Roper-Schneider did not conclusively determine which approach was superior. The groups did not differ on reading words from their own basal but did differ in reading unknown words from the other basal. The researchers concluded that text type influenced the transfer of letter-sound knowledge and strategy use and that the use of decodable books with beginning readers for a short period of time can improve children's reading. While these studies are concerned with readers' responses to decodable texts, the focus is on word recognition and accuracy.

What Are Predictable Texts?

Predictability is a concept that grows out of a sociopsycholinguistic view of reading. Sociopsycholinguistics is grounded in miscue analysis research that demonstrates that proficient readers effectively and efficiently integrate their knowledge of language cues (syntactic, semantic, and graphophonic) and reading strategies (e.g., predicting, correcting) as they transact with and make sense of texts in their sociocultural contexts (Goodman, 2003). Beginning readers with limited experience in reading benefit from the highly predictable texts that support their learning to integrate language cues and strategies (Bridge, Winograd, & Haley, 1983; Leu, DeGroff, & Simons, 1986; Rhodes, 1981; see also Brown, Goodman, & Marek, 1996). While all authentic, meaningful, functional language is predictable, allowing readers to anticipate what will come next, the degree of predictability varies with the format and content of the text. Readers predict based on what they know about language and how it works, what they know about the world in relation to the content of the text, and what they know about the world of books, their format, and their print (Goodman, 1993; Smith, 1994). Texts are easy or difficult, depending on how predictable they are for a specific reader (Goodman, 1993). What is predictable for one reader (such as books on nuclear physics or mechanical engineering) may not be predictable for another.

In highly predictable texts for young readers, factors such as patterns of words, syntactic structures, concepts, vocabulary, illustrations, page format, story structure, repetition, rhyme, and rhythm are used in different combinations to varying degrees. These features highlight language cues and increase the redundancy that make books predictable and allow readers to orchestrate the overall developing meaning of the text. As they revisit the patterns in the text, readers integrate the less print-dependent cues, such as context, syntax, and their knowledge of story, with their developing use of the cues in the print with which they are least familiar (Barrs & Thomas, 1991; Smith & Elley, 1997). With each revisiting, readers learn to use and integrate the relevant cueing systems with a focus on constructing meaning, strengthening their developing strategies, including their graphophonic strategies (Goodman, 1993).

Studies grounded in a sociopsycholinguistic view of reading have analyzed students' readings of predictable texts and compared those with the same students' readings of decodable texts. Kucer (1985) asked Susan, a third grader having difficulties with reading, to read and retell a predictable folktale and a decodable story with similar readability levels. Using miscue analysis, Kucer found that Susan was a more effective and efficient reader, stayed closer to the author's meaning, made more high-quality miscues, and had a stronger retelling with the predictable text than with the decodable. He concluded that predictable books support students' developing effective reading strategies. Martens (1999) also used miscue analysis to analyze the readings and retellings of predictable and decodable texts read by Lydia, a first grader. Her findings support those of Kucer. Martens also found that Lydia's reading of the decodable text improved the farther she got into the text, but she read the predictable text more efficiently and effectively immediately. Goodman,

Goodman, and Martens (2002) analyzed predictable and decodable texts and readings of first and third graders. Again, the children read the predictable texts more effectively and efficiently than the decodable ones. They also examined the readers' miscues in relation to language issues involved in producing decodable texts. They found that it is the compromises in language that writers and publishers must make in order for decodable texts to be readable that allow readers to make sense even of awkward decodable texts.

The Influence of Decodable and Predictable Texts on Readers' Meaning Construction Strategies

The current popularity and mandated use of decodable texts for reading instruction makes it all the more critical that teachers, administrators, and parents be knowledgeable about the influence different texts have on readers and their strategy use. To deepen these understandings and facilitate discussions, we examined five first graders' readings of decodable and predictable texts (Goodman et al., 2002). We used miscue analysis as the window for this investigation (Goodman, 1970) because it reveals patterns in readers' miscues across the text. By analyzing how efficiently and effectively readers integrate the language cueing systems and reading strategies across a text, researchers learn, for example, the readers' concerns for producing syntactically acceptable (or grammatical) structures that are semantically acceptable (make sense) in the context of the story (Goodman, Watson, & Burke, 1987).

Method

The five first graders we worked with were experiencing difficulties in reading two months into the school year. They left their classrooms each day to spend two hours in the reading resource room in a class of ten children. The reading program in the school was Open Court, in which the children daily received phonics instruction and read decodable texts. To ensure the decodable text selected for the children to read was appropriate, the teacher provided the next leveled text in the sequence that the children would be reading in class, *Sis the Cat* (Decodable Book 14). The "story" tells of the different antics of a cat named Sis, with an instructional focus on a review of the short vowels *a, i,* and *o*. Because this book was longer than most of the other decodable books, two predictable books, both leveled at first grade (Fountas & Pinnell, 1996) were used to provide a similar amount of written text for the comparative analysis. The predictable books were *All Fall Down* (Wildsmith, 1983), a cumulative sequence with a new animal added on each page, and *Rain* (Kalan, 1978), a poem, illustrated by Donald Crews, with one line on each page of the text. Combined, the two predictable books had 132 running words, compared with 127 running words in *Sis the Cat*.

Standard miscue analysis research procedures were used (Goodman et al., 1987). The texts were new and unfamiliar to the children. Prior to each reading, the children were told that if they came to something they didn't know, they should do whatever they would do if they were reading alone. In miscue analysis we do not prompt readers when they hesitate but encourage them to problem solve when they are not sure. They were also told that when they finished reading they would be asked to retell. All readings were audiotaped so they could be revisited, and we marked the miscues and analyzed them at a later time.

The readings were analyzed using a miscue analysis procedure that examines each sentence as the reader finally resolves it (Goodman et al., 1987). In this procedure the sentences, or when necessary as in some poems, linguistic units, are coded for syntactic and semantic acceptability and, when the sentence is fully acceptable, for meaning change. A sentence coded fully acceptable includes (1) miscues that are acceptable within the sentence and story, or (2) miscues that are unacceptable but self-corrected, or (3) no miscues.

We calculated each readers' miscues per hundred words (MPHW) and their correction rate. MPHW includes all miscues except for repeated miscues (i.e., identical substitutions for, or omissions of, the same text item). Corrections are calculated as the percentage of coded miscues that the reader self-corrects. Retellings are given a holistic score, with 5 being a very complete retelling and 1 a minimal retelling.

Findings

Figure 7–1 contains miscue analysis scores for the decodable (DC) and predictable (PD) texts. Each reader produced sentences with higher syntactic (grammatical) and semantic (meaning) acceptability and fewer MPHW in the predictable books than in the decodable book. The stark differences are influenced by the children's repeated miscues on *Sis*, which made up 21.2 percent of the running words in the decodable book. Repeated miscues, identical miscues across a text, are not counted after the first occurrence to avoid inflating the data. No child ever read *Sis* as expected; the children consistently substituted "Siz," "sit," or "sits." If a reader read "sits" for *Sis* nine times, for example, we counted the miscue only once. We did, however, code each sentence for acceptability. The children's consistent miscues on *Sis* caused a cumulative effect of unacceptability.

The percentage of correction for three of the first graders increased in the predictable book. In the two cases where it decreased, the children had the

First-Grade Readers	Damian		Derrick		Earl		Latarsha		Serrina	
	DC	PD	DC	PD	DC	PD	DC	PD	DC	PD
Syntactic Acceptability	7%	88%	26%	92%	15%	96%	19%	96%	93%	96%
Semantic Acceptability	7%	80%	22%	88%	15%	96%	15%	92%	89%	96%
Miscues per Hundred Words	9	4	20	9	34	6	13	10	8	5
Correction	9%	0%	0%	8%	5%	25%	6%	8%	50%	17%
Retelling (Holistic)	1/5	4/5	3/5	4/5	1/5	4/5	4/5	4/5	4/5	4/5

Figure 7–1. *Statistical Comparisons of First Graders Reading Decodable (DC) and Predictable (PD) Texts*

lowest MPHW. The retelling scores for each reader equaled or increased in the predictable books compared with the decodable book. The design features of each kind of text are different, and simple comparisons between children's comprehension of such texts are not easy to make. There is a lot more to talk about in the predictable texts with well-developed and cyclical events and characters, the use of cohesive devices to create textuality, and strong story lines. While these are characteristics that differentiate them from decodable texts, the scores may not only reflect more success by the readers in comprehending but greater opportunities to comprehend. The synthetic structures of decodable texts may provide learners with the notion that certain texts are not expected to make sense nor do they necessarily have to contain acceptable grammatical patterns of English.

Miscues as Windows: Taking a Closer Look

To more closely examine the children's strategies with the different texts, we will look more deeply at representative samples of Earl's and Serrina's readings of *Sis the Cat* (decodable) and *Rain* (predictable).

Earl

Earl's reading sample from *Sis the Cat* (see Figure 7–2) reveals the challenges he had with this text. Only 15 percent of his sentences were syntactically

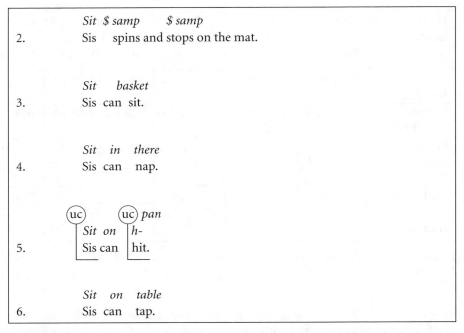

2. *Sit* $ *samp* $ *samp*
   Sis spins and stops on the mat.

3. *Sit* *basket*
   Sis can sit.

4. *Sit* *in* *there*
   Sis can nap.

5. (uc) (uc) *pan*
   Sit on | *h-*
   Sis can | hit.

6. *Sit* *on* *table*
   Sis can tap.

Figure 7–2. (A Sample of Earl's Reading of Sis the Cat Miscue markings: substitutions are written above the text; $ indicates a nonword; a circle containing UC connected to a line indicates a regression resulting in an unsuccessful attempt to correct the miscue)

(grammatically) acceptable and only 15 percent were semantically (meaning) acceptable (see Figure 7–1). He had thirty-four MPHW and a correction rate of only 5 percent. While at first glance it may appear that Earl was randomly saying words, a closer examination reveals how hard he was searching for clues to make sense as he read.

The name *Sis* was unfamiliar, particularly for a cat, to all of the children and created problems immediately. In addition, *Sis* was not always in the subject position; *Sis* was also, for example, the object of a preposition. For experienced readers this does not present a problem, but it can cause difficulties for inexperienced readers (Smith, 1976).

Earl substituted "sit" throughout his reading. "Sit" didn't make sense but was a word that had meaning for him that also had close graphic and sound similarity to *Sis*, indicating Earl's use of phonics cues. Children's stories often use imperative words to start sentences and he may have had experience with this. Continuing in line 2, he substituted a nonword, "samp," for *spins* and *stops*, which is not syntactically or semantically acceptable but again demonstrates use of phonics cues. Aware that his reading wasn't making sense, Earl used clues from the illustrations in lines 3–6. The function word *can* is in each of these sentences and Earl read it as expected in line 3, followed by "basket" from the illustration. It is possible that he knew *sit*, but since he had already substituted "sit" for *Sis*, he may have realized he couldn't read it again ("Sit can sit.") Regardless, when "Sit can basket" didn't make sense to him, he abandoned *can* and substituted prepositions in lines 4–6 that made sense with a place to sit. In English we would include a noun marker such as *the* before "pan" (line 5) and "table" (line 6), but if Earl had a sense of wordness and was relating his oral reading of words to the written words, he knew the noun marker wasn't there.

Earl wanted his reading to make sense. He tried to use phonics to decode, as he was taught, but when he had difficulty making meaning, he drew on his knowledge of language, using syntactic, semantic, and graphophonic cues, in combination with the illustrations, to predict and construct meaningful sentences. Not surprisingly, Earl's retelling was weak, with a holistic score of 1. He listed Dad, kids, kitty cat, basket, hat, and blocks as being in the story.

Figure 7–3 contains a sample of Earl's reading from *Rain*. Here he looks like a very different reader. In his reading of both predictable texts, Earl had 96 percent for both syntactic and semantic acceptability, six MPHW, and a correction rate of 25 percent (see Figure 7–1). The authentic language integrated with the illustrations in *Rain* supported Earl in using his knowledge to draw on syntactic, semantic, and graphophonic cues to predict and construct meaning. The poem is written in phrases that do not contain verbs. Because this was an unfamiliar structure to Earl, he consistently predicted and inserted the verb "is." When he realized "is" wasn't in the text, however, he actually self-corrected by saying "no" in response to his prediction. Earl's retelling of this poem, a holistic score of 4, included more description and details about the rain and where it fell.

Serrina

Serrina was the strongest of the five readers. The sample of her reading of *Sis the Cat* in Figure 7–4 reveals she had much less difficulty than Earl. Her miscue analysis scores substantiate that also: a syntactic acceptability score of 93 percent and semantic acceptability score of 89 percent, with eight MPHW and a 50 percent correction rate (see Figure 7–1).

Serrina picked out the *is* in *Sis* and substituted "Siz" for *Sis* throughout the story. Noticeable in this representative sample of her reading is the sounding out, or blending, that she did, characteristic of how she had been taught to use phonics to decode. She blended in 70 percent of the sentences in the story, sometimes on words she'd previously read or successfully blended. Her

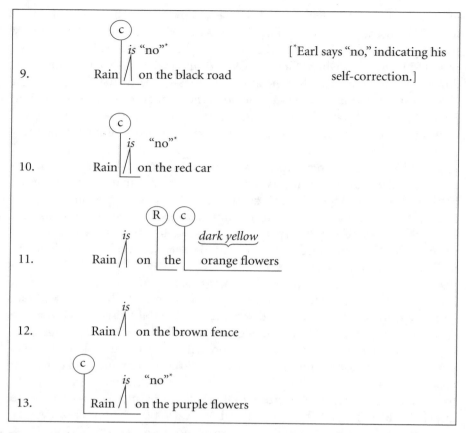

9.

      (c)
      is "no"*   [*Earl says "no," indicating his
   Rain | on the black road   self-correction.]

10.

      (c)
      is "no"*
   Rain | on the red car

11.

      (R) (c)
     is   *dark yellow*
   Rain | on | the | orange flowers

12.

     is
   Rain | on the brown fence

13.

   (c)
     is "no"*
   Rain | on the purple flowers

Figure 7–3. (A Sample of Earl's Reading of *Rain* Miscue markings: insertions are indicated with a carrot; a circle containing a C connected to a line indicates a regression resulting in the correction of the miscue; an R in the circle indicates a straight repetition of the text)

retelling was fairly complete, with a holistic score of 4 out of 5. She named the characters and told some of the things Sis did.

  In *Rain*, however, Serrina too looks like a different reader (see Figure 7–5). She blended a few times but used the multiple cues after that to read more fluidly. She did not correct her substitutions of "orange flower" for *brown fence* (line 12) but while it repeats line 11 it still makes sense. Serrina's miscue analysis scores corroborate her effective and efficient reading: 96 percent for both syntactic and semantic acceptability and five MPHW. Her correction rate of 17 percent is lower than her correction rate in the decodable text but she had fewer MPHW and all but one miscue made sense, making correction unnecessary. Her retelling score of 4 out of 5 indicated her strong understanding of the story.

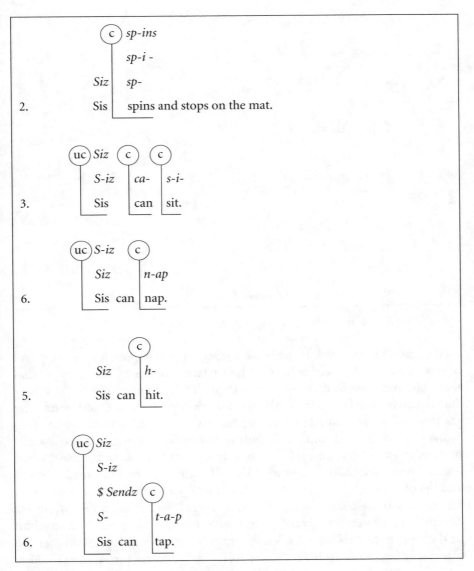

Figure 7-4. *A Sample of Serrina's Reading of* Sis the Cat

Learning from Readers: Decodable or Predictable Texts?

In their readings of these texts, these first graders have much to teach us about the influence of decodable texts on readers and reading. First, the children demonstrate that texts matter. Readers look and sound different depending

Figure 7–5. *A Sample of Serrina's Reading of* Rain

on the texts they are reading, with some texts supporting efficient reading and others getting in the way of it. On the surface, decodable texts appear that they should be easy to read because of their short, simple syntactic structures and small words. However, both Earl and Serrina were inefficient in their readings of *Sis the Cat*. Throughout the text Earl made substitutions that didn't make sense and continued reading without correcting, and Serrina had numerous sound outs, even for words she'd already read. In contrast, when reading *Rain*, the children sounded like different readers. Both read this text and the other predictable text more efficiently. The natural language patterns, repetitive syntactic sequences, redundancy between print and illustrations, and match between their own backgrounds and the conceptual background of the text supported them in demonstrating strategies that allowed them to integrate cues, solve problems, and predict and construct meaning (Rhodes, 1981). That the longer, more complex structures in *Rain* did not pose a problem for Earl, Serrina, and their classmates is not surprising. Miscue analysis research has demonstrated that students can read complex sentences when the grammatical functions and meanings of words are familiar, phrases are familiar, phrases are in a predictable order within and between sentences, and word order is predictable (Allen & Watson, 1976). Texts influence readers. When readers are struggling and using inefficient strategies, their difficulties often stem from the text.

Earl's and Serrina's transactions with the texts also teach us that reading is not about decoding or attacking words; it is a process of integrating language cues and strategies with what the reader knows about language and the world to predict and construct meaning across the text. In the predictable text, since no attempt was made to limit the use of particular letters and sounds or syntactic patterns, the children had multiple cues on which to draw. They sampled the print, syntax, and semantics and predicted with a focus on constructing meaning and used efficient strategies.

The decodable text, however, because of its construction, constrained the readers' opportunities to use multiple cues and their knowledge of language. With about 60 percent of the types of words (i.e., different words as opposed to running words) being decodable in sentences that averaged 4.4 words, it focused the readers on words and graphophonic cues. Earl, particularly, had difficulty. While it might seem his graphophonic knowledge was weak, such was not the case. If words and graphophonic patterns had been the issue, he would have consistently miscued on particular words and phoneme/grapheme patterns throughout the texts, but he didn't. He miscued on *nap*, for example, by substituting "there," but in other places in all the texts he used those particular graphophonic cues (i.e., /n/, /a/, /p/) without a problem. In addition, before he started miscuing on *can*, he read it correctly. Rarely are phonics problems consistent across a text (Goodman et al., 2002).

Earl's awareness of and attention to graphophonic cues are evident in his one-to-one matching of his substitutions with text items and in his self-corrections while reading *Rain* when he realized "is" wasn't part of the text. He abandoned relying on graphophonic and word cues in *Sis the Cat* when those strategies didn't lead to meaningful reading, as in his reading "Sit can basket," and used cues in the illustrations to come up with language that made more sense, such as "Sit on pan."

A final lesson we learned from these first graders is that decodable texts are readable. The children all read and, to varying degrees, understood them. Serrina and Latarsha even understood the decodable text as well as they did the predictable texts. The issue, then, isn't that decodable texts are unreadable; the issue is what decodable texts teach children about reading and themselves as they read them.

Margaret Meek (1988) states that "texts teach." Even decodable texts teach. While predictable texts teach readers to focus on constructing meaning by integrating the variety of language cues in the text and the world around them, decodable texts teach readers to focus on words and graphophonic cues and not trust what they know about language and the world. Predictable texts teach children that they are capable readers who know how to make sense; decodable texts teach children that they have to work hard at reading and that the written language of books can be awkward and not sound like language.

We believe that a major goal of any reading program should be to develop independent readers who see themselves as capable readers, enjoy reading, and choose to read. To reach this goal, children need opportunities to read texts that foster their growing independence by supporting their integration of cues to predict and construct meaning. Our years of experience with miscue analysis with readers of a range of ages, abilities, and language variations reading a range of materials tell us that texts teach and that readers become better and stronger readers by reading a wide variety of authentic and meaningful texts through which they learn to integrate reading strategies effectively and efficiently (Krashen, 1993; Smith & Elley, 1997).

References

Adams, M. (1990). *Beginning to read: Thinking and learning about print.* Cambridge, MA: MIT Press.

Allen, P. D., & Watson, D. (Eds.). (1976). *Findings of research in miscue analysis: Classroom implications.* Urbana, IL: ERIC Clearinghouse on Reading and Communication Skills and National Council of Teachers of English.

Allington, R. L. (Ed.). (2002). *Big brother and the national reading curriculum.* Portsmouth, NH: Heinemann.

Allington, R., & Woodside-Jiron, H. (1998a, spring). Decodable text in beginning reading: Are mandates and policy based on research? *ERS Spectrum,* pp. 3–11.

Allington, R., & Woodside-Jiron, H. (1998b). Thirty years of research in reading: When is a research summary not a research summary? In K. Goodman (Ed.), *In defense of good teaching* (pp. 143–157). York, ME: Stenhouse.

Barrs, M., & Thomas, A. (1991). *The reading book.* Portsmouth, NH: Heinemann.

Bridge, C., Winograd, P., & Haley, D. (1983). Using predictable materials vs. preprimers to teach beginning sight words. *The Reading Teacher, 36*(9), 884–891.

Brown, J., Goodman, K., & Marek, A. (1996). *Studies in miscue analysis: An annotated bibliography.* Newark, DE: International Reading Association.

Ehri, L. (1995). Phases of development in learning to read words by sight. *Journal of Research in Reading, 18,* 116–125.

Fountas, I. C., & Pinnell, G. S. (1996). *Guided reading.* Portsmouth, NH: Heinemann.

Garan, E. M. (2001). What does the report of the National Reading Panel really tell us about teaching phonics? *Language Arts, 79*(1), 61–70.

Goodman, K. S. (1970). Behind the eye: What happens in reading. In K. Goodman & O. Niles (Eds.), *Reading: Process and program* (pp. 3–38). Urbana, IL: National Council of Teachers of English.

Goodman, K. S. (1993). *Phonics phacts.* Portsmouth, NH: Heinemann.

Goodman, K. (2003). Reading, writing, and written texts: A transactional sociopsycholinguistic view. In A. Flurkey & J. Xu (Eds.), *On the revolution of reading: The selected writings of Kenneth S. Goodman* (pp. 3–45). Portsmouth, NH: Heinemann.

Goodman, Y., Goodman, K., & Martens, P. (2002). Text matters: Readers who learn with decodable texts. In D. Schallert, C. Fairbanks, J. Worthy, B. Maloch, & J. Hoffman (Eds.), *51st Yearbook of the National Reading Conference* (pp. 186–203). Oak Creek, WI: National Reading Conference.

Goodman, Y., Watson, D., & Burke, C. (1987). *Reading miscue inventory: Alternative procedures.* Katonah, NY: Richard C. Owen.

Grossen, B. (1997). *30 years of research: What we now know about how children learn to read (A synthesis of research on reading from the National Institute of Child Health and Human Development commissioned by the Center for the Future of Teaching and Learning with funding support from the Pacific Bell Foundation).* Santa Cruz, CA: Center for the Future of Teaching and Learning.

Hiebert, E. (1998). *Text matters in learning to read* (CIERA Report No. 1-001). Ann Arbor, MI: Center for the Improvement of Early Reading Achievement.

Hiebert, E. (1999). Text matters in learning to read. *The Reading Teacher, 52,* 552–566.

Hoffman, J., Roser, N., Salas, R., Patterson, E., & Pennington, J. (2000). *Text leveling and little books in first grade reading* (CIERA Report No. 1-010). Ann Arbor, MI: Center for the Improvement of Early Reading Achievement.

Hoffman, J., Sailors, M., & Patterson, E. (2002). *Decodable texts for beginning reading instruction: The year 2000 basals* (CIERA Report No. 1-016). Ann Arbor, MI: Center for the Improvement of Early Reading Achievement.

Juel, C. (1995). The messenger may be wrong, but the message may be right. *Journal of Research in Reading, 18*(2), 146–153.

Juel, C., & Roper-Schneider, D. (1985). The influence of basal readers on first grade reading. *Reading Research Quarterly, 20,* 134–152.

Kalan, R. (1978). *Rain.* New York: Mulberry.

Krashen, S. (1993). *The power of reading: Insights from the research.* Englewood, CO: Libraries Unlimited.

Kucer, S. B. (1985). Predictability and readability: The same rose with different names? In M. Douglass (Ed.), *Claremont reading conference forty-ninth yearbook* (pp. 229–246). Claremont, CA: Claremont Graduate School.

Leu, D., DeGroff, L., & Simons, H. (1986). Predictable texts and interactive-compensatory hypotheses: Evaluating individual differences in reading ability, context use, and comprehension. *Journal of Educational Psychology, 78*(5), 347–352.

Martens, P. (1999, December). Prediction and inference: The reader, the text, and the context. Paper presented at the National Reading Conference Annual Meeting, Orlando, FL.

Mason, J., Stahl, S., Au, K., & Herman, P. (2003). Reading: Children's developing knowledge of words. In J. Flood, D. Lapp, J. Squire, & J. Jensen (Eds.), *Handbook of research on teaching the English language arts* (pp. 914–930). Mahwah, NJ: Lawrence Erlbaum.

Meek, M. (1988). *How texts teach what readers learn.* Avonset, Bath: Thimble.

Mesmer, H. (1999). Scaffolding a crucial transition using text with some decodability. *Reading Teacher, 53*(2), 130–143.

Mesmer, H. A. (2001a). Decodable text: A review of what we know. *Reading Research and Instruction, 40*(2), 121–142.

Mesmer, H. (2001b). Examining the theoretical claims about decodable text: Does decodability lead to greater application of letter/sound knowledge in first-grade readers? In J. V. Hoffman, D. L. Shallert, C. M. Fairbanks, J. Worthy, & B. Maloch (Eds.), *50th yearbook of the National Reading Conference, 50,* 444–459.

National Reading Panel. (2000). *Teaching children to read: An evidence-based assessment of the scientific research literature on reading and its implications for reading instruction.* Washington, DC: National Institute of Child Health and Human Development.

No Child Left Behind Act of 2001 (H.R.1). (2002, January 8). 107th Congress. Available: *http://thomas.loc.gov*

Pressley, M. (2002). Effective beginning reading instruction. *Journal of Literacy Research, 34*(2), 165–188.

Rhodes, L. K. (1981). I can read! Predictable books as resources for reading and writing. *The Reading Teacher, 34*(1), 511–519.

Smith, F. (1994). *Understanding reading.* Hillsdale, NJ: Lawrence Erlbaum.

Smith, J., & Elley, W. (1997). *How children learn to read.* Katonah, NY: Richard C. Owen.

Smith, L. A. (1976). Miscue research and readability. In P. D. Allen & D. J. Watson (Eds.), *Findings of research in miscue analysis: Classroom implications* (pp. 146–151). Urbana, IL: ERIC Clearinghouse on Reading and Communication Skills and the National Council of Teachers of English.

Snow, C. E., Burns, M. S., & Griffin, P. (Eds.). (1998). *Preventing reading difficulties in young children.* Washington, DC: National Academy Press.

SRA/McGraw-Hill. (n.d.). *Open Court Reading 2002.* Retrieved June 10, 2004, from *www.sraonline.com/index.php/search?keywords=decodable+texts*

SRA/McGraw-Hill. (2000). *Open Court Teacher Edition.* Columbus, OH: SRA/McGraw-Hill.

Stanovich, K., & Stanovich, P. (1995). How research might inform the debate about early reading acquisition. *Journal of Research in Reading, 19*(2), 87–105.

Stein, M., Johnson, B., & Gutlohn, L. (1999). Analyzing beginning reading programs: The relationship between decoding instruction and text. *Remedial & Special Education, 20*(5), 275–288.

U.S. Department of Education, Office of Elementary and Secondary Education. (2002). *No child left behind: A desktop reference.* Retrieved April 27, 2003, from *www.ed.gov/offices/OESE/reference.pdf*

Yatvin, J. (2002). Babes in the woods: The wanderings of the National Reading Panel. *Phi Delta Kappan, 83*(5), 364–369.

Wildsmith, B. (1983). *All fall down.* New York: Oxford University Press.

8

Invisible Teacher/Invisible Children: The Company Line

RICHARD J. MEYER
University of New Mexico

While critics of the Bush Administration's energy policies have pointed repeatedly to its intimacy with the oil and gas industry . . . few education critics have noted the Administration's cozy relationship with McGraw-Hill. At its heart lies the three-generation social mingling between the McGraw and Bush families. (Metcalf, 2002, pp. 19–20)

Stephen Metcalf's deconstruction of the relationships between a large corporation, President George W. Bush, and legislation that influences what teachers may do in schools with children is quite chilling. Appearing in the popular press, Metcalf's critique goes on to explain the ways in which research on reading appears "disinterested and rigorous," but in reality is based in the interests of a large corporation rigorously working to increase its profits (p. 22). During his first presidential campaign, Bush held up the Texas Miracle as the model that could be used to fix all the reading problems in the United States. That *miracle* involved the supposed raising of all test scores in the great state of Texas. The reality was that although scores increased on the state-level test, the state's performance on the National Assessment of Educational Progress (NAEP) was basically unchanged. The miracle was a myth (Coles, 2003), manufactured for the sake of electing Bush while profiting a corporation. The heyday for corporations with roots in Texas spread as they waited for opportunities to sell their wares around the country. The corporate infiltration of schools is growing as reading and phonics programs, test-preparation materials, tests, and scoring and interpretation of tests appear in schools in response to the demand that the corporations themselves were instrumental in creating. These materials and services can be reduced to one word: profit.

Profits Soar as Context Is Ignored

Although the damage caused by the No Child Left Behind legislation and the reading policies born of it is becoming clear in classrooms (Coles, 2003; Allington, 2002), policy makers seem to be barely budging. Corporations are becoming richer as more and more of their materials are ordered for use by teachers and children. The remarkably powerful part of this dynamic is what I refer to as *nonstick surfaces.* No matter what literacy researchers and teachers in a particular context (such as a city or state) find, our evidence does not seem to stick in policy makers' minds in any way that substantially alters what is being imposed upon teachers and children.

In New Mexico, the context in which I presently work, here's what does not stick. In NCLB and in Reading First, we hear a lot about scientifically based research. In terms of reading, that means the report of the National Reading Panel (2000). That report includes no studies of diverse or second language learner groups. Apparently it does not matter (or stick in the minds of policy makers) that 51.4 percent of the students in New Mexico schools are Hispanic; 11.2 percent are Native American; and fewer than 33 percent are Anglo. Diverse students total at just under 70 percent. It does not matter (or stick) that dropout rates for those first two groups are 7.76 percent and 5.81 percent respectively (New Mexico Public Education Department, 2004). In other words, our state, the first state to be a majority of minorities, is *not* represented in the "science" being used to make our children and teachers seem defective. But we continue to pay millions to companies to supply us with materials that are sold as *scientifically based reading research.* This is bad science (Coles, 2000) being used for profit on the backs of the children of this state.

In New Mexico, more than one-fourth of our children live in poverty by U.S. census standards; more than 47 percent of our students receive free lunch; the free and reduced total is 57 percent. A recent report looking at the social health of the state, by the Fordham Institute for Innovation in Social Policy (2004), placed New Mexico at the bottom in the nation. This is our second year with this status. We earned the lowest marks in child poverty and insured children. We earned an F in graduation rates, unemployment, wages, suicide, drunken-driving deaths, teenage drug abuse, and homicides. More than 26 percent of New Mexico kids live in poverty; in contrast, in Maryland the rate is 7 percent.

Another recent demographic report, the Kids Count study (Annie E. Casey Foundation, 2003) rated New Mexico in the pits; 11 percent of our children live in extreme poverty. Child poverty, health insurance, and graduation rates must be neatly factored out of the scientifically based work we're to rely upon in teaching, teaching teachers, and research. The numbers don't stick, so they don't matter; they don't influence policy or decisions about curriculum, student learning, and teacher agency. But the corporations get richer.

There are other issues contributing to a low quality of life in New Mexico, as we are last in social health policies; forty-ninth in homicides; and forty-fourth in drunken-driving deaths (is it any wonder residents self-medicate?); and only 65 percent of eligible households receive food stamps. We are sixth in child abuse in the United States; and we earned an F in suicide. Brian Street (1995) points out that being able to read is not a prerequisite to fixing poverty and the complicated issues around it. In fact, reading is not at the center of these social issues, a basic fact ignored by the National Reading Panel and the authors of NCLB. Children will learn to read when they are not in pain, when their families are not in crisis, and when they are provided with medical and dental care. I'm not interested in anecdotes about a state legislator who "pulled himself up by his bootstraps" to leave poverty. That's an *n* of one. I am interested in the children that are left behind in neighborhoods where they are in too much physical, emotional, and spiritual pain to learn. I'm concerned that their needs and interests cannot be considered by their teachers because of policies and mandates that are hurtful.

Lois Meyer (2003) compiled two sets of data that suggest the complexity of corporation-ignored issues influencing children's success in school. In 2003, ten Albuquerque elementary schools were rated exemplary, exceeds standards, or meets standards by the New Mexico Public Education Department. Let's consider those ten; they have

- less than 27 percent students who receive free or reduced-price lunch (one as few as 2 percent)
- more than 55 percent Anglo students (six have more than 70 percent)
- no more than 35 percent Hispanic students (four have less than 15 percent)
- fewer than 7 percent Native American students (four have less than 2 percent)
- no bilingual education programs (some do not appear to have ESL programs, either)

Meyer then considered ten Albuquerque elementary schools that were rated probationary or have barely missed being rated probationary at least once in the last three years; they have

- at least 88 percent students who receive free or reduced-price lunch (five have more than 96 percent)
- less than 12 percent Anglo students (six have less than 5 percent)
- more than 73 percent Hispanic students (six have more than 90 percent)
- less than 10 percent Native American students (six have less than 2 percent)
- bilingual programs

It is frightening that some individuals might interpret these numbers to mean that being an English language learner is a deficit and probably the cause of reading difficulties. But that's what is happening as bilingual programs are under so much heat that they are evaporating via legislation or public opinion being shaped by individuals like Ron Unz (Crawford, 2004). The tiny three-year learning window to master English as dictated by NCLB in order to be tested in English effectively diminishes and debilitates bilingual programs. Programs won't demonstrate success when they are forced into unrealistic time frames for language learning.

It is time to consider poverty as a significant problem and diversity as a relevant issue. It's difficult for a nation, state, or city to face what such consideration means, but a corporation can find virtually no profit motive for honestly addressing issues of poverty, language, and culture. For example, in the Albuquerque area, Intel, with profits in the billions, is but a few miles from inner-city poverty that is beyond sad; it's embarrassing. Cornel West (2004) admonishes industry for its extreme wealth in light of social issues such as this. He argues, and I agree, that ethics and morality demand that industry assume responsibilities beyond distant shareholders to the place where the industry thrives. This idea is met with more nonstick attitude. The corporations continue to show up at district offices throughout the state and at the legislature, offering scientifically based solutions to problems they refuse to consider in any significant depth, scientific or otherwise (and here *otherwise* includes moral responsibilities).

The previous description is the context in one state. Now let's shift our attention to a wonderful, caring, smart, and reflective teacher whose teaching life and students are embedded in such a profit-motivated context. The teacher's perceived vulnerability, which is quite accurate, demands that I give few specifics about where she teaches.

Karen

Karen described her primary classroom as a "joyous" place because of her district's trust in her decision making about teaching and learning. Daily reading and writing workshops provided evidence of what her children knew, and Karen's use of assessments such as miscue analysis (Goodman, Watson, & Burke, 1987) helped her decide what she needed to teach. Each piece of her students' writing (in journals, stories, and other genres) suggested what children were coming to understand and what they might benefit from learning more about in strategy lessons Karen tailored to their needs. Grand conversations (Peterson & Eeds, 1990) about texts and discussions about connections to other texts, grammar, vocabulary, and phonics arose in response to Karen's and her students' questions and needs. They read, discussed, and wrote about many topics, including their identities as White, Black, Asian, and Hispanic Americans. More than one-fourth of the children received free or reduced lunch, and poverty was also a topic of discussion reflective of some of the literature Karen chose to read with her students. Karen explained that she taught phonics "all day!" She said, "We always talk . . . about letters, sounds, rhymes, and more." I wanted to learn more about how the children in her classroom became literate, so I initiated a study there.

The study began as an investigation into the uses of predictable texts in the teaching and learning of reading. During the study, the district shifted its stance on reading curriculum. Second-grade test scores had been reported in the local newspaper and the drop in scores led to an outcry in many forums, most notably from a few business groups. I could not trace the direct path, but based upon what Metcalf (2002) discussed in his article, conjecture leads me to believe that connections via the Business Roundtable quickly connected the district with a corporation that would "solve" the problem.

The district responded to the pressure being exerted by adopting and mandating the use of a systematic, direct, intense phonics instruction program. The types of texts used in Karen's reading instruction shifted from predictable books to phonetically regular texts that were referred to (by the publisher) as predictable and decodable but actually consisted of phonetically regular words organized into sentences that strain young readers' sense making (see Chapter 7 in this volume). Teachers were told that they were to follow verbatim the scripted lessons of the phonics program. Karen described the change:

> I was told by [a district reading administrator] that for too long teachers in this district have thought that their job was to create curriculum. I was told that is not our job. Our job is to "deliver" [*making quote signs in the air with her fingers*] curriculum.

Life in the classroom changed in response to the phonics mandate because the lessons consumed time. Karen said, "My students need to hear stories. They need to be involved with real literature . . . although [now] I always feel like I'm battling the clock" because phonics takes so long. She explained that the mandated program is so oriented to preciseness that her students are less willing to take risks as readers and writers. That, in combination with less time for authentic reading and writing, makes Karen wonder about all the possibilities that are lost: possibilities for teaching, for learning, and for young readers and writers to express themselves, their ideas, their hopes, their dreams, and their imaginations.

Each day, Karen is required to do one lesson of this systematic, direct, intense phonics program. One day, after I observed an entire lesson, Karen dismissed the children for lunch. After they left, I commented, "That took a long time." Karen explained that when she told a district reading administrator that phonics was taking up to ninety minutes on some days, she was told that she had a "personal problem." Again, she made little quote signs in the air when she said *personal problem*. "What does that mean?" she asked, looking at me.

"I don't know," I told her, because I had no idea.

The total time spent on phonics on this day was sixty minutes. The entire lesson is described in depth elsewhere (Meyer, 2001), but I'll recap the main events of the lesson here.

The Phonics Lesson (in Brief)

The phonics lesson began at 10:00. Karen read the script almost without interruption and verbatim because she has been warned about serious repercussions if she fails to do so. The children were on the rug, in a clump, facing Karen as she sat on a chair with the corporation-provided teachers guide in her lap and a dry-erase board behind her. She read a story from the script, but at every fifth word (or so), she read the phonemes in place of the word. The children then had to say the word. Karen said /k/-/r/-/o/ for *crow*, /t/-/r/-/ee/ for *tree* and so on. They didn't stop to discuss the story because the instructions did not say to. The story took five minutes and then Karen, without explaining the shift to her students, turned to the board and wrote *superman* on it. A precocious reader screamed out the word. Many of the children echoed it. Karen erased the *n* in *superman* and replaced it with a *d* to make *supermad*. A child said "supermad" and a few others echoed. One of the children asked what *supermad* means. Karen was about to explain that it's not a word, but one of the children suggested that if you are very mad at someone, you "are supermad at them."

Karen went through this process of changing real words to nonsense, changing *superman* again, this time to *supermand*. "What is *supermand*?" asked a child after some children said it, others echoed it, and others were silent.

Karen said, "It is not a word."

Then, she followed the guide and had the children read other words that she changed: *baboon* to *baboot*, *alphabet* to *alphabed*, *schoolbus* to *schoolbun*, and *recess* to *reced*.

With none of her usual (and expert) explanation about transitioning into a new activity (because the script provided no such explanations), Karen took out a puppet and used a slightly different voice to articulate phonemes that the children had to combine to say a word. For example, the puppet said /t/-/r/-/u/-/ck/ and the children said "truck". They did this with a long list of words, with some children saying, some echoing, and others remaining silent. Without discussion or segue, Karen moved to holding a large poster of the letter *d* and read the script, which told the children to write it in the air with their fingers. Some air-wrote, others mimicked the air writers, and others air-scribbled.

It was 10:14, and I looked around at the group of young children. Some were watching Karen; others were not. One child had carefully rolled up one leg of his jeans and was working at unraveling his sock. He was making a little ball with the string of elastic as he unwove it. Since he was unweaving only the threads that were parallel to the sole of his foot, he was leaving a sort of skeleton of his sock that started to slip down his leg as he unwrapped it further. A few of the children were rocking back and forth, seemingly not paying particular attention to Karen (although at this point in time it is conjecture to suggest they were not paying attention merely because they were not looking at her). One child was quietly making the sounds of bombs dropping ("eeeeyowwwwwww plichhhh") as he moved his hand above the rug and dropped it slowly down. One of the children was picking his nose; another was playing with her ears; one was rubbing her hands up and down her braids (later she undid and redid them).

The children were then required to say the isolated sound of /d/ as Karen read a story with that letter in it. The story was projected onto a screen so all could see. Without discussion, Karen moved to the part of the script that required her to read a list of words to the children so they could tell her if each began with *d*. The children were restless, exaggerating the behaviors described earlier, so Karen interrupted the script and read them a book from the school library. The bizarre behaviors stopped as the children listened to, responded to, and discussed the book. She dismissed them to write in their journals for a few minutes and then told them to return to the rug "for more phonics." Karen won't call the lessons *reading*, she explained, because the children aren't reading when they grunt, groan, and say nonwords.

Karen followed the scripted instructions for work on the board with initial consonant substitution (making *dad* into *mad*) for about ten words.

Then she gave the children letter cards with *m, n, c, d,* and *a* on them (one letter per card) and asked them to make words. A child suggested that he could make *candy* if he had a *y*. Karen said, "That is harder than we're supposed to make." This was the only time during the lesson that she looked over the children at me. Her eyes filled with water. Later, when I asked Karen about her feelings when she responded to that child, she explained that the program underestimates some children and confuses others. "It's just not for every child," she said with a sigh. But every child must sit through each lesson. No one leaves; no special help, no pullout teachers, and no interruptions of any kind are permitted during phonics.

The lesson ended with the distribution and reading of a piece of paper that was folded in half to form a four-page book about a cat. The cat's owner was illustrated as being annoyed at the cat's choices of places to nap. All of the words (except some sight words) supposedly had the sound of /a/ as in *cat*. The only words in the book were *the, cat, had, nap, on, a, mat, pad, in, pan,* and *cap*. Following the script cost the children and their teacher one hour of uninterrupted literacy time.

Who Owns What?

Karen's implementation of the program is monitored by her principal, who can stand in a corner of the first-grade pod (four classrooms with walls that an adult can see over) and observe the four first grades at one time. This is an eerie place to stand because as each teacher administers the program, an observer hears the same exact words coming out of the four first-grade teachers' mouths just slightly out of unison. The scripted voices sound like the teachers', but they are *owned* by the company. The following questions and responses examine issues of ownership underlying the mandated phonics program.

Who Owns the Definition of Reading?

The company does.

Karen's students are learning what reading is by the way it is operationally enacted day to day in school and out. The focus here is *in* school. Although Karen refers to it as phonics, the children are learning (from the script that constantly says "read . . . ") that reading is making sounds. They are learning that reading is the production of something orally so that we can move on. Say *reced* or *schoolbun* and move on. Although we heard the children's quest to find meaning in some of these words, the intention of the program is to have children string together sounds. The final consonant substitution activity teaches children to expect nonmeaning as an accepted reality of reading. Say *baboot* and move on. Remember, Karen told a child, "It's not a word," when that child asked about *supermand*. Being told to *read* a word (by the script) and that what they read is not a word (by their teacher) is confusing at best and may, in a larger sense, be teaching children that their reading is not supposed to make sense and that they are not meaning makers (Wells, 1986).

Willis (1997) suggests that the various views in the ongoing debates about reading fall into one of three categories: (1) seeing reading as a skill that can lead to success; (2) seeing it as something you have to do to succeed in school; and (3) seeing it as needed to read the word and the world (Freire & Macedo, 1987) by transacting (Rosenblatt, 1978) with texts. The phonics lesson fits into Willis' second category. And the appearance of that category in Karen's classroom occurred because she was forced to defer her definition of reading to the one explicitly presented by the program in her classroom daily. The very essence of what reading is has been appropriated by the company that supplied the program, turning Karen into a conduit for a delivery of that definition of reading. This stands in sharp contrast to the lessons Karen teaches throughout the rest of the day, when her goal is that children appropriate important questions readers ask themselves, such as *Does it make sense?* and *What does it mean?*

We do not yet know the impact of such conflicting definitions of reading. We do know that Karen's students now write less, read less, and listen to fewer high-quality pieces of literature because there's just no time.

Who Owns and Distributes Professional Knowledge?

The company does.

When she asked the district reading administrator about this crucial issue of the definition of reading, Karen heard a strong and clear response. "Teachers in this district have acted as though they are self-employed and they are not self-employed and they need to stop acting as though they are," the administrator told her.

"What does that mean?" I asked her.

"It means," Karen said, her eyes once again filling with tears, "that we are not allowed to think for ourselves or make decisions."

This program leaves no decisions in the minds of the teacher. The teacher cannot decide who needs such intense work with sounds, how much, and for how long each day. The district demands that all teachers do it every day. Karen explained that when a teacher asked at an inservice about the usefulness of the program for her entire class, the company representative said,

"Trust me. This program is good for every child in your class." Karen does not have that kind of trust because she is a smart teacher. But her district and the company do not trust her knowledge. Her decision-making rights have been stripped away by the district's withdrawal of trust in her as an informed professional. The company is heralded as the expert and teachers' knowledge is not honored, sought, or welcomed.

Who Owns (by Identifying and Responding to) Children's Needs?

The company does.

Karen is a "systematic observer" (Taylor, 1993, p. 34) of children; she is smart about child development, teaching, and learning. But her smartness is bracketed during phonics, when the corporation usurps her power to respond to what her children's behaviors are telling her. Some children follow the lesson, some echo what others say, and others are silent or call out anything they have on their minds. This doesn't matter; the lessons continue, line by line, page by page, day by day for the entire school year. What occurs during the daily lessons substantiates (for all children) what Fine and Weis (2003) write about minority children:

> The intellectual, social, and emotional substance that constitutes minority students' lives in this school was routinely treated as irrelevant, to be displaced and silenced. Their responses, spanning acquiescence to resistance, bore serious consequences. (p. 26)

The *serious consequences* are yet to be determined as we watch these children during the coming years. Presently, the children's behaviors indicate their responses to the content of the lesson. Finding phonics cognitively and affectively barren, many initiate and communicate (by their actions) a search for stimulation, contact, and meaning (Snell & Brown, 2000). They find it in their noses, along their ears, and in their clothing. They find it as they suck a bracelet or touch a friend. Their behaviors communicate the mismatches between learners, curriculum, and the interactions children expect in a social learning setting (Durand, 1990). The phonics lesson forces kids to have "tunnel vision" (Smith, 1997, p. 25) about reading as they focus on sounds rather than read to construct meaning.

Since the children's diverse needs are bracketed during the phonics lessons, Karen tolerates some of the children's aberrant behaviors at this time of the day. She explained that she cannot in good conscience ask them to focus on something that is void of meaning. That's one reason she looked up at me teary-eyed during the lesson. She understands that the bracketing of her knowledge is also the bracketing of her students' learning because she is not available to them to help address their cognitive, social, and spiritual needs.

Who Owns Curriculum?

The company does.

Curriculum, according to Dewey (1938), is *what happens* in classrooms. It *may* be enriched by the many relationships that thrive at the intersections of definitions (teacher's and students') of reading, teaching, learning, language, cultures, and experiences. It *may* be multiple voices that join for a moment in an infinite conversation that began long before the moment and will continue long after it (Bakhtin, 1996). Curriculum *may* be a setting for multiple possibilities of expression (Short & Burke, 1991). The phonics program, with its views of teachers as incapable and children as needing intense lessons about the sounds of the language, limits what *may* happen in school. The view of children as needing tiny bits of language, just a little at a time, with abrupt and frequent changes, and little regard for sense making, limits the possibilities of children's understanding and uses of language.

Karen and her students are being held hostage by the corporation's curriculum because she fears being fired for noncompliance. She and other teachers were coerced into compliance with the program when their jobs were threatened with comments such as the administrator's remark about self-employment. Such coercion is a form of violence (Stuckey, 1991) because Karen's professionalism was systematically reduced by threats and intimidation (violent tactics). Relying on the manufactured panic about reading scores (Berliner and Biddle, 1995), corporations moved into this district with strategic plans for convincing teachers (and many others) that the company's program would rescue the students. As the publisher gets rich, the mandated program "dismiss[es] the possibilities of teaching and learning that exist as potentials waiting to be realized" (Meyer, 2001, p. 82) in favor of profit and the promise of homogeneous results.

The curriculum, with its "good for all" message, is essentially about compliance. Teachers are forced to comply with the script. Students are forced to comply with a meaning-void view of reading that teaches them to act like learners in a situation that lacks the essence and substance of what readers do and why readers read. I could find no one in the district with decision-making power that found it objectionable that one of the "pedagogical implications" (Perrone, 1991, p. 24) of the phonics program is that it teaches compliance. The company's de facto curricular goals are at odds with demands for higher performance and better readers who can become responsible and active members of a democracy (Strauss, in press).

Who Owns the Power over Whether to Provide Culturally Responsive Teaching?

The company does.

Culturally relevant pedagogy (Ladson-Billings, 1994) means that teaching and curriculum are constructed with, from, and for students. This brief section is a discussion of cultural relevance and responsiveness in the phonics program.

There is none.

The corporate program does not take into consideration the differences among and between learners' languages and cultures. It does not take into consideration the needs of English language learners, who in past years in Karen's classroom benefited from learning through culturally responsive thematic units and inquiry (Freeman & Freeman, 2000). The program ignores or dismisses the complexities of teaching in a diverse society.

Some might argue that for one hour a day children might very well benefit from focusing on the sound system of the English language. As Karen explained at the beginning of this article, she taught that all day before the mandate. She taught phonics in contexts that were meaningful to her students and respectful of their linguistic (including dialectical) and cultural diversity. She taught it in specific response to their needs as she assessed those daily. For an hour each day, Karen is now forced to ignore the individuality of her students and the specificity of instruction she *could* provide. Her students read less, write less, and find their identities less integrated into their classroom. The long-term effects of this remain to be seen.

Invisible and Silenced Laborers

Teachers like Karen teach all over the United States. Children like the children in New Mexico live and go to school in a variety of places all over the United States. A problem emerges when outside companies, unfamiliar with and not responsive to the individuality of a given school or classroom, work to make a profit on the backs of children and teachers. The corporatization of our public schools is a reality. As children sit in classrooms, they labor on materials created far from the children's lives and experiences. The children labor through workbooks, worksheets, and nonsensical (supposedly decodable) texts. Physically, their bodies labor to behave and focus on tedious work that leaves their minds weary from lack of stimulation and their bodies aching from the physical act of investing their energies in meaningless and uninteresting activity. Our schools are becoming corporate-dominated sweatshops where children are at the lowest level of labor and teachers are low-level management whose job is to keep the laborers involved in the task.

Reflective, sensitive, and informed teachers, like Karen, understand what they are doing and they are pained by it. They are pained because they know that their students' needs and interests are bracketed and dismissed in order to serve the corporation. They labor and suffer under coercion and threats of losing their jobs if they fail to comply and if they fail to force children to comply. And the corporation gets richer.

Quite honestly, I'm confused and angered by this situation, yet it is becoming increasingly commonplace for me to visit a school and witness a preservice or new teacher becoming indoctrinated into the culture of compliance. I'm confused because I just don't understand how (or don't want to believe that) anyone with a sense of consciousness about issues of social justice could play a part in this culture of compliance. I'm angered when I consider the possibility that I have failed my own students in my college of education because I have not brought these issues sufficiently to their consciousness nor have I equipped them to deal with what they are being forced to do. They leave my classroom with such hope and passion, but less than a year later, in their first year of teaching, they succumb to the culture of curricular oppression (Meyer, in press).

More than thirty years ago, Paulo Freire (1970) taught us that reading is a complex process that involves much more than reading the word. Freire's ideas about "reading the world" focus on a process of "conscientization," or consciousness raising, about the distribution of power, wealth, access, justice, and equity. Working with adult students on their basic literacy skills, Freire began teaching reading through an understanding of the questions that readers brought into the classroom. Words and worlds were part of the curriculum because the curriculum was rooted in the words and worlds in which the students lived. Freire's sense of democracy was strong and urgent and he knew that for citizens to be productive and participatory members in a democracy, they must read both the word and the world.

Karen's students are being denied access to thinking about or acting upon their worlds, and their reading of the word is often tainted with nonsense. If we teach that the word is nonsense, then perhaps for some students it is not much of a leap to believe that the world is nonsense. The world is nonsense if children are taught that they have no agency in it. It is nonsense if they are taught to believe that they have no control over their thinking and if they are taught that schools exist to teach one to comply. It is nonsense if school becomes a place to focus on form, or what Bloome (1983) calls procedural display, rather than substantive content.

The corporation gains by such a configuration of school because questions are not asked. The children stop asking questions, the teachers stop asking questions, and the corporation produces a new edition of the program that is marketed as even more effective than the last. The new boxes arrive, the new editions are distributed, the new workbooks and worksheets are completed, and our children leave school learning that school is not a place to learn. More fortunate children return home to rooms full of books, family members with time to read to them and listen to them read, and all the rich stuff of quality literacy lives. Less fortunate children return home to environments that may be rich in literacies, but not the literacy valued by the mainstream or measured by standardized tests (Taylor & Dorsey-Gaines, 1988). The more fortunate students learn in spite of school; the less fortunate are ultimately blamed for not learning and forced into special needs programs or forced out of school. They are the ones pushed into silence (Fine & Weiss, 2003), anger, depression, and the highest category of risk: the risk of not caring.

I do not mean to create a scenario that is simply dichotomous, suggesting that the rich get richer and the poor get poorer. There are exceptions, of course. And the literacy landscape is more complicated than a simple dichotomy. But as I survey that landscape, driving around New Mexico, I wonder how many Karens are crying as they drive home from school, how many children find school irrelevant and empty of meaningful content, and how many billions of dollars corporations are making in a context that they helped to create and work feverishly to protect.

The children in Karen's classroom, the children of New Mexico, and children and teachers around the country are becoming invisible and silenced laborers in the corporate-created factories that used to be schools. Reflective teachers are forced into management roles that focus on delivering a standardized curriculum; thoughtful school leaders are reduced to administering ill-conceived corporate models of teaching and learning; and at the bottom of this weighty pyramid are the flattened minds, bodies, and souls of our children. They are being crushed as their creativity is replaced by a sweatshop mentality in which they *do the work* but reap none of the profits.

References

Allington, R. (2002). *Big brother and the national reading curriculum: How ideology trumped evidence.* Portsmouth, NH: Heinemann.

Annie E. Casey Foundation. (2003). *Kids count.* Retrieved March 24, 2004, from *www.aecf.org/kidscount/databook/*

Bakhtin, M. M. (1996). The problem of speech genres (V. McGee, Trans.). In C. Emerson & M. Holquist (Eds.), *Speech genres and other essays* (pp. 60–102). Austin: University of Texas Press.

Berliner, D. C., & Biddle, B. J. (1995). *The manufactured crisis: Myths, fraud, and the attack on America's public schools.* Reading, MA: Addison-Wesley.

Bloome, D. (1983). Reading as a social process. *Advances in Reading/Language Research, 2,* 165–195.

Coles, G. (2000). *Misreading reading: The bad science that hurts children.* Portsmouth, NH: Heinemann.

Coles, G. (2003). *Reading the naked truth: Literacy, legislation, and lies.* Portsmouth, NH: Heinemann.

Crawford, J. (2004). *Anti-bilingual education initiative in California.* Retrieved March 20, 2004, from *http://ourworld.compuserve.com/homepages/JWCRAWFORD/unz.htm*

Dewey, J. (1938). *Experience and education.* New York: Collier, Macmillan.

Durand, V. M. (1990). *Severe behavior problems: A functional communication training approach.* New York: Guilford.

Fine, M., & Weis, L. (2003). *Silenced voices and extraordinary conversations: Re-imagining schools.* New York: Teachers College Press.

Fordham Institute for Innovation in Social Policy. (2004). *The social health of the states.* Retrieved March 24, 2004, from *www.fordham.edu/general/Graduate_Schools/The_Fordham_Institut7298.html*

Freeman, D., & Freeman, Y. (2000). *Teaching reading in multicultural classrooms.* Portsmouth, NH: Heinemann.

Freire, P. (1970, May). The adult literacy process as cultural action for freedom. *Harvard Educational Review, 40*(2), 205–225.

Freire, P., & Macedo, D. (1987). *Literacy: Reading the word and the world.* Westport, CT: Bergin & Garvey.

Goodman, Y., Watson, D., & Burke, C. (1987). *Reading miscue inventory: Alternative procedures.* New York: Richard C. Owen.

Ladson-Billings, G. (1994). *The dreamkeepers: Successful teachers of African American children.* San Francisco: Jossey-Bass.

Metcalf, S. (2002, January 28). Reading between the lines. *Nation,* pp. 18–22.

Meyer, L. (2003, April). Presentation at the Albuquerque Teachers Federation, Albuquerque, NM. Meyer cites her source as *www.greatschools.net.*

Meyer, R. (2001). *Phonics exposed: Understanding and resisting systematic direct intense phonics instruction.* Mahwah, NJ: Lawrence Erlbaum.

Meyer, R. (in press). The differences a reading methods course made: Lessons from a beginning teacher. *Journal of Reading Education.*

National Reading Panel. (2000). *Teaching children to read: An evidence-based assessment of the scientific research literature on reading and its implications for reading instruction. Report of the subgroups.* Washington, DC: National Institute of Child Health and Human Development.

New Mexico Public Education Department. (2004). *Factsheets.* Retrieved March 24, 2004, from *www.ped.state.nm.us/div/ais/data/fs/state/st. factsheets.html*

Perrone, V. (1991). *A letter to teachers: Reflection on schooling and the art of teaching.* San Francisco: Jossey-Bass.

Peterson, R., & Eeds, M. (1990). *Grand conversations: Literature groups in action.* New York: Scholastic.

Rosenblatt, L. (1978). *The reader, the text, and the poem: The transactional theory of the literary work.* Carbondale and Edwardsville: Southern Illinois University Press.

Short, K., & Burke, C. (1991). *Creating curriculum: Teachers and students as a community of learners.* Portsmouth, NH: Heinemann.

Smith, F. (1997). *Reading without nonsense* (3rd ed.). New York: Teachers College Press.

Snell, M., & Brown, F. (2000). *Instruction of students with severe disabilities* (5th ed.). Upper Saddle River, NJ: Merrill/Prentice Hall.

Strauss, S. (in press). *The linguistics, neurology and politics of phonics: Silent "E" speaks out.* Mahway, NJ: Erlbaum.

Street, B. (1995). *Social literacies: Critical approaches to literacy development.* New York: Longman.

Stuckey, J. E. (1991). *The violence of literacy.* Portsmouth, NH: Boynton/Cook.

Taylor, D. (1993). *From the child's point of view.* Portsmouth, NH: Heinemann.

Taylor, D., & Dorsey-Gaines, C. (1988). *Growing up literate: Learning from inner-city families.* Portsmouth, NH: Heinemann.

Wells, G. (1986). *The meaning makers: Children learning language and using language to learn.* Portsmouth, NH: Heinemann.

West, C. (2004). *An hour with scholar, philosopher, and theologian Dr. Cornel West.* Retrieved March 24, 2004, from *www.democracynow.org/article. pl?sid=03/07/21/1537235&mode=thread&tid=25*

Willis, A. (1997). Focus on research: Historical considerations. *Language Arts, 74*(5), 387–397.

Note: Sections of this chapter are excerpted from Meyer, R. (2002). Captives of the script: Killing us softly with phonics. *Language Arts, 79*(6), 452–461.

9

Basal Reading Programs and the Culture of Literacy

NANCY JORDAN

Towson University

In the classroom illustrated in Figure 9–1, where the Reading Mastery program (Engelmann & Bruner, 1995) is required, the teaching of reading is a one-way transmission of knowledge and ideology from the teachers manuals and reading materials to the teachers and from the teachers to the students. Reading in these classrooms means learning by rote the knowledge provided by the basal reading program. What becomes valid knowledge is what is in the program. The teacher's role is to be a mouthpiece for this knowledge and ideology, not a reinterpreter. The children are expected to unquestioningly ingest this knowledge. But what is this knowledge and ideology that the children are ingesting?

From the beginning of public education in the United States, there was purpose behind forced schooling—a purpose different from the one that many parents, students, their teachers, and their communities envisioned for their schools. A purpose that Thomas Jefferson anticipated and argued against in 1779:

> The most effectual means of preventing (the perversion of power into tyranny are) to illuminate, as far as practicable, the minds of the people at large, and more especially to give them knowledge of those facts which history exhibits, that possessed thereby of the experience of other ages and countries, they may be enabled to know ambition under all its shapes, and prompt to exert their natural powers to defeat its purposes. (Coates, 1995–2001)

This purpose has been forged by the powerful political and economic elite based on its needs for financial domination (Goodlad, 2004; Kozol, 1991; Kohn, 2002; Karp, 1980). This powerful elite saw public schools as the training

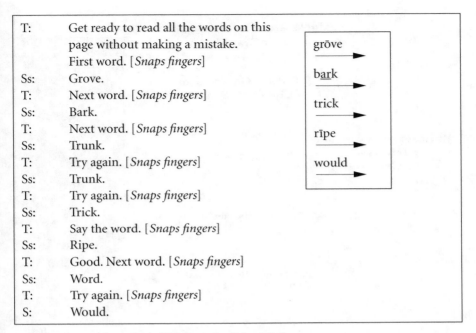

T:	Get ready to read all the words on this page without making a mistake. First word. [*Snaps fingers*]
Ss:	Grove.
T:	Next word. [*Snaps fingers*]
Ss:	Bark.
T:	Next word. [*Snaps fingers*]
Ss:	Trunk.
T:	Try again. [*Snaps fingers*]
Ss:	Trunk.
T:	Try again. [*Snaps fingers*]
Ss:	Trick.
T:	Say the word. [*Snaps fingers*]
Ss:	Ripe.
T:	Good. Next word. [*Snaps fingers*]
Ss:	Word.
T:	Try again. [*Snaps fingers*]
S:	Would.

Figure 9–1. *Second-Grade Reading Exercise (May 2001)*

grounds for its future workers that would maintain the social order. In fact, in 1909 Woodrow Wilson said, "We want one class to have a liberal education. We want another class, a very much larger class of necessity, to forgo the privilege of a liberal education and fit themselves to perform specific difficult manual tasks" (Schneider, 2004). By 1917, American schools were for all intents and purposes controlled by the interests of such people as John D. Rockefeller and Andrew Carnegie, and they came from institutions such as Princeton, Harvard, Stanford, and the National Education Association. This group formed the Education Trust and one of the principal objectives of this group was to "impose on the young the ideal of subordination" (Kidd, 1918).

And what has changed since 1918? Maybe some of the names. In addition to a new Education Trust (2004), we also have groups, such as the Business Roundtable, whose economic interests helped create the No Child Left Behind Act of 2001 and who now encourage members to "influence," "testify," "lobby," and "leverage," to ensure that each state effectively implements the law (Business Roundtable, 2002).

Who are these people that belong to the Business Roundtable? Mostly, they are white and male. Some own the newspapers. Others (like the former CEO of Enron) make outrageous profits as their investors lose their life savings and their employees lose their jobs. And yet others (such as Harold

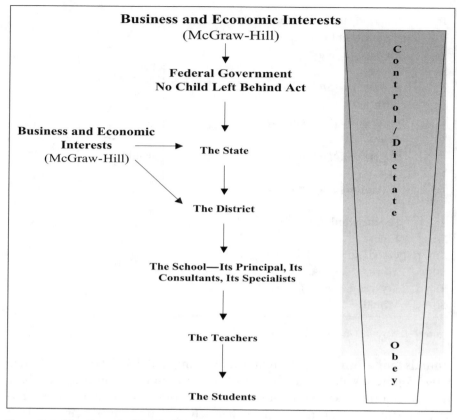

Figure 9–2. *The Control of Public Classrooms*

McGraw) own the companies that publish the mandated programs, such as Reading Mastery II and Open Court. And these programs, as these mostly white male business executives "influence," "testify," "lobby," and "leverage," are being mandated by one school district after another, predominantly for poor minority students and poor students with "limited English speaking skills." Power flows from business and economic interests through several layers of the public school system and ultimately to the classrooms of low-income "failing" schools (See Figure 9–2).

In contrast, let's look at another classroom in a wealthy school district.

Second Grade (June 2002) (O.C. = observer comments, T = teacher, S = students)

O.C.: I arrive during reading time. The children are reading many different books. Books include ones from the Goosebumps series, *Animal Jokes*, an assortment of Clifford books, *Amelia Bedelia*, and the Harry Potter books. Some are sitting in the book area in comfortable chairs. The desks are set up to make tables. All children are reading. Books are in baskets all over this room. There are at least three hundred books on shelves and in baskets. The teacher is also sitting and reading a book to herself. Some children sit on the floor in the reading area. Sixteen children are in this class. Children's work is displayed on every spare space in this classroom. One child has just finished reading a book to herself. She takes another book from a basket at the side of her desk and continues reading. Another child completes a Clifford book and chooses another from the pile on his desk . . .

[*The children read for twenty-four minutes.*]

T: Please take out your reading logs and respond to the reading that you have done today . . .

Later in the day . . .

O.C.: On the board, under the title "Word Work," the teacher has arranged cards with one word on each. The words include *firefighter, cloverleaf, rainbow, highlight, nighttime* . . .

T: Look at our words. Think which words have a long vowel sound in the first word of the compound word. Pick a word with a long sound in the first word and explain why you picked it.

S: I picked *firefighter* because in the first word, *fire*, the *i* is long. The silent *e* at the end tells you that it is a long *i*.

(Ethnographic observations)

In this classroom, like those in many high socioeconomic districts, learning to read is considered to be an active process of meaning construction. Reading instruction begins with the children's interests. Even during phonics instruction, as this lesson illustrates, children are encouraged to actively create their own understandings. Instead of having them passively recite reading lessons, teachers encourage children to use their background knowledge to relate new information to prior knowledge. Children are encouraged to predict, infer, and problem solve as they read. They are taught to use semantic, syntactic, and graphophonemic cues to construct meaning from text; and they are given time to practice these skills while reading authentic and privileged texts of the elite (Altwerger et al., 2001).

Because they live in this wealthy district, the children participating in this lesson, even though they are in a low socioeconomic school, have been receiving the same curriculum as the class privileged for a "liberal" education. No one would ever consider eliminating from the curriculum of the elite the higher-level thinking skills, such as problem solving, creative explorations, hands-on experiments, and other such components that have proven to be central to learning.

And yet the superintendent of this district has just decided that he will begin a phonics initiative and adopt a phonics program to help struggling readers, especially those with "limited English speaking skills." All children, not just students with limited English-speaking skills, in schools that receive Title I money will receive this intensive instruction, even though the county's kindergarten current initiative has showed that its program has helped low-income students "master early reading skills" on the same level as their peers in more affluent schools ("Schools to Start," 2002). In fact, this superintendent has targeted his phonics initiative only for schools with low-income students and not for schools that enroll their more wealthy peers with equivalent reading skills. I wonder which phonics program is being proposed? Open Court? Reading Mastery? Whose and what purpose is being served? If Thomas Jefferson could see us now!

Although many studies (see, for example, Chapters two, three, six, and nine in this book) examine the efficacy of using programs like Open Court and Reading Mastery for teaching reading, very little has been written describing the underlying social and political ideology these particular commercial reading programs dispense. (Please note that studies in the 1980s—Luke, 1988; Anyon, 1980—describe the underlying social and political ideology of school texts and curriculum, but not these particular texts.) In what follows, I will describe how the basal reading programs Open Court and Reading Mastery reproduce and perpetuate a white androcentric ideology and how, through their prescribed practices, they socialize children into submissive and passive roles, roles that leave them, if they are not of the elite, imprisoned in the institutional world of schooling—a world that will continue to leave them disadvantaged. Through analyzing basal-directed classroom dialogue and lessons; describing the themes in basal texts; describing how characters are signified in these texts; examining how language is used in the texts; and describing the reality that these texts reflect, I will show how children are being socialized through the "lenses" of white "androcentrism," racial/ethnic/"gender polarization," and "biological essentialism" (borrowing from and building on Bem's [1993] terminology and work on gender).

This is not an exhaustive description, in that I mostly examine the texts and lessons from *Reading Mastery II, Storybook 2* (Engelmann & Bruner, 1995) and from *Open Court, Level 2, Books 1* and *2* (2000) and *Collections for Young Scholars, Volume 2, Books 1* and *2* (2000). The stories in *Open Court, Books 1* and *2* are essentially the same as the stories in *Collections for Young Scholars, Books 1* and *2*. Even though I look only at the second-grade programs, I will reveal a general pattern found in these basal series at all grades.

What do I mean by white androcentrism, racial/ethnic/gender polarization, and biological essentialism? For me, the lens of white androcentrism is not just white male centeredness. It includes the notion that white males and their definitions, experiences, and conceptions are the norm—the unbiased standard. For example, capitalism is viewed as an unbiased norm. The "others" (nonwhite males and all females) and their experiences are seen as specific departures from that norm. It is not that white males are considered to be superior and others to be inferior, but that white males are described as human and others as "the other." The lens of racial/ethnic/gender polarization is not that white men and the others are seen to be basically dissimilar from each other, but that this perceived dissimilarity becomes central to the way the social life of the culture is ordered. This dissimilarity also permeates so many facets of the social world that a cultural connection is cemented between race, ethnicity, gender, and virtually every other aspect of human experience, including ways of speaking, social roles, status, schooling, occupations, and economic conditions. Then, through the lens of biological essentialism, white androcentrism and race/ethnic/gender polarization are rationalized and legitimized. They become the natural and predestined consequences of the intrinsic biological natures of white men and the others. And power flows accordingly. Why else would the No Child Left Behind Act be based on and derive its name from the correlation between social class and educational achievement? And public schooling becomes what this unbiased white androcentric norm makes it (see Figure 9–1).

The Program as Ritual

The lesson from Reading Mastery II that begins this chapter typifies this particular program. Children sit through hours and hours of these repetitive reading lessons. They recite and chant to the teachers' snaps. They answer questions in unison or individually about texts, such as What is Sid doing? What is the name of the shop? and Who was very sad? These questions can most often be answered with one word. And there is always a snap and a recitation. Speed and accuracy are drilled. And most importantly, everyone is expected to stay on task—no thinking, no questioning, and no opinions—the silencing within ritual. Now let's look at dialogues that typify Open Court lessons:

Second Grade, April 2001

T: Let's blend these words. All together. *K-i-ck*. What's the word?

S: Kick.

T: Next. All together. *P-i-ck*. What's the word?

S: Pick.

T: Next. All together. *T-i-ck.* What's the word?

S: Pick.

T: . . . Something you can do with a ball.

S: Kick.

T: A word that rhymes with sack.

S: Back.

[*Also*]

T: Read the title and look at the pictures on pages 23 and 24. What do you think will happen in the story? Who do you think is in the story? What do you think will happen? Where does the story take place? Why did the story happen?

[*And*]

T: Now students, you need to get out your anthologies. Yesterday, I read *Follow the Dream* [1995] to you. Today, we will reread it together. Let's begin. . . . Let's see if we can remember some things about the story. What was Columbus' dream?

S: To sail across the ocean.

T: Good. How many ships?

S: Three.

T: Good. What are the names?

S: Pinta, Nina, and Santa Maria.

T: Yes. Pinta, Nina, and Santa Maria. What was the thing called that he wrote in?

S: A diary.

T: No. We might call it a journal. On a ship it is called a log. What year did this happen?

S: Fourteen ninety-two.

T: Good. What sailed in 1492?

S: Columbus.

T: OK. Close the books.

[*Later the students will take an Open Court test with similar questions.*]

As these lessons demonstrate, the Open Court program differs from the Reading Mastery II program in that students are taught to ask questions, to predict and confirm, to use background knowledge, and to make inferences as they read. Yet, like Reading Mastery II, these lessons are part of a ritual. Each lesson becomes a chant. Again, children sit through hours and hours of these repetitive reading lessons—new words, different stories, the same chant. The Open Court program appears to give students voice, but ultimately there is only one correct answer—a one-word correct answer. So while students are encouraged to give voice to their ideas, those ideas are ultimately silenced by the program. I'm not sure which is worse, never to have voice or to be given voice and to then have it rejected. And, as with Reading Mastery II, accuracy and fluency (speed) are at the core of the program.

And what are the children learning through the rituals of both of these programs? Are they learning to tolerate repetitive tasks, to be accurate, to be quick, to be obedient, to be compliant, and, most significantly, to be silent? Are they learning to be docile? It could be argued that these are the most necessary skills for low-wage jobs in twenty-first century capitalistic society. And whose children are most likely to receive these lessons?

The Themes

"The Seed Shop" in *Reading Mastery II, Storybook 2* opens with a man at work in a seed shop. When the boss leaves, she instructs the man to watch the shop and take care of a pile of notes on a table. The man reads the first note but reads it incorrectly because he has not learned to read words with the consonant-vowel-consonant-final *e* configuration. He reads the vowel as a short sound. Consequently, the man follows the directions incorrectly and makes a mistake. This continues through notes with key words such as *pine*, *pane, cone, slope*, and *tape*. As can be imagined, the boss returns to quite a few problems. She then decides that she needs to teach her employee to read. And now when a note tells the man to do something, "he does it." This makes the man and his boss happy. Thus, being good means being able to read to follow the boss' directions.

Permeating *Storybook 2* is the overarching theme that learning to read makes you a good person (see Figure 9–3). Eight out of twenty stories have this theme, and in six out of these eight stories, learning to read is further defined as learning to read directions. This is portrayed as necessary for making you a good employee, a good helper, and, if you are the best reader, a teacher. The other themes in *Storybook 2* are doing good deeds makes you a good person—be kind and nice (four out of twenty stories); working hard makes you a good person (four out of twenty stories); if you are good you will live in a nice house, have a nice car, have a lot of cash, and have a dog (two out of twenty stories); and if you are pretty and have nice clothes, you will be liked (two out of twenty stories). Throughout, these stories drill the concept that learning to follow the rules makes you a good person. And ultimately these stories preach docility—don't wish to be anyone else; be happy with who you are.

8 of 20 Stories	4 of 20 Stories	4 of 20 Stories	2 of 20 Stories	2 of 20 Stories
Learning to read makes you a good person. ↓ Learning to read directions makes you a good and nice person. ↓ Purposes for learning to read: • To become a good employee • to become a good helper • to get things done • if you are the best reader, you can be a teacher	Doing good deeds makes you a good person—be kind and nice.	Working hard makes you a good person.	If you are good, you will • live in a nice house • have a nice car • have a lot of cash • have a dog	You will be liked if you • are pretty • have nice clothes

Figure 9–3. *Themes from* Reading Mastery II, Storybook 2

As with the texts in Reading Mastery II, the enveloping theme of the texts in Open Court and Collections for Young Scholars is also being good. The texts in Open Court, however, are organized into units around the topics of being brave, the virtues of being rich or poor, kindness, and dinosaurs. (See Figure 9–4.) Stories in the Being Brave unit include the adventures of Frog and Toad in *Dragons and Giants* (Lobel, 1971), the legends *A Hole in the Dike* (Green, 1974) and *The Legend of the Bluebonnet* (dePaola, 1983), a photo-essay about Sally Ride (Behrens, 1984), and a realistic fiction story titled *Molly the Brave and Me* (O'Connor, 1990). Being brave in these texts connotes being good, and being good means being a good friend, doing good deeds, working hard, and sacrificing for others. Likewise, in the Kindness unit, kindness connotes goodness and goodness means being a good friend, doing good deeds,

Being Brave/ Being Good	Rich and Poor	Kindness/ Goodness	Dinosaurs
• being a good friend • doing good deeds • sacrificing for others	• being a good and kind leader leads to riches • being virtuous and honest is better than being rich • being poor and giving is better than being rich and greedy • working hard and caring about what you do is more important than riches	• being a good friend • doing good deeds • working hard • sacrificing for others	

Figure 9–4. *Collections for Young Scholars, Vol 2 Book 1*

working hard, and sacrificing for others. Rewards and awards are also conferred on those that give (goodness) in this unit in stories such as *The Elves and the Shoemaker* (Littledale, 1975), *Clara Barton: Red Cross Pioneer* (Grant, 1974), and *Music, Music for Everyone* (Williams, 1984). Similarly, in the Rich and Poor unit, goodness can also lead to rewards and awards in such stories as *The Simple Prince* (Yolen, 1978) and *Cinderella* (Perrault, 1977), where goodness and kindness lead to riches. Yet, even more persistently, goodness is specified through themes that include being virtuous and honest is better than being rich; being poor and giving is better than being rich and greedy; and working hard and caring about what you do is more important than riches. In other words, being honest, caring, doing good deeds, working hard, and self-sacrificing are reward enough and will make you happy. You might be working for minimum wage, homeless, and hungry, but you'll be happy.

It might seem simplistic to render these stories, many of them all-time favorites and written by distinguished authors, to such a reductionist conclusion, but layered together, these stories, as with the stories in Reading Mastery II, reinforce and socialize students into being "good," compliant, and docile. Where are the stories where goodness encompasses such character descriptors as adventurous, creative, ingenious, aggressive, ambitious, assertive, confident, enterprising, steady, and strong? Are these the stories for the elite? With a steady diet of goodness as defined by these programs, students are socialized into the roles for the other. Their stories are left untold. Their voices are silenced as they learn the connotations for *good*—connotations that leave them disempowered and docile in the institutional world of schooling.

The Story Characters

Returning to "The Seed Shop" in *Reading Mastery II, Storybook 2*, the man, Sid, does not read "the right way." He wants to be good and follow his boss' orders, but his reading prevents him from correctly completing these orders. Sid, though, takes his work seriously and, using his knowledge of the consonant-vowel-consonant configuration, creates his own interpretations of his boss' notes. He actually tries to make written instructions, such as "Send a cone to Sam's tree farm" and "Send ten pine trees," make sense. Remember, this is a seed shop and not a garden center. Sid is proud of his work. But when his boss returns, he learns that he made bad mistakes. He is bad. Sid, as the pictures denote, is Hispanic. After screaming and yelling at Sid, his boss teaches him to read "the right way" and he becomes a "good" employee. If a note tells him to do something, "he does it." Thus, the signification for Sid (who is bad) is the cultural code for being a Hispanic male, the other, as defined by white androcentric ideology. Learning to read "the right way," and *compliantly* following orders reclassifies Sid as "good." Consequently, in becoming good, Sid becomes impotent. The others in *Storybook 2* succumb to similar fates. Figure 9–5 reveals the denotations for character by race and gender in *Reading Mastery II, Storybook 2*.

White males are the dominant characters. These white males over-whelmingly take on the cultural code for white men in a white androcentric ideology—the white men/good denotation. The others, as I have shown, do

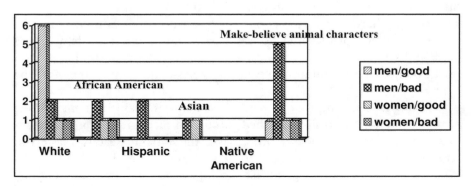

Figure 9–5. *Characters in* Reading Mastery II, Storybook 2

not fare so well. If they are male, they are bad or are not represented in the stories. Except for one white female, the others have not learned to read the right way, to work hard, and to be obedient. This white female has, so she can be a teacher. The others are bad until they conform to the cultural code for the other. In addition, the make-believe characters predominantly take on the men/bad cultural code. It could be surmised that these characters serve to further teach lessons of docility without the attachment of race, even though these stories are not gender neutral. The female characters are left to perpetuate the roles for being female in an androcentric ideology—nice, pure, weak, dependent, bossy, silly, evil, self-sacrificing, and so on.

In contrast, the stories in *Collections for Young Scholars, Volume 2, Book 1* are primarily about white males and their experiences (see Figure 9–6). These white male characters mostly conform to the men/good cultural code. White females are also represented in the stories. As with the females in Reading Mastery, the connotations for being white and female are nice, pure, weak, dependent, silly, hardworking, and self-sacrificing. For example, the story about the life of Sally Ride predominantly describes her as hardworking and hard playing in sports. Her hard work led her to be the "best qualified" (p. 60). By the end of the story the word *determination* was also applied to signify Ride. It seems to me that in order for a woman to be a pioneer in any field, she would need to be more than just hardworking or even determined.

Similarly, in *Clara Barton: Red Cross Pioneer* (p. 200), Barton is portrayed as the definitive caregiver—self-sacrificing, caring, hardworking, an angel, and devoted to others. According to these stories, through hard work and self-sacrifice, these women triumphed, never confronted or negated by discrimination. These two texts list events in the lives of Ride and Barton rather than develop them as subjects who, it could be surmised, had to overcome great obstacles to obtain their success in a male world. Their lives are

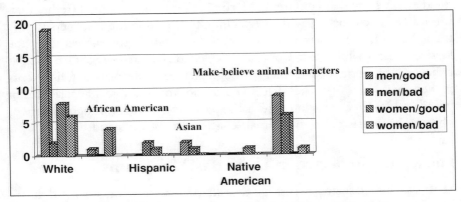

Figure 9–6. *Characters in* Collections for Young Scholars, Volume 2, Book 1

left signified by the following items and questions: "Where did Sally Ride grow up? What was Sally's favorite school subject? How did Sally learn about the astronauts? How long did Sally's astronaut training last?" ("Comprehension Checkpoints," p. 13) and "Number the events in Clara Barton's life; When did Clara Barton find out about the Red Cross? How old was Clara Barton when she died? Which word best describes Clara Barton? a. caring, b. selfish, c. proud" (p. 45). By sticking with the facts about the lives of the others and delineating their lives to such questions, even when they achieve fame, these exercises rendered the others as lifeless, docile. And what of the others and their actual life experiences? Mostly nonexistent (see Figure 9–6).

Likewise, in *Collections for Young Scholars, Volume 2, Book 2,* the story about the life of Squanto becomes the story of the Pilgrims: "Why did the first group of Englishmen come to America? What month did the first Pilgrims arrive in America? What happened to the Pilgrims during their first winter in America? Who was Squanto? Squanto could speak to the Pilgrims because he spoke . . . Why did the Pilgrims have the first Thanksgiving?" (p. 78). And what are the readers expected to learn about Squanto? That he learned the Englishmen's language? That he belonged to the Patuxet people? A life silenced by comprehension questions.

Other types of questions further connote the others. Consider the questions asked about Martin Luther King Jr.: "Was Martin Luther King, Jr., a good leader? Why do you think so?" Asking if the character is a good leader assumes that he could also be considered a bad one, and the children have the option of coming to that conclusion. Contrast these questions with the one asked about Abraham Lincoln: "What do you admire most about Abraham Lincoln?" This question implies that there is so much to admire about Lincoln that the children can just pick the characteristic they admire most. And in our culture, being admirable as opposed to good implies strength. It could even be argued that framing Martin Luther King Jr. as good (rather than admirable) is consistent with the connotation of goodness so persistently applied to others in *Book 1* (see Figure 9–4), in which the subject takes the passive role. So, while Open Court and Collections for Young Scholars look as if they tell the stories of the others through pictures and stories that list events in their lives, the stories are lifeless and do not touch the real experiences of their subjects. Their questions likewise appear to be written through the lens of white androcentrism. The white male continues to be the standard.

The Reality Reflected in These Basal Programs

At this point, it seems necessary to ask: Who writes the stories that are found in Reading Mastery II and the Open Court programs? The authors

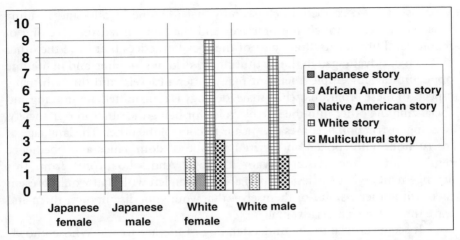

Figure 9–7. *Authors of the Stories in* Collections for Young Scholars, Volume 2, Book 2

of the stories in *Reading Mastery II, Storybook 2* are Siegfried Engelmann and Elaine Bruner (1995). They are both white. As I have discussed, the stories in Open Court have been written by different authors and organized into themes. The pictures, the topics, and the events in the texts appear to represent the lives and experiences of many different groups of people. Yet these stories are mainly authored by white writers, both male and female (see Figure 9–7).

And when classroom lessons and dialogues, themes, character descriptions, and the language in the stories are considered along with the authorship of the stories, these stories become the stories of a white androcentric ideology. This white androcentric control is symbolized through the basal assignments, its stories, its tests, and its quiet classrooms with the teacher in front lecturing. In fact, the focus is on control and who has it and who should learn to not have it.

In Conclusion

It appears that layer after layer, from the lessons to the texts themselves, and most aspects of their literacy learning in school, are teaching these children what it means to be the other. The programs aligned with federal and state mandates determine that they will read only what they are allowed to read, imagine what they are allowed to imagine, and become what they are allowed to become. It is no wonder that many resist learning to read or that the instruction fails them. Where are the voices of the others—their realities?

As I have described, in classrooms that use Open Court and Reading Mastery II, even though the practices and the texts differ, the teaching of literacy and literacy itself are part of the social practices that leave the other children disadvantaged in the institutional world of schooling and in lifetime opportunities for employment. At many different levels, and through many aspects of these programs, white male ideology is transmitted, reinforcing and socializing the other into the narrow roles for being the other in our society. Reading instruction becomes the means to control the other. The language of instruction, both spoken and written, is one of dominance and obedience reminiscent of the master-servant ideology. And who profits from this arrangement? What stories (scripts) are children left with that would present them with other visions for themselves that would not disempower them and leave them at such a disadvantage?

It seems crucial to the understanding of literacy to ask: Whose knowledge and doctrines are maintained through literacy instruction? Whose programs are used and why? Whose stories can be told? And who benefits? Do they really want no child to be left behind? As educators, we must challenge the structures that allow the perpetuation of these programs. Maybe then all children will have the opportunity to use literacy to build their own lives, and with our help, envision new ways of being.

References

Altwerger, B., Arya, P., Jin, L., Lang, D., Laster, B., Martens, P., Pitcher, S., Renman, N., Wilson, P., & Wiltz, N. (2001, December). The impact of reading programs on second graders' reading. Symposium conducted at the annual meeting of the National Reading Conference, Miami.

Anyon, J. (1980). Social class and the hidden curriculum of work. *Journal of Education, 162,* 67–91.

Bem, S. L. (1993). *The lenses of gender: Transforming the debate on sexual inequality.* New Haven, CT: Yale University Press.

Business Roundtable. (2002). *Business Roundtable tool kit: Action steps.* Retrieved from *http://brt.org/toolkit/ActionSteps.html*

Coates, E. R. (1995–2001). *Thomas Jefferson on politics and government.* University of Virginia Library. Retrieved September 11, 2004, from *http://etext.virginia.edu/etcbin/ot2www-jeffquot?specfile=/web/data/ jefferson/quotations/www/jeffquot.o2w&act=surround&offset=853547& tag=39.+Educating+the+People&query=The+most+effectual+means+ of+preventing*

Collections for Young Scholars, volume 2, book 1. (2000). Chicago: Open Court.

Collections for Young Scholars, volume 2, book 2. (2000). Chicago: Open Court.

Education Trust. (2004). Retrieved from *www.edtrust.org*

Engelmann, S., & Bruner, E. (1995). *Reading Mastery II: Storybook 2.* Columbus, OH: SRA Macmillan/McGraw-Hill.

Goodlad, J. (2004). *A place called school: Twentieth anniversary edition.* Columbus, OH: McGraw-Hill.

Karp, W. (1980, May). Textbook America: The teaching of history. *Harper's Magazine.* Retrieved from *www.sourcetext.com/grammarian/textbook2.html*

Kick, R. (2003). The educational system was designed to keep us uneducated and docile. *The memory hole: Rescuing knowledge, freeing information.* Retrieved from *www.thememoryhole.org/edu/school-mission.htm*

Kohn, A. (2002). The 500-pound gorilla. *Phi Delta Kappan, 84*(2), 112–119.

Kozol, J. (1991). *Savage inequalities.* New York: Crown.

Luke, A. (1988). *Literacy, textbooks, and ideology.* Philadelphia: Falmer.

Open Court Reading, level 2, book 1. (2000). Columbus, OH: SRA.

Open Court Reading, level 2, book 2. (2000). Columbus, OH: SRA.

Schneider, C. E. (2004) Birthday reflections. Retrieved January 10, 2005, from *http://www.aacu-edu.org/liberaleducation/le-wi04presidentsmessage.cfm*

Schools to start phonics initiative: Plan aims to close English skill gap. (2002, October 3). *The Washington Post,* p. MN3.

Story Book References

Behrens, J. (1984). *Sally Ride, Astronaut: An American First.* New York: Scholastic.

dePaola, T. (1983). *The Legend of the Bluebonnet.* New York: Putnam Publishing Group.

Grant, M. (1974). *Clara Barton: Red Cross Pioneer.* New York: Children's Press.

Green, N. (1974). *The Hole in the Dike.* New York: Scholastic.

Littledale, F. (1975). *The Elves and the Shoemaker.* New York: Scholastic.

Lobel, A. (1971). *Dragons and Giants.* New York: Harper Collins.

O'Connor, J. (1990). *Molly the Brave and Me.* New York: Random House.

Perrault, C. (1977). *Cinderella.* Germany: Nord-Sud Verlag.

Williams, V. (1984). *Music, Music for Everyone.* New York: Greenwillow.

Yolen, J. (1978). *The Simple Prince.* New York: Parent's Magazine Press.

10

An Open Look at the
Open Court Program

POONAM ARYA, BARBARA LASTER, AND LIJUN JIN

"Initial reading instruction relies on explicit teaching of sounds, blending of sounds into words, and on the leverage of using this knowledge for reading and writing" (*Open Court Reading, Level 2, Book 1,* 2000, p. 15 TE). The philosophy of the Open Court program (2000) for initial reading instruction is evident in this statement. According to the Open Court program, the focus in grades K–1 is on the alphabetic principle, the development of print and book awareness, phonemic awareness, sound-letter association, sound-spelling association, and fluency. Each skill of decoding is taught systematically and explicitly. Teachers are advised to follow a set instructional plan for both word study and compre-hension. In grade 2, the program gradually shifts the emphasis from decoding skills to developing reading fluency and comprehension (2000, p. 18). The focus is on literal and inferential comprehension that is teacher directed.

This philosophy was examined in a study of two sites that used the Open Court program. The two schools, OC School and BLOC School (Balanced Literacy–Open Court) both used Open Court for two and one-half years before the study commenced. The BLOC School added a balanced literacy initiative to the Open Court program during the year of the study.

Background

Teachers, researchers, and policy makers are exploring what it means to be a reader, how written words are identified and learned, and how reading is learned and taught (Allington, 2002; Garan, 2001; NRP, 2000; Pressley, 2002; Snow, Burns, & Griffin, 1998; Yatvin, 2002). Studies have addressed these questions in relation to the Open Court Reading program. Specifically, Foorman, Francis,

Fletcher, and Schatschneider (1998) compared three reading approaches that "took place in a print-rich environment with a significant literature base" (p. 37). The three approaches were Open Court, called DC or direct code; EC or embedded code, which involved the teaching of a specific list of onsets and rimes, guided reading, and other comprehension-focused activities; and IC or implicit code, which mirrored a whole language approach. Students, all of whom were first and second graders receiving Title I services, were given a variety of assessments. Those in the Open Court/DC classrooms did statistically better on measures of decoding, phonological processing, and word reading than students in the other classrooms. There were, though, no statistically significant differences in comprehension among the groups, as measured by a cloze test that determined understanding at the sentence level. Another measure of comprehension aimed at understanding of narrative and expository passages was deemed to be too difficult for many of the children in the study. Foorman et al. suggest that future studies examine the connection of early explicit decoding instruction and later reading comprehension instruction. They also recommend further exploration of the nature of explicit decoding instruction, specifically, the role of scripted teacher instruction versus more flexible teacher instruction.

Barrett (1995) examined classrooms in which Open Court phonics was embedded in a "balanced literacy" curriculum. He evaluated the reading achievement of first-grade students in three groups: Open Court phonics materials integrated with a district's language arts curriculum, phonics instruction in the context of guided and shared reading, and a control group. Posttests revealed the Open Court and phonics-in-context groups outperformed the control group.

The study described in this chapter was designed to add to the knowledge base about the impact of the Open Court program on young children. The specific research questions were

1. What strategies do second graders at two Open Court sites use to construct meaning from text?
2. What is the impact of the Open Court program on students' knowledge of the reading process?
3. What are the views of teachers who use the Open Court program?

Methodology

Participants

Participants in the study were drawn from two urban elementary schools in a large Mid-Atlantic city. The two schools, OC School and BLOC School, were located in urban working-class neighborhoods and had similar demographic characteristics. Specifically they each had a high percentage of free and reduced lunch (87 to 92 percent) and at least 98 percent of the students were African American. All of the students in the study were fluent English speakers, did not receive special education services, and had attended the same school from kindergarten through second grade.

The original sample consisted of thirty second graders at each school—ten high, ten average, and ten low readers, as designated by the school personnel. Because of attrition, at the end of the study, there were forty-nine participants: twenty-two at BLOC and twenty-seven at OC. Attrition was attributed to absenteeism and scheduling conflicts. At OC School students were homogenously grouped in classes for reading instruction while at BLOC School students were heterogeneously grouped.

Data Sources

Materials

Children read one of twenty-four texts that were selected for use in the study. All reading materials represented authentic literature (authored trade books) with an identifiable story grammar. The researchers broadly followed Fountas and Pinnell's (1996) system for leveling the books. They ranged from preprimer to grade 4. To give students some choice in the books they read, three texts at each level were provided. To make sure that students were reading material that was somewhat challenging to them, students read texts that fell within a predetermined range for miscue frequency and retelling performance. The researchers also made sure that none of the texts was being used for instruction at the two sites and that students had not read them previously. In taping the readings and retellings, standard procedures for miscue analysis were utilized.

Retelling outlines were developed for each selected story, following Leslie Morrow's guidelines (2001). Oral retellings of the texts were used to ascertain each student's comprehension score. The retelling outlines contained the elements of setting, characters, plot episodes, story cohesion, and inferences, themes, and connections. Each retelling outline was reviewed independently by at least two researchers before finalizing the form to be used for data collection.

The Burke Reading Interview (Goodman, Watson, & Burke, 1987) was used in order to discover students' understandings of the reading process and perceptions of themselves as readers. (See appendix at end of chapter.) To determine the students' phonic and structural analysis skills in decontextualized contexts, a standardized phonics test, the Word Attack subtest of the Woodcock-Johnson Psycho-Educational Achievement Battery (Woodcock, 1998), was also administered.

Finally, an open-ended interview with nine prompts was given to each of the six teachers involved in the study. These interviews were aimed at providing data about views of the Open Court program as well as views about reading instruction in general.

Procedures

A team of researchers worked with each student on a one-on-one basis in administering the miscue analysis. After students read the text out loud, they were asked to do an oral retelling of the story. They were also administered the Woodcock-Johnson Word Attack subtest and the Burke Reading Interview. The collection of data was counterbalanced in that half of the students read the text and did the retelling first and half took the Word Attack subtest and the reading interview first. Reading sessions were audiotaped for later analysis. To triangulate the student data, the researchers conducted interviews with the teachers. These sessions were also audiotaped for later analysis.

Data Analysis

Students' readings were analyzed according to Miscue Analysis Procedure I (Goodman et al., 1987) to learn about their strategy use and their skill in comprehending (constructing meaning while reading). All miscues were coded by two researchers. Interrater reliability of .90 was established for coding of all miscues. Researchers also analyzed the retellings of texts for inclusion of story elements, sequencing, inferences, and cohesiveness. Each element was scored on a scale of 0 to 2, with a score of 0 indicating no evidence and a score of 2 indicating strong evidence. Each retelling was analyzed by two researchers and in cases of disagreement, a third researcher resolved the differences. An interrater reliability of .95 was established.

Phonics scores, in terms of percentiles, and standard scores were computed using the methods described in the Woodcock-Johnson Psychological Battery. The metacognitive interviews were also independently coded and scored for strategy use.

Descriptive statistics were used to identify patterns of reading at each site. In addition, multivariate statistics enhanced the understanding of relationships of groups within sites and across sites. Data were triangulated so that multiple data sources (miscues, retellings, phonics in and out of context, and interviews) supported conclusions.

Findings

There are two major components of the findings: (1) reading behaviors of students (individual students' phonic scores, oral reading miscues, retellings, and metacognitive reports); and (2) interviews of teachers.

Reading Strategies of Students

Although there were no statistically significant differences between the two schools, there were interesting variations regarding accuracy, construction of meaning while reading, and comprehension after reading. These will be reported as well.

Phonics in Isolation

The children at the two schools displayed strong phonic knowledge, as reflected in their standardized scores for decoding isolated nonwords. At OC School, children's mean standard score was 111.65, and at BLOC School it was 115.18. This is at the very upper end of the average range for second graders (average is equivalent to 100 with a range of 85 to 115). It is notable that at both schools the designated grouping of the children as high, middle, or low readers followed the pattern of this particular skill of pseudoword reading, although all fell within the second-grade range. (See Figure 10–1.)

Reading Strategies

A careful examination of miscues made by students when reading orally was done to better understand students' use of in-process reading strategies. Analysis of the miscues of students at the two sites showed students' high use of graphic and sound cues. The children at the two Open Court schools used graphic and sound knowledge on average about 88 percent of the time to decode, with a focus on initial and/or ending parts of words. It is interesting to note that they did not have a high number of nonwords among their miscues; they generally substituted real words in the sentences, whether or not they made sense. See Figure 10–2 for two examples.

Group	OC	BLOC
High	133.25	134.57
Middle	108.00	116.42
Low	92.71	97.12

Figure 10–1. *Phonics Standard Scores*

Child 71
Student: silently
Text: "All right," said Peter <u>slowly</u>, "bring it out now."

                                        —*A Letter to Amy* (Keats, 1998a)

Child 74
Student: nighttime   stand   caused
Text: But the <u>nightmare</u> tried to <u>sneak</u> back down the stairs. So I <u>chased</u> it.

                          —*There's Something in My Attic* (Mayer, 1988)

Figure 10–2. *Substitutions*

The examples in Figure 10–2 also illustrate the use of syntactic cues by students at the two sites. They often substituted words that were the same part of speech as the text. For OC School, children's syntactic acceptability (either yes or partial) was 71.5 percent, and at BLOC School, children's syntactic acceptability was 69.6 percent. The pattern of miscues called grammatical strength (the relationship between syntactic, semantic, and correction miscues) indicates that children used their knowledge of language structure in phrases and sentences. Children at OC School had 41.3 percent and at BLOC School 39.2 percent, which shows that many times the children kept the structure of the English language in mind when reading.

The miscue data indicates that while the children relied on their graphophonic and syntactic knowledge, it was often at the expense of meaning. It is noteworthy that 38 percent of the miscues made by children at BLOC and 40 percent of the miscues made by children at OC were not semantically acceptable. This was particularly true of the low readers at both of the schools. For example, a low reader at BLOC produced the miscue in Figure 10–3.

Although children sometimes used some semantic cues to make sense of part of a sentence (semantic acceptability partial—OC 27.7 percent and BLOC 29.9 percent) or make sense of an entire sentence (semantic acceptability yes— OC 30.5 percent and BLOC 32.9 percent), they did not consider the entire story

---

Child 2
Student: straight necklace
Text: One evening Father Goat asked, "Has anyone seen my <u>striped</u> <u>necktie</u>?"

                          —*Gregory, the Terrible Eater* (Sharmat, 1983)

Figure 10–3. *Use of Syntax*

> Child 25
> **Student:**   **changed**
> **Text:**   Peter <u>chased</u> it this way and that.
>
> *—A Letter to Amy*

Figure 10–4. *Making Sense at the Sentence Level but Not the Story Level*

meaning. This point is illustrated in one student's reading of *A Letter to Amy* (Keats, 1998a). In the text, a sentence describes how a letter is blown in the wind. In the next sentence, the student read the miscue shown in Figure 10–4.

Students at both schools also had very few partial corrections, unsuccessful attempts to correct miscues (OC 6.0 percent and BLOC 3.2 percent). This indicates an unwillingness to take risks in trying to correct, or a lack of awareness when miscues did not make sense.

Book Level and Comprehension

Although the students at the two schools had similar miscue patterns, they exhibited some differences in the book level they could read and in comprehension of the stories. While most of the students at both schools read stories considered to be appropriate for second or third graders, students at OC School read books somewhat less challenging (average level of 4.7) than students at BLOC School (average level of 5.5). (See Figure 10–5.)

All but five out of forty-nine children read authored trade books within the second-grade level. Seven readers read the most difficult book available, which was at a late third-grade/early fourth-grade level. The contrast between the two schools was especially evident in the top and low groups. The mean book level read by children in the top group at BLOC was 7.6 in comparison to a mean level of 6.5 read by the top group at OC. The difference was just as

School/ Book Level	1	2	3	4	5	6	7	8
OC N = 27	3	0	3	3	7	6	2	3
BLOC N = 22	0	2	1	3	3	8	1	4

Figure 10–5. *Number of Students Reading Books at Each of Eight Levels*

Child 75

"Story about brother Titch. Where his brother and sister had something um . . . and he told them wrong um . . . in her drink."

—Titch

Figure 10–6. *Retelling Sample by OC Student*

evident with the low group, at BLOC the low group read on the mean level of 3.6 and the low group at OC read on the mean level of 2.5. The middle groups were not as different, with the BLOC middle group reading on the 5.6 level and the OC group reading on the 5.1 level.

Another area of analysis was the children's retellings of the stories they read. The retelling scores ranged from 23 percent to 93 percent at BLOC School and from 1 percent to 86 percent at OC School. The students at BLOC School had a mean retelling score of 56.8 percent and those at OC School had a mean retelling score of 53.4 percent. When looking more in depth at the retellings of children at OC School, researchers found they sometimes lacked cohesiveness and made fewer inferences and connections than the children at BLOC School. Especially true for the children in the low group was that their retellings sometimes consisted of disjointed events from the text or included information not present in the text. For example, Figure 10–6 shows what one child said about *Titch* (Hutchins, 1971).

However, at BLOC School the students, even in the low group, often demonstrated that they understood the structure of a story. A typical retelling of a student from BLOC School demonstrated more inferences and connections about the books read (see Figure 10–7).

The difference between the two sites with respect to retellings may have been due to curriculum extensions offered by the balanced literacy initiative, which was introduced to BLOC school students at the beginning of the school

Child 3

"Um, it was about a boy named Peter and he wanted his baby chair. He didn't want it to paint it pink and he moved outside. He got all his stuff and he put it in neat, he packed it up neat and he, and then he hide. His mother thought he hide under the curtains but his shoes was right there. And then he popped out all over."

—Peter's Chair (Keats, 1998b)

Figure 10–7. *Retelling Sample by BLOC Student*

year (but not fully implemented until January 2001). Added to the daily schedule were interactive read-alouds, literacy centers, and accountable talk (for example, teachers asked students to support their answers from the text and/or to state why they agreed or disagreed with another student about what they had read.) Furthermore, classroom libraries and word walls were added to every classroom. Before the balanced literacy initiative, students read independently using the decodable books as prescribed by Open Court; later, classroom libraries were expanded significantly. They offered a variety of books for the students to choose from depending on their interests; there were also books from a variety of levels on the same topic. Students read independently for a specific time—twenty minutes per day—and they read during their lunch period and when they finished their other work early. This was a change in practice from the regular Open Court program. Literacy center activities, which engaged the children in many different forms of reading and writing, replaced skill centers. Writing was integrated with reading rather than isolated as in the Open Court model. Even though there were some major curricular changes, the short duration of this new initiative may explain why the difference in retellings between OC and BLOC students was not dramatic.

Designated ability groups seemed to have little relationship to the retellings. Interestingly, this is reflected in the fact that the low and middle groups of children at OC School scored higher than the high group on retelling. Similarly, at BLOC School the low group scored higher than the middle group on retelling.

Student Interviews

The metacognitive interviews offered other insights into student approaches to reading. In response to the question When you are reading and you come to something you do not know, what do you do? most of the children said, "Sound it out." This was true for all of the children at both schools. Some of the other responses were "Ask my mother" and "Skip it." Furthermore, at BLOC School, students shared that they used the "ABC cards" on the wall, demonstrating the use of the classroom environment (a strategy stressed by the teachers). The students' responses highlight the fact that they were focusing on the word level of processing.

Teachers' Stance

To further understand the children's reading behavior, researchers interviewed teachers. Most of the teachers shared that they liked the Open Court program because of the availability of the program materials. Also, since their school system had many children moving from school to school, the Open Court program was perceived as providing consistency to the primary reading program in the system. At OC School, one teacher was ambivalent about the Open Court program. Referring to the anthology, the teacher said, "First of all, it is not leveled. And everybody in second grade is expected to read on second-grade level. And I don't think that's fair, because in the reading class I have the lowest students." This teacher felt that the texts were not appropriate for her students. Another teacher stated that the anthologies were good for the children "but were kind of boring."

Although all of the Open Court components were evident in the classrooms at BLOC, teachers reported being supported by the principal to move away from strictly following the program. For example, instead of using read-aloud only in the limited way suggested by the Open Court program, teachers enlarged the read-aloud activity because of the balanced literacy initiative. One teacher at BLOC School focused on reading aloud for fluency and helping children become independent in their reading:

> I really didn't realize how important read-aloud was until maybe about the beginning of the year when I saw the students, I would have them do a read-aloud instead of me and they began to read with so much expression. So every morning we do read-aloud. And phonics is the second most important to me. Because it helps them to sound out the words when they are reading. So we have phonics every day. That's including the Open Court program. . . . We have reading circles where the children can pick books that they want to read and share them with the class.

All of the teachers at BLOC participated in professional development and the principal bought books, materials, and supplies to develop literacy centers in the classrooms. The teachers at BLOC School shared that they were doing more comprehension strategy instruction while using the anthology. The teachers used the concept board recommended by Open Court (but only sparsely before the balanced literacy initiative) for comprehension development and more consistently emphasized that the children should analyze the stories, looking for clues, problems, and wonderings. One teacher shared that during this year she felt more comfortable going beyond the Open Court teacher manual, and as an example, she explained how after one story, they "went out into the hallway, kicked [their] shoes off in order to predict the weather and then . . . incorporated math into it." In another classroom, students were so motivated that they formed their own book clubs. When asked what good readers do, five out of six teachers emphasized using strategies and expression when reading a story.

Most teachers also discussed that good readers "get information from the story" and "reread." Some teachers focused considerable attention on the technical aspects of reading, such as "phonetic base, sight words, parts of speech, constant review," instead of focusing on what occurs during the reading process, helping students become aware of the reading process in a more global way, or developing proficient, independent readers. Teachers' perspectives were influenced by a variety of factors including the instructional leader of the reading program in their particular school.

Discussion and Implications

To answer the questions about what strategies students used to construct meaning and what they knew about the reading process, we examined in detail children's miscues and their responses to a metacognitive interview. The second-grade children at these two Open Court sites were focused on word recognition. They used multiple cueing systems with a heavy focus on syntactic and graphophonic cues. The miscue analysis revealed that these children were trained to focus on both the sound features and the graphic features of words. The high scores on the pseudoword test could be attributed to the emphasis on phonics in the Open Court program; this was similar to the findings of Foorman et al. (1998) and Barrett (1995). Thus, the children demonstrated use of phonics skills both in and out of context.

What the children did not use was the power of semantics across sentences. They still were predominantly focused on word recognition at the word, phrase, or sentence level without using the larger meaning to inform their reading of a text. Their strong base in phonics did not enable them to get to the main focus of reading: comprehending while reading and responding to texts after reading.

While overall comprehension did not differ significantly, the children at BLOC School compared with those at OC School demonstrated a pattern of greater use of inferences and making connections. This may be explained by the extended time spent discussing texts at BLOC School. Overall, what may have been missing in both the pure Open Court program and the BLOC School program was greater opportunity to respond critically and creatively to books and stories.

Grouping is a related issue. In these two schools, when the teachers designated high, middle, and low readers, they seemed to base those decisions solely on children's skill in graphophonics. Such practices ignore students' competencies in semantics and comprehension. At OC School, students were placed in homogeneous classrooms for reading instruction based on their word-level accuracy scores rather than their comprehension of texts. This is in contrast to what many teachers said were the most important aspects of the reading process. At BLOC School, students were placed in heterogeneous groups for reading instruction. However, when teachers were asked to designate high, middle, and low readers, they did not base their distinctions on comprehension; rather, they grouped students only according to accuracy of word recognition. So even though the instruction was in heterogeneous groups, teachers' perceptions of what makes a good reader were skewed toward word identification skills.

A similar focus on decoding was evident in the children's metacognitive interviews. They focused on the word level when talking about good readers or strategies for reading; for example, many mentioned "sound it out" as their primary strategy. Many of the children actually used strategies—such as syntax—that went beyond just graphophonics when they were reading but still voiced a proclivity to look only at the word level. The self-reports may have been limited by the children's ability to articulate what they actually did. These same self-reports probably do echo what was discussed in their classrooms.

In terms of the views of teachers, the Open Court program seemed expedient but limited. Teachers were expressive when asked about their views of teaching reading and how the Open Court program furthered or hindered their practice. The teachers, in general, were satisfied with the Open Court program. A high rate of student mobility was cited as one impetus for a districtwide program that "keeps all on same page." Most teachers, though, supplemented both the materials and the instruction. One teacher commented: "I've used Open Court writing. But also I have a lot of my own writing skills." Overall, the teachers liked the Open Court program because it was convenient rather than because it provided sufficient instruction to promote competent readers.

In conclusion, the Open Court program did have an impact on children's reading strategies. Students in these classes did not verbalize many of the components of successful reading, nor did they demonstrate some of the key strategies that good readers use. Rather, the students came to view reading as decoding. In the case of Open Court, real reading of expository and narrative literature is sparse and many of the materials are contrived rather than authentic. Teachers feel a need to supplement the commercial program in order to give their students more opportunities to develop their comprehension and writing skills. It is true that prepackaged programs may be attractive: all of the materials are readily available; materials may seemingly match a school district's curriculum goals; and they are easy to explain to the public. Yet experienced teachers often find them to be constraining. Our data suggests that the Open Court program is systematic but not necessarily comprehensive.

References

Allington, R. L. (2002). *Big brother and the national reading curriculum: How ideology trumped evidence.* Portsmouth, NH: Heinemann.

Barrett, T. J. (1995). *A comparison of two approaches to first grade phonics in the Riverside Unified School District.* East Lansing, MI: National Center for Research on Teacher Learning. (ERIC Document Reproduction Service No. ED393061)

Foorman, B. R., Francis, D. J., Fletcher, J. M., and Schatschneider, C. (1998). The role of instruction in learning to read: Preventing reading failure in at-risk children. *Journal of Educational Psychology, 90,* 37–55.

Fountas, I., & Pinnell, G. (1996). *Guided reading: Good first teaching for all children.* Portsmouth, NH: Heinemann.

Goodman, Y., Watson, D., & Burke, C. (1987). *Reading miscue inventory: Alternative procedures.* Katonah, NY: Richard Irwin.

Garan, E. M. (2001). What does the report of the National Reading Panel really tell us about teaching phonics? *Language Arts, 79*(1), 61–70.

Morrow, L. (2001). *Literacy development in the early years: Helping children read and write* (4th ed.). Boston: Allyn & Bacon.

National Reading Panel. (2000). *Teaching children to read: An evidence-based assessment of the scientific research literature on reading and its implications for reading instruction.* Washington, DC: National Institute of Child Health and Human Development.

Open Court Reading, level 2, book 1, Teacher Edition. (2000). Columbus, OH: SRA/McGraw-Hill.

Pressley, M. (2002). Effective beginning reading instruction. *Journal of Literacy Research, 34*(2), 165–188.

Snow, C. E., Burns, M. S., & Griffin, P. (1998). *Preventing reading difficulties.* Washington, DC: National Academy Press.

Woodcock, R. W. (1998). *Woodcock reading mastery tests—revised examiner's manual.* Circle Pines, MA: American Guidance Services.

Yatvin, J. (2002). Babes in the woods: The wanderings of the National Reading Panel. *Phi Delta Kappan, 83*(5), 364–369.

Children's Books

Asch, F. (1985). *Bear shadow.* New York: Scholastic.

Hutchins, P. (1971). *Titch.* New York: Simon & Schuster.

Keats, E. J. (1998a). *A letter to Amy.* East Rutherford, NJ: Puffin.

Keats, E. J. (1998b). *Peter's chair.* East Rutherford, NJ: Puffin.

Mayer, M. (1988). *There's something in my attic.* New York: Puffin.

McKissack, P. (1986). *Flossie & the fox.* New York: Scholastic.
Sharmat, M. (1983). *Gregory, the terrible eater.* New York: Scholastic.
Ziefert, H. (1997). *A new house for mole and mouse.* East Rutherford, NJ: Puffin.

Appendix

Reading Inventory

1. When you are reading and you come to something you don't know, what do you do? What else do you do?
2. Who is the best reader you know? What makes this person a good reader?
3. If you knew that someone was having difficulty reading, how would you help him or her?
4. What would a teacher do to help that person?
5. How did you learn to read?
6. Who helped you to learn to read? How did they help you learn?
7. Do you think that you are a good reader? What makes you think so?
8. What would you like to do better as a reader?
9. Do you read at home? What do you read? What is your favorite thing (book, magazine, etc.) to read at home?

11

Teachers' Perspectives on Open Court

KATHARINE DAVIES SAMWAY AND LUCINDA
PEASE-ALVAREZ

> *Open Court was implemented in a completely top-down way. Every-*
> *thing was dictated from the top. There was no trust in teachers, and*
> *teachers, many of whom had been excellent teachers for years, were*
> *scolded and treated disrespectfully.*
>
> —MANDY

Increasingly, in response to political and public perceptions that children aren't achieving at desirable levels and that teachers aren't doing their jobs well, school districts are mandating prescriptive reading programs that emphasize skills instruction. Teachers aren't expected or encouraged to exert their professional knowledge; instead, they are frequently expected to follow the textbook manual and not deviate from it. In California, this movement has gained momentum since the statewide adoption of two reading textbook series for the elementary grades, Houghton Mifflin and Open Court (McGraw-Hill). Interestingly, the California Instructional Resources Evaluation Panel (the committee that makes recommendations regarding textbook adoption) recommended that the 1995 version of Open Court *not* be placed on the textbook adoption list (Moustafa & Land, 2002).

McGraw-Hill, the publisher of Open Court, describes its program in the following way:

> Open Court Reading is a research-based curriculum grounded in systematic,
> explicit instruction of phonemic awareness, phonics, and word knowledge,

comprehension skills and strategies, inquiry skills and strategies, and writing and language arts skills and strategies. (2003)

Features of Open Court include the following: detailed directions in the teaching manuals, a heavy emphasis on whole-class instruction, and a spiraling curriculum that is used to justify whole-class instruction. Despite challenges to the supposed benefits of Open Court, by January 2000, Open Court was being used in one in eight elementary schools in California (Moustafa & Land, 2002).

In the many public discussions about adopting Open Court that we were privy to as teacher educators working with preservice and practicing teachers, we were struck by the absence of teachers' voices. In our contacts with hundreds of teachers, we didn't hear teachers clamoring for a textbook series. What we heard was anguish on the part of teachers who were alarmed that they would have no choice over the materials they would be obliged to use, regardless of the needs of their students. Later, after district adoptions had been made, we heard teachers expressing frustration at how they couldn't teach the way they thought they should teach. It was at this point that we decided to investigate the impact of a mandated reading program on the beliefs and practices of teachers. We decided to focus on Open Court, as this was the program that appeared to be adopted by school districts with the lowest high-stakes test scores and the largest numbers of historically underserved students.

Our Research Project

In this chapter, we will report on findings from a small-scale study that is part of a larger ongoing study of teachers' views and perspectives about Open Court. Our goal in the larger study is to investigate how teachers in different schools and districts in Northern California are making sense of Open Court. Interviews from teachers working in the first school that we approached constitute the data we refer to here.

As we consider the views and practices that teachers refer to in our interviews as manifestations of their emerging understandings as learners, we have approached this research project as a study of teacher learning. The perspective on learning and understanding that frames our study conceives of these processes as socially and culturally constituted (Cole, 1996; Heath, 1983, 1989; Lave & Wenger, 1991; Ochs, 1988; Rogoff, 2003; Wenger, 1998). Through their involvement with others in a variety of contexts, including the workplace, teachers actively construct their roles, responsibilities, and understandings. While agency, as it relates to the roles teachers play in the learning process, is an important aspect of the sociocultural perspective that frames our work, it is also important to remember that teacher agency is shaped by the social and power relationships that define their engagement with others (see, for example, Pacini-Ketchabaw & Schecter, 2002).

The teachers we report on here teach in the same elementary school in a large urban school district in the San Francisco Bay Area where almost a third of the students are English language learners (ELLs). The district adopted Open Court in order to improve test scores and address the reality that students often move from school to school during the school year (i.e., the district argued that having one reading program throughout the district would mean that children would have access to consistent and continuous instruction). The elementary school, Orchard Elementary, is midsize and ethnically mixed. According to the district website, although 45 percent of the students are African Americans, there are also many students from Asian, Latino, and Caucasian backgrounds. Almost 20 percent of the children are ELLs. The teaching staff is very experienced, stable, and highly regarded by parents, many of whom have gone to great lengths to ensure that their children can attend the school. Until the Open Court mandate, the school had been moving toward what teachers referred to as balanced literacy at all grade levels. For example, they had begun to implement guided reading in both the primary and the intermediate grades.

In selecting interviewees, we sorted the teachers into primary and intermediate groups and then randomly selected five teachers from each group. Half the teachers we interviewed were of color. Interviews lasted from one to two hours. We used an inductive, iterative approach to data analysis, which involved reading through and discussing the transcribed interviews and posing questions that shaped our analysis. Key findings include the following:

1. Open Court had affected teachers' sense of agency.
2. Teachers felt there was a much diminished role for informed teacher decision making.
3. Teachers valued some of the teaching ideas and materials in Open Court, but were highly critical of key features.
4. There had been some subtle acts of resistance.

Open Court Affected Teachers' Sense of Agency

One of the most compelling findings was how all the teachers felt a lack of control over what and how they teach and consequently felt undermined and disrespected. The teachers were unequivocal about the fact that Open Court was forced on them, regardless of their experience, knowledge, or worth as teachers, and they weren't happy about it. Carol, a veteran teacher, captured how the mandated program undermined her in the following comment:

My spirit has been broken. And I said, you know, after twenty-five years or whatever it was, you know, my heart was taken from me. My soul . . . And I understand that the district had pressure put down on administrators. Everybody. For scores to go up. But we're people. We're not things and that's why I went into education. Because we're people. We have feelings. We have, you know, it's a give and take. And we're human. We're not a thing. We want people to react with us. We want to see things grow. And you know, you don't do that the way that was put upon us.

The teachers commented at length about the disrespectful, top-down way in which the program was implemented. For example, Mandy said, "Open Court was implemented in a completely top-down way. Everything was dictated from the top. There was no trust in teachers, and teachers, many of whom had been excellent teachers for years, were scolded and treated disrespectfully." Teachers also commented on how the professional development that was offered in conjunction with the adoption was problematic. They tended not to find workshops helpful, particularly when run by staff developers who had little or no experience with Open Court. They were also outraged by the way in which staff identified by the district office as instructional facilitators visited classrooms in order to check on whether the teacher's were implementing the program as mandated. For example, Carl commented, "She [the instructional facilitator] wanted us to [recite] the teachers manual. And if it says, 'Sh,' you're supposed to say it. . . . She's a former teacher in the district. And it built a lot of animosity." Although the teachers had many concerns, they did not feel that they could raise them, such as with their principal or with district office personnel. For example, Mandy commented, "At school meetings and at trainings, we were not allowed to say negative things. We were encouraged to give positive testimonies on what was 'working.' . . . And we were told that we had no choice and negative comments about Open Court were not acceptable."

Open Court Led to Less Decision Making on the Part of Teachers

Although most of the teachers we interviewed were experienced, two were relatively new to the profession. Regardless of how much experience the teachers had, they expressed profound concerns about the way in which their professional decision-making capacities had been undermined by the adoption of Open Court. Mandy commented on how it undermined her notions of what it means to be a good teacher:

> My teaching changed a lot. Previously I had been an early childhood teacher and also an art teacher. And I had learned about being a good teacher. I had learned to teach very differently, through a child-centered philosophy. Open

Court was an extreme way for me to become an elementary school teacher. I felt like I had to throw out everything I had ever learned about being a good teacher. It all boiled down to classroom management and being a dictator, especially at the first-grade level; it felt like I was forcing the kids to jump through hoops.

Pru, a thirty-two-year veteran who expressed a willingness to comply with district mandates, was nevertheless concerned that her know-how as a teacher was not recognized and that she wasn't trusted to be able to make instructional decisions that would benefit her students:

> I don't get the feeling like I'm considered a smart enough person to know that it's OK to pick and choose. . . . And from my experiences for thirty-two years, I know that there are some excellent things that we have dropped just because the trend has changed, and that certain things that I have done have worked with children, different children. That I should be allowed to use that experience to make decisions on how I'm going to teach in the classroom. Certainly I can have the Open Court format, but if I can see that this group of children do not learn well that way or that they are totally turned off by this rote, let's say.

While the majority of the teachers we interviewed (eight of ten) thought that all teachers in the district should use Open Court because it was a district mandate, the two teachers who argued against the mandate did so for pedagogical reasons, saying that one must use one's knowledge of learners when making instructional decisions. One of these teachers, Betty, said, "I just don't think all teachers should [have to use] anything. . . . You have to use what is going to be appropriate for your students."

Even those teachers who were not opposed to the district mandating Open Court nevertheless argued for greater flexibility in its implementation because they didn't think it should be used with all children, a sentiment that Pru captured when she said, "That's the thing I don't like about Open Court . . . it can't be for everyone. It really can't. I don't think anything can be one solution to solve everyone's problems."

In addition to commenting on how the district's decision to implement Open Court had compromised their decision making, teachers told us that their students had negative attitudes toward Open Court. For example, Pru talked about how both successful and less successful readers reacted negatively to the program. She said, "I'm definitely speaking from the comments that children made. My top children two years ago totally were upset and said so. 'This is boring. I want to move on. I want to do other things. Why do I have to read with the rest of the group?' You know what I mean? And yet I have also the slow group that says. . . . You know, you can see they can't keep up. And they get turned off from it." Mandy spoke of how her first graders reacted: "When I used it with first graders who had not been introduced to it before, it felt terrible. These children had been used to fun, developmentally appropriate kindergarten. They were miserable. They were restless and complained. In the beginning, some would fall asleep. Several boys would fall out of their chairs (and their shoes!) constantly. Some would cry. Later in the year, when we didn't do blending every day, the kids would ask, 'Do we have blending today?' If I said, 'No,' they would say with a huge, snappy voice, 'Thank you!'"

Strengths and Weaknesses of Open Court

None of the teachers whom we interviewed discounted Open Court in its entirety, although they all were very critical of various features and were deeply offended by the manner in which it had been implemented. In the interviews, we asked teachers to comment on strengths and weaknesses of the program, and all of the teachers were able to identify some strengths in the program (see Figure 11–1). Strengths included that the structure of the program is familiar to both students and teachers (five teachers); it makes instructional planning easier (four teachers); it facilitates teacher-teacher collaboration (three teachers); it meets the needs of students, such as struggling primary readers (two teachers), mid-level children (two teachers), and English language learners (one teacher); it facilitates teacher growth (three teachers); and the theory behind Open Court is strong (one teacher). However, the most dominant strength mentioned by the teachers was the provision of useful materials and activities (seven teachers). The teachers referred to a range of materials (e.g., phonemic awareness and phonics materials and decodable books) and activities (e.g., rereading and proofreading strategies).

When talking about strengths, the teachers frequently appeared to be searching for something positive to say about the program, but when it came time to talk about weaknesses, they rapidly and in great detail described weaknesses they saw in the program; not only were they more facile at discussing weaknesses, but they also mentioned many more weaknesses than strengths. As Figure 11–2 illustrates, many of their expressed weaknesses addressed implementation issues, such as themes not being linked well to standards or themes not being well developed (six teachers), the word study component being weak (three teachers), and too much emphasis on phonemic awareness and phonics (two teachers). They also talked about concerns grounded in a lack of focus on the specific needs of students, including that students don't like Open Court (five teachers), there is too much whole-class instruction (four teachers), it doesn't meet the needs of English language learners (four teachers), and it isn't developmentally appropriate (four teachers).

Strengths of Open Court	Number of Respondents	Percent of Respondents
Some good activities and useful materials, including • phonics/phonemic awareness/ decodable books • themes • stories/anthologies • rereading strategy • proofreading • big books • word wall • research articles	7	70%
Familiar structure for students and teachers	5	50%
Instructional planning is easier	4	40%
Meets the needs of students: • struggling (primary) readers • mid-level children • ELLs	2 2 1	20% 20% 10%
Facilitates teacher-teacher collaboration	3	30%
Facilitates teacher growth	3	30%
Theory is strong	1	10%

Figure 11–1. *Teachers' Views on the Strengths of Open Court*

However, the two most frequently mentioned weaknesses were writing (nine teachers) and pacing (nine teachers).

The teachers expressed concern that writing was all but ignored and/or was not addressed well in Open Court. For example, Sam said, "Their writing program is very underdeveloped. It's like they spent all this time on the reading part, but the writing was just kind of piecemeal." Another teacher, Mandy, indicated that she was not happy with the writing component and relied on her coach for writing support: "The writing area was terrible. I was fortunate that my first coach had been a Reading Recovery teacher, because she taught me some good reading and writing techniques that I would not have learned otherwise."

Although Open Court identifies time designated for independent practice, when teachers are advised to address the needs of individual students, the

Limitations of Open Court	Number of Respondents	Percent of Respondents
Weak program components:		
• writing gets short shrift	9	90%
• themes not linked well to standards/themes are poor	6	60%
• word study component weak	3	30%
• too much emphasis on phonemic awareness/phonics	2	20%
• literature poor/too little time for good literature	2	20%
• expository reading poorly addressed	1	10%
• too much grammar instruction	1	10%
• too little time for other curricular areas	1	10%
• lot of busywork	1	10%
Lack of focus on student needs and interests:		
• pacing—not learner-centered instruction	9	90%
• students unhappy with Open Court	5	50%
• too much whole-class instruction/too teacher-centered	4	40%
• not meeting the needs of ELLs	4	40%
• developmentally inappropriate	4	40%
• not meeting needs of African American children	1	10%
• not a rich program	1	10%
Limited and inappropriate view of what reading is	3	30%
Lack of differentiated staff development/ ongoing support	2	20%
Disorganized materials/too many materials for teacher	1	10%

Figure 11–2. *Teachers' Views on Weaknesses of Open Court (other than implementation issues)*

teachers said that they never had time for this as they felt enormous pressure to keep up with the program. Pacing was a huge concern mentioned by the teachers. They did not agree with what they believed were the program's underlying assumptions that all learners must begin at the same point, progress at the same rate, and/or learn in the same way. The Open Court program, as implemented by the district, did not provide room for differentiated instruction, for guided reading, or even for teachable moments, and these are issues that the teachers commented on. Because it did not allow for teacher decision making, teachers felt shackled to the pace inherent in the program, as Marge indicated:

> The pace has to move on, but your kids haven't gotten, you know, the difference between fiction and nonfiction, or adverbs or what have you. . . . I'll slow down my whole program and go over it and over it and lose the pace of the whole thing. That's a big problem I have with Open Court, pacing.

The teachers were aware that the district mandate not to deviate from the Open Court program was fueled by a desire to improve test scores and show growth, and they were skeptical of that goal, as Sam's comment illustrates:

> For example, take the pacing . . . sometimes I feel like we are on this treadmill. And we're going faster and faster and faster. And the kids are just, like, being bombarded. And I tell them to slow down. So I don't want to feel like we're just constantly in motion. I think there needs to be kind of [*inaudible*] stop and take a breath and just kind of relax. But there's so much pressure to raise test scores, to show growth. And sometimes that growth, I don't think can be reflected in test scores. I think it may take a year or two.

Other teachers explored the importance of taking learning styles into account and how that wasn't possible with the pacing of the program, as Chris revealed in this comment:

> Sometimes with Open Court they forgot the learning styles of kids . . . I really think learning styles are important . . . but there's no time to delve and say, "How can I get this artistic kid to get through these words?" . . . There isn't time to kind of delve into learning styles . . . there's no chance, no opportunities.

One of the underlying principles of Open Court is the notion of a "spiraling curriculum" in which concepts and skills are taught and then revisited later on so that if students don't acquire that knowledge when originally taught, they will have other opportunities to learn it. Of course, this is a contentious notion because it raises the important issue of whether curriculum or the needs of learners should be driving instruction. The spiraling curriculum and pacing were clearly connected in the minds of the teachers whom we interviewed. For example, Chris related how she shared her concerns with an Open Court staff developer, who told her that the students would "pick up" the skills later on:

> I think there are some skills that are just too soon to teach kids, and . . . Open Court says, "No, just give it to them anyway. If they don't get it, who

cares, they're confused, just give it to them." And I don't agree with that. Maybe there's research that says that's OK . . . I haven't seen it yet . . . I talked to an Open Court person . . . I said, "Wait a minute. Why am I teaching these different spellings, four spellings for the short *e* sound?" You know, they're not going to remember that, and the thing was, "Well just . . . expose them to that, and later on down the line, they'll pick up those spellings." . . . So even now, with some of the concepts, I don't know if I should, I kind of skim over them and do them later, just because I think they're introduced too soon.

Subtle Acts of Resistance

As we listened to the teachers talk about their experiences with Open Court over a two-year period, we were struck by how dispirited they sounded. We wondered why these experienced, highly regarded teachers had succumbed to a heavily scripted program that appeared to undermine their professional self-respect. We had been expecting to hear about open acts of resistance but rarely heard of any. We heard of symbolic acts of resistance, such as when a teacher attended a staff development event dressed in clothes that were reminiscent of military fatigues. We know of some teachers who have left the district or have moved into a middle school because of their dissatisfaction with Open Court. Sam also commented on this:

Sam: They [the district] didn't anticipate the backlash that they would get . . .

Interviewer: You mentioned a backlash. . . . Has the backlash had an impact on the district?

Sam: Yeah, I think some teachers have chosen to leave. We have one teacher.

Interviewer: Leave the district?

Sam: Leave the district. That's one way I think teachers have opposed Open Court.

Although we almost never heard of open, public acts of resistance on the part of the teachers we interviewed, Sally was an exception. She told us how she eventually refused to be a bad teacher and resisted her principal's request not to rock the boat:

> I was expecting the principal to come and say something to me because she's trying to keep everything nice and watertight. And I am punching holes in it. But she didn't say anything. And the odd thing is that I got to a point where there was no way I would do it. There's not any way. You'd have to fire me. You'd have to fire me. There's no way.

As we reread the interviews, we realized that although the teachers didn't talk about overt or very public acts of resistance, they did comment on more subtle forms of resistance. In fact, all the teachers talked about adaptations they had begun to make, particularly after the first year. For instance, some teachers commented on how they had reduced or eliminated the phonemic awareness and phonics activities or used some of the mandated time designated for Open Court for guided reading. Other teachers talked about how they augmented the writing component or replaced themes they thought were inappropriate.

How Did Teachers Construct Their Pedagogical Understandings and Practices?

The teachers whom we interviewed were in a state of flux. Their prior views of teaching had been seriously challenged by the Open Court mandate. They accepted authority to varying degrees and conformed to the district mandates even when troubled by them. In many cases, their comments indicated that they thought they should do what superiors told them to do, even if the demands made of them were at odds with their own pedagogical beliefs.

When the implementation of the program became intolerable, the teachers did not refuse to use it; instead, they tweaked it based on prior experiences and understandings about what good teachers do, as the following comment from Sally illustrates:

> I did what a good teacher is supposed to do, where somebody says try this, and I will pick and choose, and the first year I did. Well, well I said, OK. Decodables, for example. OK, I'll try it. We'll see. We'll see what happens. OK, but then also as a good teacher, you know when to push the jettison button. You don't have a lot of time, you don't waste your time with the stuff that you know is bullshit and the stuff that you know goes against all that you already know. For real. From experience. My process with Open Court has been one of, you know, slicing off stuff. OK. I'm not going to use that. That, I might. That I like. That I like. Everything else, I'm not doing. . . . And I want to treat it like a program, like I treat any other program that's offered to me. Or any other thing. I'll pick the best of what I need. And what I think my kids need.

An unexpected finding was that negative experiences with Open Court had led some teachers to revisit and reaffirm their commitment to what mattered in their work with children. Sam became increasingly unhappy with the degree to which her teaching had become teacher centered and said:

> There needs to be a balance. Yeah. Too much for the last two years, I feel like I have dictated. . . . There are small opportunities of choice. . . . I feel like

I was always still in the driver's seat. I was always in control of their learning. Rather than being a partner with the child, with the student. And it's interesting that I'm coming back now to some of the things, thinking about . . . some of the things I was doing earlier in my career.

In a similar vein, Sally told us how her experience with Open Court clarified what was important to her as a teacher and enabled her to be more courageous in her teaching:

It has really deepened my commitment to what I already knew. It's made me militant about it. It really made me be really daring with my teaching and to risk. It really crystallized things for me. It made things more clear.

The teachers had clearly been grappling with their views and practices vis-à-vis Open Court. This is a complex process, and this complexity is evident in several contradictions in what they said. For example, several interviewees said that they believe in learner-centered teaching, but they were implementing a program that pays scant attention to the needs of individual learners. Also, interviewees indicated that teachers should follow district policy and implement it, but all of the teachers we interviewed were adapting it. This point is further illustrated by a comment by Carl, who indicated that teachers should obey mandates but have more control over what and how they teach:

They adopted Open Court; we're supposed to follow it. I'm going to have some faith that it's a good program. You know, it's not bad. . . . You have to kind of put your ego aside and I think that's one of the difficulties for some teachers. [*Later in interview*] I think teachers want to have more control. They want to have that responsibility. They are willing to have that control, responsibility. But the infrastructure within the school site doesn't allow you to do that. So, I'd like to see something more . . . inquiry-based research, teacher action research. They really take responsibility.

Conclusions

Our data indicate that Open Court had an impact on teachers' instructional practices and decision making. Most noticeably, it led to teachers becoming markedly demoralized; they felt undervalued as knowledgeable professionals and were resentful of the top-down way in which the program had been implemented. Despite these highly charged responses to Open Court, only one teacher stated that she refused to implement the program. Instead of engaging in open acts of resistance, the teachers reported tweaking or adapting the program. From our vantage point, these subtle acts of resistance are revelatory of the power relations that define the working lives of teachers and ultimately the learning opportunities available to their students. These teachers, like so many, work within a system that provides them with little or no respect for their professional autonomy. Their agency is negotiated and situated within an ecology characterized by mandates that do not acknowledge their experience and know-how. It is possible that, over the long term, transmission-oriented approaches to learning and teaching will be more firmly entrenched in the minds of teachers who work in schools where Open Court has been mandated by district and school-based administrations.

This perspective on learning and teaching may also limit opportunities for students to partake in classroom communities that draw on their needs, interests, and experiences. And, as we and others have argued, this aspect of classroom pedagogy is particularly important in enhancing the educational opportunities available to ethnic minority children from diverse linguistic, cultural, and racial backgrounds (e.g., Moll & Greenberg, 1990; Samway & Alvarez, 1987; Tharp & Gallimore, 1988; Vasquez, Pease-Alvarez, & Shannon, 1994). Through their acceptance of programming like Open Court, teachers like the ones we interviewed (who have serious reservations about this program) are co-opted by current reform[1] efforts aimed at enforcing one-size-fits-all pedagogies. Within this climate of reform, educational equity may be better served by those who resist curricular mandates such as Open Court and commit to and enact instructional programming that acknowledges the needs, interests, and experiences of all students. This demands that we, as teacher educators, must focus on ways to support practicing and prospective teachers in resisting harmful policies and mandates that are increasingly defining what teachers can and cannot do in their classrooms. To do otherwise is to abandon the children who are often most in need.

References

Cole, M. (1996). *Cultural psychology: A once and future discipline.* New York: Cambridge University Press.

Heath, S. B. (1983). *Ways with words: Language, life, and work in communities and classrooms.* New York: Cambridge University Press.

Heath, S. B. (1989). The learner as cultural member. In M. L. Rice & R. L. Scliefelbusch (Eds.), *The teachability of language* (pp. 333–350), Baltimore: Paul H. Brookes.

Lave, J., & Wenger, E. (1991). *Situated learning: Legitimate peripheral participation.* New York: Cambridge University Press.

---

[1] We are using the term *reform* to indicate a change in policy rather than an improvement in a phenomenon.

McGraw-Hill. (2003). *Open Court Reading.* Available: *www.sraonline.com /index.php/home/curriculumsolutions/reading/ocr/622*

Moll, L. C., & Greenberg, J. B. (1990). Creating zones of possibilities: Combining social contexts for instruction. In L. C. Moll (Ed.), *Vygotsky and education: Instructional implications and applications of sociohistorical psychology* (pp. 319–348). New York: Cambridge University Press.

Moustafa, M., & Land, R. E. (2002). The reading achievement of economically-disadvantaged children in urban schools using Open Court vs. comparably disadvantaged children in urban schools using non-scripted reading programs. In *Yearbook of the Urban Learning, Teaching, and Research Special Interest Group of the American Educational Research Association* (pp. 44–53).

Ochs, E. (1988). *Culture and language development: Language acquisition and language socialization in a Samoan village.* New York: Cambridge University Press.

Pacini-Ketchabaw, V., & Schecter, S. (2002). Engaging the discourse of diversity: Educators' frameworks for working with linguistic and cultural difference. *Contemporary Issues in Early Childhood, 3*(3), 400–414.

Rogoff, B. (2003). *The cultural nature of human development.* New York: Oxford University Press.

Samway, K. D., & Alvarez, L. P. (1987). Integrating language arts instruction for language minority students: One teacher's experiences. *Educational Horizons, 66*(1), 20–23.

Tharp, R. G., & Gallimore, R. (1988). *Rousing minds to life: Teaching, learning, and schooling in social context.* Cambridge: Cambridge University Press.

Vasquez, O. A., Pease-Alvarez, L., & Shannon, S. M. (1994). *Pushing boundaries: Language and culture in a Mexicano community.* New York: Cambridge University Press.

Wenger, E. (1998). *Communities of practice.* New York: Cambridge University Press.

12

The Rich Get Richer;
the Poor Get Direct Instruction

CURT DUDLEY-MARLING

Boston College

PAT PAUGH

University of Massachusetts–Amherst

During the latest period of educational reform, there has been renewed interest among the media (Stossel, 1995; Whitmire, 1999) and educational reformers (Olson, 2000) in Direct Instruction (DI), a rigidly sequenced, highly scripted approach to teaching reading. ABC's news program *20/20*, for example, portrayed Direct Instruction as a "method of teaching children how to read that [is] simple and work[s] every time" (Stossel, 1995). More recently, DI has been given a further boost by the passage of the federal No Child Left Behind (NCLB, 2001) legislation, which, in turn, was strongly influenced by the publication of the *Report of the National Reading Panel* (National Reading Panel 2000). NCLB, drawing on the *Report of the National Reading Panel*, attempts to reform reading instruction in the nation's schools by emphasizing "scientifically-based reading instruction" (Coles, 2003). In practice, this has meant a strong push to get schools to embrace skills-oriented, commercial reading programs like DI (Manzo, 2002) that emphasize the explicit teaching of letter-sound relationships in early reading instruction, often to the exclusion of reading connected text (Allington, 2002; Coles, 2003).

It seems, however, that in practice, directive pedagogies like DI are still most attractive to people working with students deemed to be at-risk for educational failure (Haberman, 1991), that is, poor and minority children, especially children from single-parent households, and students with disabilities (Ayers, 1993). Whether this prescription is good for them is the focus of this chapter.

We begin by situating the emergence of DI in Lyndon Johnson's war on poverty in the 1960s. We then briefly review relevant research addressing the efficacy of Direct Instruction as an approach to beginning reading instruction. Finally, we consider the harm we believe is done when instructional programs like DI define educational failure as a technical or personal problem removed from the social, cultural, and political contexts within which students make sense of their lives.

Direct Instruction: A Historical Context

Running for reelection in the spring of 1964, President Lyndon Johnson offered his vision of a Great Society that would rest on "abundance and liberty for all . . . an end to poverty and racial injustice, to which we are totally committed in our time" (1964b). The Great Society would be a place

> where every child [could] find knowledge to enrich his mind and to enlarge his talents. It [was] a place where leisure [would be] a welcome chance to build and reflect. . . . It [was] a place where the city of man [would] serve not only the needs of the body and the demands of commerce but the desire for beauty and the hunger for community. (Johnson 1964b)

Lyndon Johnson's dream of a great society contrasted sharply with the reality of a racially and economically divided country in which millions of Americans faced "a daily struggle for even a meager existence" (Johnson, 1964a). It was in this context that President Johnson called for a national "war on poverty."

Sounding very much like a contemporary politician, Johnson declared that the war on poverty was not "simply to support people, to make them dependent on the generosity of others"; rather, it was "a struggle to give people a chance" (Johnson, 1964a). Ultimately, Johnson believed, the poor would lift themselves out of poverty by acquiring the skills demanded by a complex society. Therefore, one of the places where the Great Society would be built was in the classrooms of America. "Our society will not be great until every young mind is set free to scan the farthest reaches of thought and imagination," Johnson told a campaign audience.

Early education programs like Head Start and Project Follow Through, an extension of Head Start, were evidence of the federal government's commitment "to give people a chance" to share in the nation's riches by improving the schooling of disadvantaged children (House, Glass, McLean, & Walker, 1978). Although a range of pedagogical practices was enacted in Head Start and Follow Through classrooms, these programs were firmly rooted in the discourse of *cultural deprivation* (Ladson-Billings, 1999) that explains "disproportionate academic problems among low status students as largely being due to pathologies or deficits in their sociocultural background (e.g., cognitive and linguistic deficiencies, low self-esteem, poor motivation)" (Valencia, 1986, 3). From the gaze of cultural deprivation theory, disadvantaged children are unable "to profit maximally from the opportunities that the schools provide" (Bereiter & Engelmann, 1966, p. 25) because they have been deprived of stimulating cultural experiences shared by middle-class children.

In 1966, Bereiter and Engelmann, the authors of DISTAR, reported that poor black children lacked the ability to use language "to explain, to describe, to instruct, to inquire, to hypothesize, to analyze, to compare, to deduce, and to test . . . the uses [of language] that are necessary for academic success" (p. 31). They concluded that a considerable number of the children they studied could "hardly speak at all," a condition they attributed to their observation that "language is apparently dispensable enough in the life of the lower-class child for an occasional child to get along without it altogether" (p. 31). Through the lens of cultural deprivation, the lives of poor children were seen as deficient in opportunities for acquiring "the knowledge and ability which are consistently held to be valuable in school" (p. 24). Still, most educators, including Bereiter and Engelmann, shared Lyndon Johnson's optimism that "new techniques of teaching" (Johnson, 1964b) could overcome the educationally damaging effects of a culturally deprived environment.

Early intervention programs like Head Start and Follow Through continue to be seen as places where teaching techniques can be developed that will inoculate *disadvantaged* children "against the virus (of ignorance) found in their homes and communities that was inimical to their development. . . . These disadvantaged children [will] survive and thrive (academically) despite the contagions in their home environment" (Smith, 1998, p. 206). Direct Instruction was one of the instructional models that emerged to meet the needs of students from economically disadvantaged (i.e., culturally deprived) backgrounds (Becker, 1977). DI was originally marketed as DISTAR, a K–3 program for teaching mathematics and reading that was eventually expanded to other grades and subject areas (Viadero, 1999). The instructional framework of Direct Instruction underpins SRA's Corrective Reading, Journeys, Horizons, and Reading Mastery programs. Although DI emerged within the context of remedial education, its proponents argue that it is an appropriate and effective approach for all children (Fuerst, 1976). Still, DI has found its most receptive audience in the field of special education, no doubt because many special educators share the behaviorist philosophy that underpins Direct Instruction. The response of regular educators to Direct Instruction has, until recently, been less enthusiastic, however. As Engelmann himself put it: "We were sort of like the plague for regular education" (Viadero, 1999, p. 20).

No longer a "plague," DI has come full circle. Born in the context of "cultural deprivation," DI has been reborn in the age of "at-risk," what Bill Ayers (1993) has called "cultural deprivation recycled for the 1990s" (p. 29). Once again, Direct Instruction is being offered as a corrective for poverty, discrimination, severely underfunded schools, and crumbling school facilities (Gonzales, 2000). Have education experts resisted a simple, effective, research-based practice, as DI proponents have claimed (Carnine, 1999), or are there good reasons "regular education would have nothing to do with [DI]" (Viadero, 1999, p. 20)?

Simple and Effective? A Brief Review of the Research

Pointing to a research base extending over twenty-five years that demonstrates that Direct Instruction is "simple," "superior," "proven," and "effective," Siegfried Engelmann and his colleagues have often expressed their chagrin that a program that "works" with low-income children has not been more widely accepted by the educational establishment (Adams and Engelmann, 1996; Watkins, 1988). Sensing an opportunity in the recent moral panic over the putative failures of American education, the developers of DI have been working vigorously to find a place for DI as a strategy for educational reform. Indeed, DI proponents have forged close relationships with the Bush administration as well as the influential, neoconservative Fordham Foundation (e.g., Carnine, 1999) which seeks to reform education through the forces of the free market.

The research base underpinning the claim that Direct Instruction is a *simple* and *effective* approach for teaching reading is the nexus of the arguments utilized by DI supporters.

Project Follow Through and Beyond

Advantage Schools, a for-profit corporation that uses Direct Instruction in all of its schools, offers the following testimonial to the effectiveness of Direct Instruction.

> The [research] results overwhelmingly support the superiority of the DI method over all other programs. All tests of academic skills not only show the DI programs to be superior, but DI is the only program to bring these low-performing students within the national norm. In addition, the DI programs prove superior on social measures, such as measures of "self-esteem" even when compared to programs that direct their energy specifically at improving self-esteem. (Advantage Schools, n.d.)

There is a substantial body of research on Direct Instruction although the degree to which the research "overwhelmingly support[s] the superiority of the DI method" has been disputed. The "research" to which Advantage Schools and other DI proponents generally point in support of their claims for the superiority of DI (Adams & Engelmann, 1996; MacIver & Kemper, 2002; Stein, Carnine, & Dixon, 1998; Viadero, 1999) is a ten-year government-funded educational experiment called Project Follow Through (Watkins, 1988). The Follow Through design enabled comparisons of more than twenty models of early childhood education, including Direct Instruction, to address the question Which model works best? (House et al., 1978, p. 131). For DI proponents the answer to this question is clear: DI worked best. Viadero (1999), for example, concluded that "in numerous head-to-head comparisons over the years with other classroom approaches, Direct Instruction has been the winner" (p. 20). Although Viadero refers to "numerous studies" supporting DI, she, like other DI proponents, places particular importance on Project Follow Through. Given the degree to which claims for the superiority of DI continue to be linked to the Follow Through evaluation, a closer examination of Project Follow Through data is warranted.

A reanalysis of the Follow Through evaluation data by House et al. (1978) challenged the finding that Follow Through Models emphasizing basic skills (like DI) were more successful than other models (Stebbins, St. Pierre, Proper, Anderson, & Cerva, 1977). House and his colleagues conclude that, "This finding is erroneous . . . because of misclassification of the models, inadequate measurement of results, and flawed statistical analysis. . . . Participation in Follow Through classes has not been shown to be . . . superior . . . to schooling normally provided by the schools" (House et al., 1978, p. 130). Yet the proponents of Direct Instruction have continued to analyze, reanalyze, and meta-analyze the Project Follow Through data first reported in 1977 (Viadero, 1999).

In this section, we focus on three fundamental criticisms of the Follow Through study and subsequent research on DI: the uneven relationship between program goals and evaluation measures; inconsistent findings across sites; and the definition of reading underpinning evaluation measures. Readers interested in a detailed, technical critique of the Project Follow Through findings should read House et al. (1978).

And the Winner Is . . . Basic Skills

Each of the Follow Through models differed in its goals for compensatory education. Some models included social and emotional development as well as academic skills among their goals. Others emphasized language experience and personal development. Direct Instruction was among the programs that focused on *basic skills.* In an effort to contain an enormous amount of data, program evaluators categorized both the Follow Through models and the assessment measures into three categories: basic skills; cognitive-conceptual skills, and affective skills.[1] Based upon this classification scheme of instructional models and assessment measures, the program evaluators concluded that none of the models showed positive effects in the cognitive-conceptual area but that students receiving basic skills instruction scored higher on measures of self-concept (Stebbins et al., 1977). Additionally, "models that emphasize[d] basic skills succeed[ed] better than other models in helping children gain these skills" (House et al., 1978, p. 130). In other words, the models classified as basic skills (Direct Instruction, Behavior Analysis Approach) were most successful in teaching students basic skills. Of course, which skills were considered basic was a matter of judgment, in this case the judgment of the Follow Through evaluators who both selected the evaluation measures and determined which measures assessed basic skills.

Instead of concluding that Direct Instruction was especially effective at teaching basic skills to disadvantaged students, it is more accurate to conclude that DI was more effective teaching the skills the Follow Through evaluators believed to be basic than programs the evaluators did not think focused on basic skills to begin with. The important point here is that not everyone would agree with the conclusion that DI works, that is, that the DI model or the dependent measures employed by the Follow Through evaluators to assess the effectiveness of DI and other programs focus on skills that are *basic* to academic success, especially in reading, a point we will return to shortly.

DI Works "Every Time"

Both the original analysis of the Project Follow Through data and a later critique by House and colleagues (1978) highlighted the finding that the effects of the Direct Instruction model on basic skills varied dramatically across sites. "Although the Direct Instruction model had some of the best sites, it had at least one site that performed worse than every other model" (p. 154). One possible explanation for the intersite variation in Project Follow Through is that characteristics of the communities, schools, teachers, and students influenced the effectiveness of the various Follow Through models. This was certainly the view of the Project Follow Through evaluators, who observed

---

[1] According to House et al. (1978), these categories were the result of subjective judgments by the evaluators, and the evaluators themselves acknowledged that other categorizations were possible.

that "unmeasured local circumstances, including those associated with implementation . . . have more influence on results than have the philosophies of the sponsors" (cited in House et al., 1978, p. 154). Adams and Engelmann (1996), however, have dismissed the possibility that "different programs work with different students" (p. 87), preferring to blame conflicting results on external factors such as budget cutting (Adams & Engelmann, 1996; Meyer, Gersten, & Gutkin, 1983) and inconsistent implementation (Adams & Engelmann, 1996) even though Gersten and Keating (1987) point to "apathy, sarcasm, and latent hostility" (p. 31) as an explanation for unsatisfactory performance of DI students at certain Follow Through sites. DI advocates routinely attribute unsatisfactory performance at DI sites to problems with implementation. A recently completed study in Wisconsin that found that non-DI children in grades 1–3 scored significantly higher on overall reading achievement than students receiving Direct Instruction (Ryder, Sekulski, & Silberg, 2003) has been severely criticized by Engelmann because, in his opinion, the DI teachers did not follow the program's procedures (Manzo, 2004). Engelmann's criticism follows a pattern among DI advocates: whenever DI fails, teachers are to blame.

The assertion that DI "work[s] every time" (Stossel, 1995) is also challenged by longitudinal studies of students taught using Direct Instruction. In a follow-up of students who participated in the original Follow Through study, for example, Becker and Gersten (1982) reported a fairly dramatic decline in student reading achievement from the end of third grade to fifth and sixth grades. In another follow-up study of students from New York City who participated in the original Follow Through study, Gersten and Keating (1987) reported that "no differences were found in academic achievement" (p. 30) despite a general decline in the rate of student retention. Other research indicates that Project Follow Through students who received Direct Instruction outperformed comparison groups on certain measures of academic success (e.g., graduation and dropout rates, college applications and acceptance) (Darch, Gersten, & Taylor, 1987; Meyer et al., 1983), but even here the results are mixed. In the Darch, Gersten, and Taylor study, for example, significant differences were reported in dropout and graduation rates for DI students who entered first grade in 1969, but not for the students who entered first grade in 1970. However, even when longitudinal studies appear to support the positive, long-term benefits of Direct Instruction, important questions remain. Is it reasonable to claim that DI works when Follow Through students who received Direct Instruction achieve as low as the twentieth percentile (Gersten, Keating, & Becker, 1988) even if this is "significantly better" than a comparison group? Similarly, does a 40 percent dropout rate demonstrate the power of DI even if it is lower than a 58 percent dropout rate for a comparison group (Gersten & Keating, 1987)? More seriously, longitudinal studies that compare DI students with other groups whose instructional history is unknown make the error of comparing *something* with *nothing*; that is, comparing students who participated in a "special" academic intervention with students who did not.

More current data reinforces the conclusion that the effects of Direct Instruction may not last. Mabel B. Wesley Elementary School in Houston, Texas, has become a poster school for Direct Instruction. An article in the New Orleans *Times-Picayune*, for example, offers the following assessment of DI. When the principal introduced DI at Wesley, "only 18 percent of the school's third-graders could read above grade level. Five years later, that number had soared to 85 percent. By 1996, all of Wesley's third-graders passed the Texas Assessment of Academic Skills" (Lane, 1998). Similar testimonials have appeared in media outlets across the country. Yet reading scores for Wesley students, as measured by the Stanford Achievement Test, showed a decline of nearly fifty percentile rankings from first through fifth grades (Houston Independent School District, 1998). Astonishingly, as pass rates on the Texas achievement test went up, overall reading scores showed a steep decline as students moved through the grades.

Effective at What?

From a sociolinguistic perspective, reading and writing are social practices involving "specific ways of interacting with people, specific ways of using language . . . specific sets of values for various kinds of behaviors, and specific sets of interpretations for understanding and guiding behavior" (Bloome, Harris, & Ludlum, 1991, p. 22). From this point of view, people don't learn literacy as much as they learn *literacies,* and people don't learn to read once and for all as much as they learn to read particular texts in particular ways (Gee, 1996). James Gee puts it this way:

> One does not learn to read texts of type X in way Y unless one has had experience in settings where texts of type X are read in way Y. . . . One has to be socialized in a practice to learn to read texts of type X in way Y, a practice other people have already mastered. (1990, p. 43)

Simply put, reading is an incredibly complex process. How readers position themselves in relationship to texts, the meaning they make of texts, the processes they use for making meaning, and so on depend on the social and cultural contexts within which reading takes place.

Underpinning Direct Instruction is a quite different model of reading that equates reading with a set of discrete skills (e.g., phonemic segmentation, sound blending) that are assumed to be fundamental to the reading process. Assumptions about what it means to read are also embedded in the assessments that are used to determine the efficacy of programs like DI. The Project Follow Through evaluators used the Wide Range Achievement Test (WRAT), a word recognition task, and comprehension passages from the Metropolitan Achievement Test (MAT) to assess reading development. Accepting claims that Project Follow Through and other DI research *prove* that DI is a "simple and effective" means for teaching reading depends on accepting the definition of reading embedded in measures of reading achievement used by DI advocates. If we do not accept the model of reading underpinning DI and measures of reading used to prove its efficacy—and current theory in sociolinguistics, literary studies, and cultural psychology indicate that this model is a grossly inadequate representation of the reading process—then we must reject both DI and its research base.

Essentially, Direct Instruction accomplishes its own goals. It teaches what its proponents define as *basic skills*—the knowledge evaluated on standardized measures of achievement although even then there is evidence that DI is not always successful in teaching the decoding skills that are its focus (Altwerger, Arya, Jin, & Jordan, 2004; Ryder et al., 2003). Whatever its research base, by rejecting the model of reading that underlies both DI and the research base upon which DI proponents stake their claims, we firmly reject DI as a method for teaching reading to any student, including students labeled at risk for learning problems. But we go even further. Not only do we reject the efficacy claims of DI proponents, but in the section that follows, we argue that DI is harmful to students already disadvantaged by poverty and discrimination.

The Rich Get Richer; the Poor Get Direct Instruction

Underlying discussions of reading and reading instruction in the media, in state and federal legislatures, in the boardrooms of educational publishers, in academic journals, and among educational reformers, school board members, and the general public is the assumption that there exists a *best* method for teaching reading to schoolchildren and that this method can be identified through rigorous scientific research. The proponents of Direct Instruction, for example, cite a body of research they claim certifies the status of DI as the best method for teaching reading. Similar claims are made by the marketers of Open Court and Success for All. Still, in a country where progress is seen as the inevitable result of an indomitable can-do spirit, it is taken for granted that today's *best* methods will be rendered obsolete by even better approaches to teaching reading at some point in the future. Obsolescence is fundamental to the long-term financial health of any corporate entity that develops and markets products for sale and, in the context of the free market, *method* is just another product.

Direct Instruction, with its emphasis on scripts, prompts, pacing, and the *training* of teachers, may be the quintessential method. As a method, DI reduces reading and reading instruction to technique and learning failures to technical problems (Bartolome, 1994). Portraying learning failures as technical problems situates school troubles in the heads of individuals who lack the resources or experiences for school success. Equating school troubles with personal troubles (Mills, 1959) leaves no reason to consider the effects of poverty and discrimination or underfunded schools and deteriorating facilities on children's learning. As Swadener (1995) observed:

> If risk factors are conceptualized primarily as individual attributes which may lead to learning difficulties, earlier and "more effective" screening tools are often advocated, as are inoculation style early intervention programs designed to minimize later educational problems. . . . The emphasis within this framework . . . is getting the child "ready" for school, rather than getting the school "ready" to serve increasingly diverse children. (18)

In this context, diversity is uninteresting, unimportant, or, worse, a defect. Certainly, diversity is the enemy of technique (Postman, 1992), which may explain why educational reformers who view diversity as a threat to a *common* culture are so enamored of method (e.g., Stotsky, 1998). The application of standardized methods or techniques is the principal means by which schools participate in assimilative practices that seek to level the social, cultural, and linguistic differences students bring with them to school. The assumption underlying these practices is that once students adopt certain literacy behaviors, for example, they will be granted access to the nation's economic and cultural riches (Smith, 1998). However, the reality is that literacy has never been an effective "vaccine" (Smith, 1998, p. 206) for *inoculating* groups of people against the crippling effects of poverty and discrimination (Carnoy & Rothstein, 1997; Graff, 1979; Horsman, 1990).

Constructing reading instruction in methodological or mechanistic terms "dislodged from the sociocultural reality that shapes it" (Bartolome, 1994) renders students' social, cultural, and linguistic backgrounds irrelevant or, worse, *risk* factors. In the context of *method*, students' background knowledge and experience are separated from the curriculum and are unavailable as resources to support their learning. To the degree that students' knowledge and language are permitted in the classroom, they are there so that they can be evaluated for correctness.

The evidence indicates that the knowledge, language, and experiences of some students are valued in school, however. Teachers of affluent students, for example, are more likely than teachers of poor and working-class students to utilize and incorporate students' language, knowledge, and life experiences into the curriculum (Anyon, 1980; Bartolome, 1994). In affluent schools, "students are continually asked to express and apply ideas and concepts. Work involves individual thoughts and expressiveness, expansion and illustration of ideas, and choice of appropriate method and material" (Anyon, 1980, p. 79). In poor and working-class schools,

> work is following the steps of a procedure. The procedure is usually mechanical, involving rote behavior and very little decision making or choice. The teachers rarely explain why the work is being assigned, how it might connect to other assignments, or what the idea is that lies behind the procedure or gives it coherence and perhaps meaning or significance. (73)

Students in more affluent schools are given opportunities to draw on their language and experiences as means of infusing their cultural and linguistic identities into the official curriculum, what Dyson (1993) calls "staking a claim." Students in poor and working-class schools, places overpopulated by students of color, are the object of a methods fetish (Bartolome, 1994) that makes no room for their linguistic and cultural identities. The languages and experiences of students in affluent schools are resources. The languages and experiences of students in poor and working-class schools are problems. Poor and working-class students learn skills that can be used in the marketplace; students from privileged homes learn the skills they need to use the marketplace for their own ends. To students in middle- and upper-middle-class schools, we declare, "Your ways with words, your ways of being in the world are welcome here." To students already disadvantaged by poverty and discrimination, we proclaim, "Let them eat skills" (Noble, 1994). The rich get richer; the poor get Direct Instruction.

DI functions as a disciplinary technology that renders student knowledge irrelevant while cutting students off from their cultural and linguistic backgrounds. Because Direct Instruction positions "children at risk" as "lacking the cultural and moral resources for success in a presumed fair and open society" (Sleeter, 1995, p. ix), DI is an effective tool in the "struggle for power over how to define children, families, and communities who are poor, of color, and/or native speakers of languages other than English" (p. ix). Proclaiming itself an antidote to the crippling effects of poverty, discrimination, and the "savage inequalities" described by Jonathon Kozol (1991), DI situates the blame for educational failure in the language and culture of poor and minority students. Instructional technologies like DI, "by robbing students of their culture, language, history, and values," reduce students "to the status of subhumans who need to be rescued from their 'savage' selves" (Bartolome, 1994, p. 176). Further, as method extraordinaire, DI ensures that students' language and culture will not change the classroom or, more significantly, threaten society at large.

DI is emblematic of the directive, controlling "pedagogy of poverty" (Haberman, 1991, p. 290) that renders the cultural and linguistic backgrounds of poor and minority students *strange* and reduces these students "to the status of subhumans" (Bartolome, 1994, p. 176) whose worth is determined by test scores. In the context of the methods fetish it becomes reasonable to challenge the effectiveness of health and dental care and hot lunch programs, for example, because they don't impact measures of academic achievement (Adams & Engelmann, 1996). Small wonder that "the classroom atmosphere created by constant teacher direction and student compliance seethes with passive resentment that sometimes bubbles up into overt resistance" (Haberman, 1991, p. 291). Small wonder that McCarthy and Crichlow (1993) cite student alienation as the principal cause of the disproportionately high rate of failure among minority students in our schools. Small wonder, too, that students subjected to disciplinary technologies such as Direct Instruction, school uniforms, zero tolerance, high-stakes testing, grade retention, and summer school may be more likely to be involved in delinquent acts (DeVries et al., 1991). Attending schools that have little respect for who he or she is or where he or she comes from is too heavy a burden for any child to bear.

Siegfried Engelmann, one of the developers of Direct Instruction, complained that DI was a "plague" for regular educators (Viadero, 1999, p. 20) who have willfully ignored the data supporting Direct Instruction (Carnine, 1999). The question we asked here is Have education experts resisted a simple, effective, research-based practice as DI proponents have claimed? We think that theory and research in literacy education support the conclusion that DI is a plague on education and educators are right to resist it. George W. Bush has mused, "You teach a child to read, and he . . . will be able to pass a literacy test," and in this context, programs like Direct Instruction have some appeal. However, we have much more ambitious goals for literacy education, our students, and the future of participatory democracy.

References

Adams, G. L., & Engelmann, S. (1996). *Research on Direct Instruction: 25 years beyond DISTAR.* Seattle: Educational Achievement Systems.

Advantage Schools. (n.d.) *Direct Instruction.* Available: *www.advantage-schools.com/home/di.htm* [Accessed September 20, 2002]

Allington, R. L. (Ed.). (2002). *Big brother and the national reading curriculum: How ideology trumped evidence.* Portsmouth, NH: Heinemann.

Altwerger, B., Arya, P., Jin, L., & Jordan, N. L. (2004). When research and mandates collide: The challenges and dilemmas of teacher education in the era of NCLB. *English Education, 36,* 119–133.

Anyon, J. (1980). Social class and the hidden curriculum of work. *Journal of Education, 162,* 67–92.

Ayers, W. (1993). *To teach: The journey of a teacher.* New York: Teachers College Press.

Bartolome, L. I. (1994). Beyond the methods fetish: Toward a humanizing pedagogy. *Harvard Educational Review, 64,* 17–194.

Becker, W. C. (1977). Teaching reading and language to the disadvantaged: What have we learned from field research? *Harvard Educational Review, 47,* 518–543.

Becker, W. C., & Gersten, R. (1982). Follow-up of Follow Through: The later effects of the Direct Instruction model on children in fifth and sixth grades. *American Educational Research Journal, 19,* 75–92.

Bereiter, C., & Engelmann, S. (1966). *Teaching disadvantaged children in the preschool.* Englewood Cliffs, NJ: Prentice-Hall.

Bloome, D., Harris, L. H., & Ludlum, D. E. (1991). Reading and writing as sociocultural activities: Politics and pedagogy in the classroom. *Topics in Language Disorders, 11,* 14–27.

Carnine, D. (1987). A response to "False standards, a distorting and disintegrating effect on education, turning away from useful purposes, being inevitably unfulfilled, and remaining unrealistic and irrelevant." *Remedial and Special Education, 8*(1), 42–42.

Carnine, D. (1999). *Why education experts resist effective practices.* Washington, DC: Thomas B. Fordham Foundation.

Carnoy, M., & Rothstein, R. (1997, January–February). Are black diplomas worth less? *The American Prospect, (30),* 42–46.

Coles, (2003). *Reading the naked truth: Literacy, legislation, and lies.* Portsmouth, NH: Heinemann.

Darch, C., Gersten. D., & Taylor, R. (1987). Evolution of the Williamsburg County Direct Instruction program: Factors leading to success in rural elementary programs. *Research in Rural Education, 4*(3), 111–118.

Dyson, A. H. (1993). *Social worlds of children learning to write in an urban primary school.* New York: Teachers College Press.

DeVries, R., et al. (1991). Sociomoral development in Direct-Instruction, eclectic, and constructivist kindergartens: A study of children's enacted interpersonal understanding. *Early Childhood Quarterly, 6,* 473–517.

Fuerst, J. S. I. (1976). Report from Chicago: A program that works. *The Public Interest, 43,* 59–69.

Gee, J. P. (1999). *Social linguistics and literacies.* New York: Falmer.

Gee, J. P. (1996). *Social linguistics and literacies (2ⁿᵈ ed.)* New York: Falmer.

Gersten, R. & Keating T. (1987). Long-term benefits from Direct Instruction. *Educational Leadership, 44,* 28–31.

Gersten R., Keating T., & Becker W. C. (1988). The continued impact of the direct instruction model: Longitudinal studies of follow through students. *Education and Treatment of Children, 11,* 318–327.

Gonzales, R. (2000, October 16). *All things considered.* Washington, DC: National Public Radio.

Graff, H. J. (1979). *The literacy myth: Literacy and social structure in the nineteenth century city.* New York: Academic.

Haberman, M. (1991). The pedagogy of poverty versus good teaching. *Phi Delta Kappan,* pp. 290–294.

Heath, S. B. (1983). *Ways with words: Language, life, and work in communities and classrooms.* Cambridge: Cambridge University Press.

Horsman, J. (1990). *Something in my mind besides the everyday: Women and literacy.* Toronto: Women's.

House, E. R., Glass, G. V., McLean, L. D., & Walker, D. F. (1978). No simple answer: Critique of the Follow Through evaluation. *Harvard Educational Review, 48,* 128–160.

Houston Independent School District. (1998). *Wesley Elementary School: School profile.* Available: *www.houstonisd.org*

Johnson, L. B. (1964a). *Lyndon Johnson, the war on poverty.* Available: *http://longman.awl.com/history/primarysource_29_2.htm*

Johnson, L. B. (1964b). *Speeches by Lyndon B. Johnson: The Great Society.* Available: *www.tamu.edu/scom/pres/speeches/lbjgreat.html* [Accessed January 20, 2002]

Kozol, J. (1991). *Savage inequalities: Children in America's schools.* New York: Crown.

Ladson-Billings, G. (1995). Toward a theory of culturally relevant pedagogy. *American Educational Research Journal, 32*(3), 465–491.

Ladson-Billings, G. (1999). Preparing teachers for diverse student populations: A critical race theory perspective. In A. Iran-Nejad & P. D. Pearson (Eds.), *Review of Research in Education* (Vol. 24) (pp. 211–247). Washington, DC: American Educational Research Association.

Lane, C. (1998, June 30). Reading program is controversial. *The Times-Picayune,* p. B1.

MacIver, M. A., & Kemper, E. (2002). Guest editors' introduction: Research on Direct Instruction in reading. *Journal of Education for Students Placed at Risk, 7*(2), 107–116.

Manzo, K. K. (2002). Some educators see reading rules as too restrictive. *Education Week, 21*(23), 1, 23–24.

Manzo, K. K. (2004). Study challenges direct reading method. *Education Week, 23,* 3.

McCarthy, C., & Crichlow, W. (1993). Introduction: Theories of identity, theories of representation, theories of race. In C. McCarthy & W. Crichlow (Eds.), *Race, identity, and representation in education* (pp. xii–xxix). New York: Routledge.

Meyer, L. A. (1984). Long-term academic effects of the Direct Instruction Project Follow Through. *The Elementary School Journal, 84*(4), 380–394.

Meyer, L. A., Gersten, R., & Gutkin, J. (1983). Direct instruction: A Project Follow-Through success story in an inner city school. *The Elementary School Journal, 84*(2), 241–252.

Mills, C. W. (1959). *The sociological imagination.* Oxford: Oxford University Press.

Moll, L., & Gonzalez, N. (1994). Critical issues: Lessons from research with language minority children. *Journal of Reading Behavior: A Journal of Literacy, 26*(4), 439–456.

National Reading Panel (2000). *Report of the National Reading Panel: Teaching children to read: An evidence-based assessment of the scientific research literature on reading and its implications for reading instruction: Report of the subgroups.* Washington, DC: National Institute of Child Health and Human Development.

Nieto, S. (1998). Fact and fiction: Stories of Puerto Ricans in U.S. schools. *Harvard Educational Review, 68*(2), 133–163.

No Child Left Behind Act of 2001 (H.R. 1). (2001, January 8). 107th Congress. Available: *www.thomas.loc.gov*

Noble, D. (1994). Let them eat skills. *The Review of Education/Pedagogy/Cultural Studies, 16,* 15–30.

Olson, L. (2000). Researchers rate whole-school reform models. *Education Week, 18,* 1, 14–15.

Postman, N. (1992). *Technopoly: The surrender of culture to technology.* New York: Vintage.

Proulx, E. A. (1993). *The shipping news.* New York: Scribner.

Ryder, R. J., Sekulski, J. L., & Silberg, A. (2003). *Results of Direct Instruction reading program evaluation longitudinal results: First through third grade 2000–2003.* Milwaukee: University of Wisconsin–Milwaukee.

Sleeter, C. E. (1995). Foreword. In B. B. Swadener & S. Lubeck (Eds.), *Children and families "at promise": Deconstructing the discourse of risk* (pp. ix–xi). Albany: State University of New York Press.

Smith, H. L. (1998). Literacy and instruction in African American communities: Shall we overcome? In B. Pérez (Ed.), *Sociocultural contexts of language and literacy* (pp. 189–222). Mahwah, NJ: Lawrence Erlbaum.

Stebbins, L., St. Pierre, R. G., Proper, E. C., Anderson, R. B., & Cerva, T. R. (1977). *Education as experimentation: A planned variation model.* Cambridge, MA: Abt Associates.

Stein M., Carnine, D., & Dixon, M. (1998). Direct Instruction: Integrating curriculum design and effective teaching practice. *Intervention in School and Clinic, 33,* 227–234.

Stossel, J. (1995, October 13). *20/20.* New York: ABC.

Stotsky, S. (1998). *Losing our language: How multicultural classroom instruction is undermining our children's ability to read, write, and reason.* New York: Free.

Swadener, B. B. (1995). Children and families "at promise": Deconstructing the discourse of risk. In B. B. Swadener & S. Lubeck (Eds.), *Children and families "at promise": Deconstructing the discourse of risk* (pp. 17–49). Albany, NY: State University of New York Press.

Tashman, B. (1994). Our failure to follow through. Available: *http://darkwing .uoregon.edu/~adiep/ft/tashman.htm*

Valencia, R. (1986). *Chicano school failure and success: Research and policy agendas for the 1990s.* New York: Falmer.

Viadero, D. (1999). Scripting success. *Teacher Magazine,* pp. 20–22.

Watkins, C. L. (1988, July). Project Follow-Through: A story of the identification and neglect of effective instruction. *Youth Policy,* pp. 7–11.

Welch, O. (1994). The case for inclusive dialogue in knowing, teaching, and learning about multicultural education. In S. Hollingsworth & H. Sockett (Eds.), *Teacher research and educational reform: 93rd yearbook of the National Society for the Study of Education, Part I* (pp. 52–65). Chicago: University of Chicago Press.

Whitmire, R. (1999, December 27). Parents, students can shop around as schools test-drive reform models. *USA Today,* p. D8.

13

The Impact of Reading Mastery on Children's Reading Strategies

G. PAT WILSON, NANCY W. WILTZ, AND DEBORA LANG

Towson University

Introduction

As part of a larger comparative study that looked at differences in the types of strategies used by students across four different reading programs, we looked at the reading strategies that are promoted explicitly and implicitly in an SRA Reading Mastery program (Engelmann, Bruner, Hanner, Osborn, Osborn, & Zoref, 1995).

Formerly known as Direct Instruction, the program now known as SRA Reading Mastery is used in thousands of schools nationwide (Viadero, 2002). It uses a highly structured, behavioralist-based instructional approach in an attempt to accelerate the learning of at-risk students. Curriculum materials and instructional sequences are designed to move students to mastery at the fastest possible pace. Phonics instruction is a key building block and the program employs a synthetic phonics approach to instruction based on a behavioral analysis of decoding (Kame'enui, Simmons, Chard, & Dickson, 1997). Instruction is scripted, with the teacher using a presentation that contains both the stimuli for children's responses and a script of what the teacher is to say. The lessons are fast paced, aiming for high student involvement through instructor signals and choral responses. Children work with short pieces of text. The stories in the anthology are written by program authors. Errors are addressed immediately through the use of protocols that teachers are to initiate as soon as an error is made. Questions posed by the program's script are literal at this level, with clear, short answers from the text. While early mastery of basic skills is a key element, the program also seeks to increase students' general knowledge. Overall, the program is designed to remediate deficits.

The Reading Mastery program was evaluated using the Consumer's Guide to Evaluating a Core Reading Program Grades K–3, by Deborah C. Simmons and Edward K. Kame'enui and published by the College of Education at the University of Oregon (2003). SRA/McGraw-Hill's 2002 Reading Mastery Plus program was one of seven core programs that received the highest Oregon ratings (*Final Report of the Maryland Committee*, 2003). These programs are considered acceptable for use in Reading First schools under the No Child Left Behind Act.

The School

Cicely Elementary (a pseudonym to protect the privacy of the school, its faculty, and its children) is located in the heart of a large metropolitan city on the East Coast. Ninety-five percent of the children are on free or reduced lunch; 15 percent speak English as their second language. The school has a 48 to 50 percent annual mobility rate, and the community is marked by poverty.

The second-grade reading schedule includes one and a quarter hours of daily reading instruction, during which children work with word lists, fact paragraphs, stories in an anthology, and workbooks. This time is segmented into a thirty-minute whole-group reading instruction period, fifteen minutes of vocabulary practice, and thirty minutes of independent reading and workbook activity.

During a sixty-minute language arts period, half the time is focused on grammar while the other half emphasizes paragraph writing. Another forty-five-minute afternoon reading time involves numerous and varied activities including reading assessments and revisiting morning lessons. In addition, although not part of Reading Mastery, activities such as readers theatre, independent reading from the classroom library, and teacher read-alouds were observed in the second-grade classrooms at Cicely. Teachers sought to augment the program.

Methodology

Through this study, we sought to learn how the Reading Mastery program influenced the children's reading and perceptions about the reading process. We looked at the strategies they employed, their understanding of strategies, and their comprehension.

Data Collection

All the second-grade children who had been receiving Reading Mastery instruction since at least the beginning of first grade, but were not receiving special education nor participating in English second language services, participated in the study. Twenty-seven children from three different classrooms were involved. Teachers identified children as high, medium, or low readers based on the Reading Mastery program assessments (nine high, six medium, and twelve low). Individually, the children were asked to read and then retell typical stories for their age during one session and to take a phonics test and answer questions from an interview during another session. The sessions were counterbalanced to account for the effects, if any, of order (Graziano & Raulin, 2003). Story readings and retellings were audiotaped and transcribed; standard miscue analysis procedures for data collection were employed (Goodman, Watson, & Burke, 1987).

The story readings provided a sample of children's strategy use while reading. The children read authored trade books selected from lists of leveled books (Fountas & Pinnell, 1996, 2001) that were not used as reading material in any of the classrooms. Two to three books from each of eight levels ranging from preprimary through late third grade were available for the children. We asked children to read a book we estimated they could read with at least 85 percent accuracy. When children had difficulty understanding the text or processing it while reading, they were not asked to progress to a more difficult one.

To provide a measure of comprehension, we asked students to retell the story in their own words. When children needed assistance, researchers avoided giving information about the text. Instead, they rephrased questions for clarity or used general prompts such as "And then what happened?" and "Can you tell me more about that?" (Goodman et al., 1987).

A protocol of nine open-ended questions adapted from the Burke Metacognitive Interview (Goodman et al., 1987) was administered to all students to learn the children's perceptions of the reading process and to ascertain their awareness of reading strategies. Each child was administered the Word Analysis subtest of the Woodcock Johnson Psycho-Analytic Battery (Woodcock, Johnson, & Bonner, 1990) to assess phonics using word lists of decontextualized nonsense words.

Classroom observations were conducted in the spring of 2001. Field notes described as closely as possible the actual events as they occurred, were transcribed during or immediately following each observation, and focused on the researcher's general impressions of the classroom, detailed documentation of reading instruction, and personal reflections. Audiotaped class sessions were transcribed and included in the field notes, which were organized chronologically.

An open-ended, flexible interview format (Seidman, 1991) was used to determine teachers' and the principal's understanding of SRA Reading

Mastery, how professional and personal experiences influenced the selection of and teaching of the program, and details about the reading program's strengths and weaknesses. All interviews were tape-recorded, transcribed, and included with the field notes. In addition, one-on-one and small-group informal conversations with teachers and the principal were included in the field notes.

Data Analysis

The oral reading samples were analyzed using standard Miscue Analysis Procedure II (Goodman et al., 1987) in order to learn each child's strategy use in making sense of the text. Syntactic, semantic, and graphophonic cue use was determined. In addition, rate of self-correction was calculated. The miscues were coded by a minimum of two researchers and an interrater reliability of .90 was established. Retellings were analyzed using the protocol established by Morrow (2001) to seek evidence of setting, characters, plot episodes, story cohesion, and inferences and connections in the retellings. Each of these areas was scored on a scale of 0 to 2, with a 0 meaning no evidence and a 2 meaning strong evidence. Each retelling was analyzed and scored by two researchers, and in the case of disagreement, a third researcher resolved the difference. Interrater reliability of .95 was established. For both the oral reading and the retellings, percentages were obtained to allow comparison of scores. The Word Analysis subtest of the Woodcock Johnson Psycho-Analytic Battery (Woodcock et al., 1990) was scored according to the procedures provided by the publisher to gain standard scores and percentiles. The scores were also turned into a percentage of correct responses out of total number possible in order to allow comparison with the miscue data. Multiple data sources (miscues, retellings, phonics test, interviews, observations) support the conclusions.

Results

To understand the impact of the program on children's reading, data from the principal, the teachers, and the children were considered.

Principal's Perspective

The principal made the decision to use Reading Mastery. As a former speech and language pathologist, she first saw the program used on Native American reservations to teach children with limited English proficiency.

She feels that the children at Cicely had weak language skills, limited vocabulary, and little background knowledge to apply to academics. She said, "I had a school filled with children with language and vocabulary deficits. I needed guaranteed results. We tried every approach, then found what was appropriate for these kids" (Lang, 2002, line 1269). She finds Reading Mastery meets her goal to teach children to recognize words and apply phonics knowledge to decode unknown words while increasing their vocabulary. She finds the program has weaknesses in comprehension and writing but is committed to the program because of its success in raising standardized test scores. She has teachers augment the program by adding the forty-five-minute afternoon reading block, which teachers can use for comprehension building and writing.

Teachers' Perspective

Four themes emerged from the data from the formal and informal interviews with teachers. The first was the impression that Reading Mastery works well. Teachers commented that Reading Mastery is research based and works well with children in special education. They feel it provides structure and consistency and prepares children for middle school. Comments included that children know about phonics, letter sounds, blending, sounding out, and finding patterns.

The second theme was that Reading Mastery needs to be augmented. For example, one teacher noted that she adds her own instruction when she feels the children are not learning. Another adds problem solving and critical thinking skills and more work with nonfiction. Another teacher noted the lack of writing in the program. Teachers raised concerns about children's comprehension, and one teacher noted that Reading Mastery "has skills and memory, but not much meaning" (Lang, 2002, February 27).

The third theme centered on teachers' desire that the children succeed and to know how to ensure that success happens. They want this research to show them what they should do. They are committed to expending time and effort on children's behalf.

The last theme centered on teachers' frustration. One teacher said, "The [Reading Mastery] people come in and they want their thing, the state comes in and they want something else, the city comes in and tell us to do something else. Each wants something else" (Lang, 2002, lines 1983–1987). Some teachers feel a frustration at the various pulls on their instruction and feel a lack of certainty that what they are told to do will result in benefits to children.

Children's Understanding and Strategy Use

All but three of the children read authored trade books within or above the second-grade level. Miscue analysis showed they relied heavily on graphophonic cues. On the average, 92 percent of the miscues held high or some graphic similarity while 81 percent held high or some sound similarity (see Figure 13–2). Further analysis of the words the children substituted during their oral reading indicated strength in recognition of the initial sounds and ending sounds, including suffixes, but general weakness in analysis of the middle of words. The children did well on the phonics test of nonsense words. On the Word Analysis section of the Woodcock Johnson Psycho-Educational Battery (1990) standard scores indicated average achievement, with a range from 82 to 150 and a mean of 108 (see Figure 13–2). Only one child's score fell below average.

An analysis of the semantic acceptability of the children's miscues indicated that the miscues use partially or fully acceptable in terms of meaning only about 50 percent of the time (see Figure 13–2). The children self-corrected or made an attempt to correct miscues only about one-quarter of the time ("attempts to correct" means the child gives multiple responses to a text word; see Figure 13–2 and example in Figure 13–1). The lack of attempts to correct becomes more serious when the children do not attempt to correct words that are not real words; that is, they treat nonwords the same as real words.

Use of nonwords became characteristic of many of the readers. The rate of nonword substitutions for words in the text ranged from 0 to 44 percent of

---

   $cluckled   fox ©
Then he chuckled softly, "My dear child," he

       4. disagreed
       3. disagreed
       2. disgr-
       1. disgr-
    said, sounding right disgusted, "of course I am a fox."

Child 64 (designated high reader)
Miscues: 12%
Nonwords/miscues: 21%
Correction yes plus correction partials: 48%
(Mark was one of the few children who self-corrected.)

Figure 13–1. *An Excerpt from Mark's Reading of* Flossie and the Fox *(McKissack, 1986)*

Mean percentages for the Reading Mastery Program (RM)

1A. Syntactic and semantic miscue means and corrections

	Syn. Yes	Syn. Partial	Syn. No	Sem. Yes	Sem. Partial	Sem. No	Corr. Yes	Corr. Partial	Corr. No
RM	39.1	27.2	33.5	23.2	27.7	48.2	20.1	5.7	74.0

1B. Graphophonic related

	Sound Similar	Sound None	Graphic Similar	Graphic None	Phonics Test
RM	82.1	16.5	92.4	7.7	108.0

1C. Retelling related

	Setting	Characters	Retelling Cohesion	Inferences and Connections	Overall Percentage
RM	77	97	38	32	55.30

- Syn. = syntactic acceptability; Sem. = semantic acceptability; Corr. = correction
- Sound Similar = sound similarity (high similarity + some similarity)
- Graphic Similar = graphic similarity (high similarity + some similarity)
- Phonics Score = phonics pseudowords from the Woodcock Johnson Psycho-Educational Battery–R, Achievement Word Attack subtest
- Standard Scores: based on an average standard score of 100 with a standard deviation of 15

Figure 13–2. *Miscues*

the miscues. The nonwords the children substituted usually held high graphic and sound similarity (see Figure 13–1). The tendency spanned the designated groups, with an average of 13 percent for high readers; 21 percent for middle readers; and 9 percent for low readers. The nonwords seemed to be a result of reliance on visual cues and phonetic analysis without consideration of semantic acceptability, since nonwords hold no meaning.

The children's comprehension was measured through their retellings. The mean retelling score was 55 percent. The mean score for inclusion of setting was 77 percent; for characters, 97 percent; for cohesion, 38; and for inferences and connections, 32 (see Figure 13–2). Overall, the children's retellings lacked cohesiveness and were often a series of pieces remembered randomly from the story or its pictures. Some children, when asked to retell the story, waited for questions from us; for example, when asked to retell the story he had read, one reader asked, "Why? I just read it to you," while another asked, "Aren't you going to ask questions?" Based on the program design, our observational data of classroom instruction, and the children's retellings, it is apparent not only that the children are not used to retelling as a task but that talking about stories is not part of the children's standard fare. It is not part of the program and it is rarely observed.

The following retelling excerpt is from Peter, a child designated as a middle reader, who read *Flossie and the Fox* (McKissack, 1986) with 84 percent accuracy, 12 percent nonword miscues, and 8 percent self-corrections. His overall retelling score was one of the highest, at 82 percent.

> There was this girl that was going to get some eggs to Mrs. [*inaudible*] across the woods. She had to go through the woods and she had met this fox and she didn't believe that he was a fox. And, eh, Flossie didn't believe that he was a fox. And, and Flossie went on and then he started to tell her that he had a fluffy tail and he didn't, and she didn't believe him. After that, he told her that he could walk fast and she didn't believe him and the hounds started to chase him and when they were in the woods at the water, he showed her that they had a long nose and she thought that he was a rat. And then and she thought he was a squirrel and she thought that he was a cat. So he started to cry and Flossie gave him a peach, but he didn't want one. He was crying like a baby. When he was almost at the end of the woods, he was, he kept following her until she got to Mrs. [*inaudible*] cabin . . .

Even though Peter's retelling is fairly strong, especially in inclusion of characters, setting, and plot episodes, it is only moderate in terms of cohesion and inferences and connections. This pattern of strength in characters, setting, and plot episodes was typical in the children's retellings.

While retellings give insight into comprehension, the interviews provide insight into perceptions about the process of reading and about strategy use. All but one of the second graders said that they read at home. Children designated as high readers generated longer lists of materials that they read at home than did children in the designated low groups. While books were the most popular medium, children's lists included magazines, newspapers, and recipes. The overwhelming favorite at Cicely was Dr. Seuss books, many of which were mentioned by title as well as by author.

The children at Cicely reported that parents, other family members, and teachers were instrumental in helping them learn to read. Often they said they learned to read by reading or being read to, and a few mentioned picture reading and going to the library. The children at Cicely want to read well. All but one child professed to being a good reader. For example, Tiffany said:

[I'm a good reader] because the books are special and the books are . . . fun to read. I like hard books, like chapter books, and . . . when we finish all our work we can read a book. I love to read.

When asked, "When you are reading and you come to a word you do not know, what do you do?" 76 percent answered, "Sound it out," Try to say it," or "Say the word." The second most common response was "Ask the teacher," which was also the most common response when children were asked, "When good readers don't know a word, what do they do?" Jamilah gave a more explicit answer, which typified the work ethic of the children at Cicely, as well as a shortage of effective, self-extending reading strategies:

> I raise my hand for [the teacher] to tell me. Somebody will help me and tell me the answer. And [the teacher] will say, you can do it. They will help me every time. I'll think about the word and sit there until I know the word. If I have to take it all day . . . then I will sit there and think. And if I don't know, I'll look in a book and see if I can figure out the answer.

Discussion

At Cicely Elementary, like any other school, the influence of the program, the faculty, the children, and the community contributes to the results. For the principal, a reading program that works teaches children to read despite low language skill and poverty. Our research data shows that Reading Mastery indeed works when one defines *works* according to the principal's (and program's) definition of *works*. Children are learning reading skills. Most are able to decode previously unseen grade-level authored trade books. However, children at Cicely rely heavily upon their teachers for help, are limited in alternative strategies to attack unknown words, and do not attend to meaning well. In the Reading Mastery program at Cicely, children learn what they are taught.

Teachers feel ambivalence and concern about the completeness of the program. Teachers and the principal feel the program is weak in comprehension building. Our data support this. The children often do not correct their miscues, and they frequently substitute nonwords for real words in the text. Based on children's retellings, rote-level comprehension of characters, setting, and plot episodes is evident; however, inference is not strong.

The children seem to accept the use of nonsense words when reading. When we asked the principal about children's use of nonwords, she noted, "This is to be expected. The children do not have the language to recognize all the words they read. We ask them to read above their language level; they would not be able to identify all the words" (Lang, 2002). We suspect that in this highly teacher-directed program, children take a passive role regarding judging the correctness of their reading. From the design of the program, and from our observations of its implementation, we find that children are used to waiting for the teacher to tell them whether what they read is right or wrong. They do not recognize as their role and responsibility monitoring for correctness and fixing what is read if it seems incorrect or at least asking about words they don't recognize. The children might notice that some of the words they read don't sound like words, but they aren't encouraged to act on that recognition. The program may be so teacher directed that the children do not direct themselves and do not ask questions, despite efforts from the teachers to augment and extend the program. The effect of Reading Mastery on the children's reading includes their development of a perception that reading that is accepted by their teachers might not make sense, and it is the teacher's responsibility to tell them if they made a mistake and what to do about it. It is not their responsibility.

Strong language use with rich language experiences contributes to success in reading and writing (for examples, see studies by Heath, 1986/1994). The choral responses to literally oriented questions of Reading Mastery do not promote discussion. Discussion of literacy texts would allow language to develop. It would allow children to develop skill in oral presentation, in justification of ideas, and in the general pragmatics of give-and-take in talk. Given that language mediates thinking (Moffett, 1968/1983; Smagorinsky & O'Donnell-Allen, 1998; Vygotsky, 1987; J. Wertsch, 1991; J. V. Wertsch, del Rio, & Alvarez, 1995; Zebrowski, 1994), language should be a tool of learning. Yet the scripted nature of the Reading Mastery program limits language use.

Therefore, there are three areas that prompt uneasiness on our part about Reading Mastery. First, the children rely on decoding and have limited strategy knowledge. Second, the children are dependent on their teachers and don't evaluate their reading for sensibility. Third, there is a lack of adequate language use promoted in the program.

In addition, the Reading Mastery program offers children little opportunity to choose and read books beyond those of the program and limits their interaction with thoughts and ideas beyond those sanctioned in the program. Given the choral responses to questions scripted by the program, children have little opportunity to deviate from the set program through discussion. The program places limits and controls, and teachers are not supposed to change instruction for individual children beyond a protocol dictated by the program when children make errors. The children's experience reading a variety of text and using texts as models from which to write their own texts is shunted by program constraints. All in all, opportunity to transact with text, to create and enter "text worlds" (Langer, 1995) fed by author and by reader, worlds in which imagination becomes a tool of understanding the intersection of text and life, is held in abeyance. Too little is expected of children in the Reading Mastery program. Nevertheless, Reading Mastery is one of the top-rated programs approved for use by schools receiving Reading First grants.

References

Engelmann, S., Bruner, E., Hanner, S., Osborn, J., Osborn, S., & Zoref, L. (1995). *Reading Mastery.* Columbus, OH: SRA/McGraw-Hill.

Final Report of the Maryland Committee for Selecting Core Reading programs. (2003). Baltimore: Maryland State Department of Education.

Fountas, I., & Pinnell, G. S. (1996). *Guided reading: Good first teaching for all children.* Portsmouth, NH: Heinemann.

Fountas, I., & Pinnell, G. S. (2001). *Guiding readers and writers (grades 3–6): Teaching comprehension, genre, and content literacy.* Portsmouth, NH: Heinemann.

Goodman, Y., Watson, D., & Burke, C. (1987). *Reading miscue inventory: Alternative procedures.* Katonah, NY: Richard Irwin.

Graziano, A. M., & Raulin, M. L. (2003). *Research methods: A process of inquiry* (5th ed.). Upper Saddle River, NJ: Pearson Education/Allyn & Bacon.

Heath, S. B. (1986/1994). Separating "things of the imagination" from life: Learning to read and write. In W. H. Teale & E. Sulzby (Eds.), *Emergent literacy: Writing and reading* (pp. 156–171). Norwood, NJ: Ablex.

Kame'enui, E. J., Simmons, D. C., Chard, D., & Dickson, S. (1997). Direct instruction reading. In S. A. Stahl & D. A. Hayes (Eds.), *Instructional models in reading* (pp. 58–84). Mahwah, NJ: Erlbaum.

Lang, D. (2002, February 27). Field notes.

Langer, J. A. (1995). *Envisioning literature: Literacy understanding and literature instruction.* New York: Teachers College.

McKissack, P. C. (1986). *Flossie and the Fox.* New York: Dial Books for Young Readers.

Moffett, J. (1968/1983). *Teaching the universe of discourse.* Portsmouth, NH: Boynton/Cook.

Morrow, L. M. (2001). *Literacy development in the early years: Helping children read and write* (4th ed.). Needham Heights, MA: Allyn & Bacon.

Seidman, I. E. (1991). *Interviewing as qualitative research.* New York: Teachers College Press.

Simmons, D. C., & Kame'enui, E. K. (2003). *A consumer's guide for evaluating a core reading program grades K–3: A critical elements analysis.* Eugene, OR: University of Oregon.

Smagorinsky, P., & O'Donnell-Allen, C. (1998). Reading as mediated and mediating action: Composing meaning for literature through multimedia interpretative text. *Reading Research Quarterly, 33*(2), 198–226.

Viadero, D. (2002, April 17). Studies cite learning gains in Direct Instruction Schools. Available: *www.edweek.com/ew/newstory.cfm?slug=31direct.h21*

Vygotsky, L. (1987). Thinking and speech. In R. W. Rieber & A. S. Carton (Eds.), *The collected works of L. S. Vygotsky: Problems of general psychology* (Vol. 1) (pp. 201–214). New York: Plenum.

Wertsch, J. (1991). *Voices of the mind: A sociocultural approach to mediated action.* Cambridge: Harvard University Press.

Wertsch, J. V., del Rio, P., & Alvarez, A. (1995). Sociocultural studies: History, action and mediation. In J. V. Wertsch, P. del Rio, & A. Alvarez (Eds.), *Sociocultural studies of mind* (pp. 1–34). New York: Cambridge University Press.

Woodcock, R., Johnson, W., & Bonner, W. (1990). *Woodcock Johnson Psycho-Educational Battery–R.* Itasca, IL: Riverside.

Zebrowski, J. T. (1994). *Thinking through theory: Vygotskian perspectives on the teaching of writing.* Portsmouth, NH: Boynton/Cook.

14

First Do No Harm: Teachers' Reactions to Mandated Reading Mastery

NANCY RANKIE SHELTON

Towson University

The political climate surrounding standardized test results has intensified, forcing change in literacy instruction in classrooms across the nation. While this nationwide trend stems from the federal No Child Left Behind legislation, the effects are felt more strongly in states that receive funding through the Reading First moneys attached to the legislation. Schools with low test scores face punitive measures that include having their test scores publicized, having themselves and/or their students identified for remediation, and being taken over by the state (Elmore & Fuhrman, 2001).

In Florida, the situation is aggravated by the fact that the state has placed tremendous weight on the performance of lower-achieving students in the school grading used by the Florida Department of Education. With heavy emphasis on the scores of struggling students, schools increasingly make curriculum decisions based on test score results; thus state departments of education shape education policy. As noted by Weaver and Geske (1997), "The governor's office can wield considerable influence on a variety of education policies and in particular on school funding issues" (p. 315). Florida's current governor, Jeb Bush, exercises his policy-shaping power by keeping accountability formulas and funding in a state of constant change. Florida's A+ Plan (Florida Bill CS/HB 751, 1999) mandates education policy and controls supplemental funding for education based primarily on Florida Comprehensive Assessment Test (FCAT) scores. Since the inception of the A+ Plan, the criteria for grading have been continuously revised.

In the A+ Plan, school grading criteria are critically important because of the funding attached to grade achievement. FCAT scores are used to assign school grades, and bonuses of one hundred dollars per student are awarded to A schools and to schools that improve by at least one letter grade from one school year to the next. Funding for professional development is provided to implement "proven programs" and approved staff development in struggling schools, leaving administrators with little choice but to implement government-sponsored reading programs. With mandatory retention for third-grade students who do not pass the FCAT (see *http://firn.edu/doe/commhome/progress/proghome.htm* for details) and twenty-one schools receiving an F grade in 2004 (Florida Department of Education, 2004), a frenzy has been created around low test scores, leaving school-based administrators scrambling for quick fixes. Scripted reading programs are marketed with claims of increased test scores for all who follow their programs, and within this mayhem, approved scripted reading programs have been offered to school administrators as a guaranteed road to salvation. Invariably, such programs are adopted by high-poverty schools whose students do poorly on standardized tests.

Many educators are trying to resist legislated reading instruction, but in so doing, they find themselves in perilous positions. Garan (2002) points out that the "barrage of criticism" leaves teachers unsure of their teaching, lowering their confidence to the point that they question their own pedagogical knowledge and effectiveness. Public criticism regarding low test scores has led to increased public rewards and punishments for teachers that shift the focus from intrinsic to extrinsic motivation and further exasperate the problem. As Kohn (2000) put it, "Teaching and learning alike come to be seen as less appealing when someone has a gun to your head" (p. 22). When teachers are constantly criticized for their inability to raise the test scores of their students, they often succumb to political pressure, changing their instructional practices to meet political demands. These conditions alter the emotional aspect of teaching, which, according to Graves, often identifies effective teachers (2001).

Forced change, according to the research summarized by Bascia and Hargreaves (2000), comes in the form of new programs prescribed on the basis of so-called scientific evidence. Bascia and Hargreaves report that such programs are identified and prescribed by policy makers who fail to recognize the significance of the conceptualizations of teaching espoused by teachers. Teachers have ideologies that guide their practice and those ideologies vary among the members of the profession. According to Bascia and Hargreaves, reform measures that prescribe programs force all teachers into the "technical" ideology, with detrimental effects. Despite the documented negative effects of the "dominant technical model" to teaching and learning, forced technical change continues to be a major push in education reform. In a summary of relevant research, Bascia and Hargreaves report that the persistence lies "in the systemic, contextual and political nature of public education and people's attempts to control and change it" (p. 15).

The Study

This political climate represents the environment into which the teachers whose stories are told in this chapter were forced. Research analyzing the impact of mandated literacy reform was conducted at Shoals Elementary, located in a rural community in north central Florida. A comparative case study conducted over the course of one school year included observational and interview data. The larger study (Shelton, 2003) examined the teachers' beliefs about literacy instruction, the political climate at the school, and the teachers' reactions to the mandate requiring Reading Mastery as their core reading curriculum. Formal and informal interviews of four teachers and two administrators (principal and curriculum resource teacher) resulted in 175 pages of verbatim transcripts. In addition, field notes from participant observation focused on teaching and learning in the classrooms in order to give a firsthand account of the learning environment and, when combined with interviewing data, "allow for holistic interpretation of the phenomenon being investigated" (Merriam, 1988, p. 102). The fifty-nine observations ranged in length from forty-five minutes to four hours, with the majority of the observations being approximately two hours in length.

Data analysis identified patterns in the acts of planning curriculum, teaching, and reflecting on literacy experiences in the classroom and contained evidence of the teachers' efforts to work out a balance between the conflicting forces identified in the theoretical framework that grounded the research. These forces are the political climate, the mandated reading program, the teacher's own concept of teaching, and the teacher's understanding of literacy development. Observation and interview data were used to identify evidence of the consciousness the participants had of the forces this research presumed to be present in varying degrees during the teachers' decision-making process. This chapter focuses only on the emotional toll paid by the teachers as a direct result of losing control over classroom instructional decisions.

A complete description of the teachers' understanding of literacy development can be found in the full report (Shelton, 2003); however, to fully understand how severely the mandate to teach Reading Mastery compromised the professionalism of the teachers, it is necessary to understand that their views on literacy development, though individually constructed and divergent among individuals, did not match what the reading program required in their teaching. Teachers varied in their reactions to the program because of their background experiences and beliefs about teaching and learning, but they were united in their lack of faith in the program as a panacea for reading difficulties, their resentment toward their loss of power, and the emotional toll the mandate had on them personally.

The teachers who participated in this case study were required to use Reading Mastery (Engelmann & Hanner, 1995) because of administrative decisions driven by claims that the program would help improve scores and thereby eliminate mandated retention of students based on test scores. The teachers were forced to accept the mandate and expressed that, in their professional opinions, strict adherence to the program would harm the teaching and learning environment. The teachers, who volunteered to be in this research, include two fourth-grade teachers (one white male, one black female) and two third-grade teachers (white females).

The Teachers Respond to Their Own Instruction

In many ways, the teachers at Shoals were caught in a tug of war (Buckner, 2002). They were constantly pulled back and forth between what they thought they should do because of the curriculum mandate and what they wanted to do because of their own beliefs about teaching and learning. The teachers brought their own perspectives and personal responses to teaching Reading Mastery, and despite some commonalities, the teachers' instructional responses to teaching Reading Mastery were not uniform. They entered the year with varied past experience with the program and individual opinions of the value of the program. What follows are individual characterizations of the experience for each teacher.

Mrs. Phillips: "It's Very Frustrating"

Mrs. Phillips, one of the third-grade teachers, had been teaching for eighteen years before this research was conducted. Mrs. Phillips had a master's degree in elementary education and had taught in both public and private schools. She had used a variety of methods to teach reading, including Reading Mastery for at least six years, but until this year she was not mandated to strictly follow the program. When Mrs. Phillips first started teaching the Reading Mastery program, she was working with below-grade-level students, and she found it to be a suitable program. However, more recently, she was asked to use Reading Mastery to teach above-grade-level and on-grade-level students and very strongly voiced her opinion that Reading Mastery is "not adequate at all for above-grade-level learners; they need something far different."

Mrs. Phillips described Reading Mastery Level 3 as a "transition" from the very phonics-based earlier levels to a year of vocabulary building and teaching the students to read for information. Because students at this level are learning to read for information, the reading sections and comprehension questions are all about recall of facts. The students are reading to learn facts, not to develop higher-order thinking strategies and habits. The questions in Reading Mastery are what Mrs. Phillips referred to as "right-there questions"; they ask for details given in the text and don't require synthesis, analysis, or evaluation of what is read.

Mrs. Phillips clearly stated that with grade-level and above readers, she preferred not to teach Reading Mastery. She did not agree that Reading Mastery was appropriate for all students and she did not like the homogeneous grouping that the program required. She objected more to what was not part of the reading program than what was. The absence of quality children's literature, reading comprehension strategies, and high-order thinking opportunities for the students disturbed Mrs. Phillips. She also disagreed with the rapid pace and timing of the program. The school's monitoring of the number of lessons that each reading class completed pressured her to continue forward progress at the pace prescribed by the program manuals. Because of the time required to execute the various components of the program (see the full report), Mrs. Phillips was unable to include writing instruction in her reading block as long as she taught Reading Mastery as her core program.

Relationships were important to Mrs. Phillips. In her attempt to balance her relationships with her colleagues, her students, and her administration, she found herself in conflict, which was revealed through the intense negative emotions expressed during her interviews. Mrs. Phillips often nostalgically discussed past practices that went beyond her current skill-driven instruction and included integrated thematic units. Her description of past teaching practice indicated that she did not approach teaching from a technical perspective; however, at this point in her career, her teaching was now defined as following a series of procedures. Mrs. Phillips became the technical teacher that her principal asked her to become, acting on a narrow, restricted view of teaching and learning regardless of her knowledge about teaching and her understanding of her students' needs. Her defeat became clear when asked why she did not fight to regain some of the autonomy she used to have in teaching. She replied, "I'm a cynic and I think nothing would change." Her defeat had evolved into hopelessness and frustration:

> There are people now telling us we have to do this, and we have to do it this way, and it takes the autonomy of the teacher away. . . . It's frustrating. It's very frustrating because . . . there's so much we have to cram in our curriculum now that it has taken the fun out of teaching. We used to have units that we would do that included arts and crafts activities, literature, math,

and science all within the unit. But we can't do them now. . . . [Students] don't see the connection between what they're studying and what they're going to use at all, which is frustrating.

As Mrs. Phillips saw it, the purpose and the fun had been taken out of teaching, and she did not know how to get them back. Each day she faced a room full of students with diverse needs and backgrounds. She knew that each student needed individual attention, relevant curriculum, and a little fun. However, people outside her classroom had designed her day. She had no way to regain control.

Mrs. Zeigler: "It Doesn't Teach"

Mrs. Zeigler, the other third-grade teacher, had been teaching for fourteen years and had extensive experience teaching Reading Mastery. She was a certified special education teacher who accepted her first regular education assignment the year this study was conducted. Because of her special education background, it was expected that she would be comfortable teaching Reading Mastery, as the program was designed for teaching reading to students with learning disabilities. This expectation was met on the classroom level; Mrs. Zeigler knew the procedures well and executed them smoothly. However, in reflecting on her reading instruction, she was critical of the program and believed it to have limited student benefits. While Mrs. Zeigler believed Reading Mastery was a beginning place for reading instruction because of the structure it provided, she contended that the continued use of the program lowered her students' motivation. "After a while, the kids were like, 'Okay, we're past this,' and I could see it in them, because their motivation to do it was less and less as we went on. And my motivation got less and less, and I think those two go hand in hand." She noted that the immature look of the textbook, the poor stories, and the content in the stories dampened the students' excitement.

While the program helped the students learn to answer literal comprehension questions, it never moved out of the detail questioning into higher-order thinking. "There are more right-there questions than there are any other thought-provoking, critical thinking questions. It doesn't make the kids think at all. It doesn't teach the kids." Mrs. Zeigler also saw no evidence of transfer to other content areas. For example, one lesson required the students to label various cities, states, and countries but did not include an instruction or introduction of the concepts: "They just identify it, they didn't teach it. I don't think Reading Mastery has taught very many concepts at all. It was just, 'Here it is, this is what it is. Okay, know it.'"

This model of instruction affected how Mrs. Zeigler felt about other major components of reading instruction within Reading Mastery. According to Mrs. Zeigler, vocabulary instruction was nothing more than "word attack." The students just pronounced the words; there was no phonics instruction, no decoding, and no sound pattern instruction. Mrs. Zeigler would have liked to see more relevant vocabulary instruction instead of the program just providing word definitions. The instruction did not activate prior knowledge of the vocabulary words or any discussion of known meanings. The focus was recite and repeat. This lack of instruction was a problem for Mrs. Zeigler, who criticized the program for inadequate "concept skill" and writing instruction.

Lack of writing in the program was also problematic for Mrs. Zeigler. She noted that the workbook assignments were mostly fill-in-the-blank format and the students were not required to attend to spelling when they completed the workbooks. While Mrs. Zeigler knew that some of her students "really care[d] about that and they really want[ed] to get it right" she also was aware that others "[didn't] have that intrinsic kind of motivation and [would] just write as close as they [could] get it and just go on."

Ignoring what she considered to be good practice to meet the needs of a program compromised Mrs. Zeigler's professionalism. To deviate from the script by following her understanding of good practice required defying orders from the principal. Mrs. Zeigler did what Santman (2002) found commonplace practice: "Teachers across the nation were abandoning what they knew about good teaching and learning because the ramifications for low test scores were and continue to be so deep. . . . This obsession with the test prevents thoughtfulness in teaching" (p. 204).

Like Mrs. Phillips, Mrs. Zeigler felt monitored by the administration. She repeatedly referred to the directive made by her administration that she was to "follow the script" and stated that the administration told her that her students' lack of progress the year before was a result of her not teaching the program properly.

The emphasis that the administration put on following the script prevented both of the third-grade teachers from personalizing or supplementing instruction. They felt accused of poor teaching and were unwilling or unable to draw on their professional knowledge to supplement weaknesses in the program. Mrs. Zeigler and Mrs. Phillips both shared the perception that the administration did not approve of the way they had executed the program the year before; however, their reactions to this perceived accusation produced different results in the classroom. While Mrs. Phillips simply executed the program as required, Mrs. Zeigler put forth effort to extend her teaching beyond the program. This was evident in two areas: diverging from the program to support students during the scripted correction and teaching writing.

Mr. Wright: "It Is Not a Building Block of Reading"

Mr. Wright, a fourth-grade teacher, was the youngest of the four teachers and had taught only at Shoals. In fact, he did his full-time internship at the school and had been teaching there since he had graduated from the university six years prior to the year the research was conducted. According to Mr. Wright, Reading Mastery is not a "building block of reading;" rather, "it is just one more little thing we have to get through before we read." Unlike the other three teachers, Mr. Wright often deserted Reading Mastery and infused his instruction with practices that aligned with his own beliefs, such as using literature to instill motivation to learn to read. Mr. Wright expressed that Reading Mastery taught certain skills, and then he used those skills to teach other parts of reading through shared novels and research projects. Mr. Wright did not confine his reading instruction to Reading Mastery because, he said, "Reading development varies in kids, and some kids need different things than others." Deviating from Reading Mastery allowed Mr. Wright to integrate a variety of strategies.

When Mr. Wright taught Reading Mastery, he followed the script and his lessons were very fast paced. The program promoted this pace and Mr. Wright capitalized on it to enable him to get through lessons quickly so as not to draw attention to his teaching at the times when he set the program aside. His instruction followed the script very closely even though the program created theoretical tensions for him because "sticking to the script does not allow for individual questions from the students to be addressed by the teacher." Therefore, when he deviated from the program, he worked much more closely with his students to help them develop skills that enhanced their individual literacy needs.

Another tension arose when Mr. Wright recognized inaccuracies in the scientific information included in the program and came upon other factual inaccuracies. He explained them to the students as fiction despite the apparent intention of the text. Partly because of these inaccuracies, Mr. Wright engaged his students in reading research projects.

> A lot of times I say, "Use information from the text to support your answer," and I also have the kids draw upon previous knowledge because we've studied the solar system this year and we know that half of what the [Reading Mastery] book says is only part of the truth. And so I use that to tell the kids that all the time when you read stuff you're not always getting the examples of the same truth. So the more you read, the better off your knowledge is because one book might say one thing and one might say another.

Even though he knew that both the program designers and his administration frowned upon deviating from the script to correct inaccuracies or to discuss possibly problematic elements in some of the lessons, Mr. Wright found it necessary. One unit drew attention from some of his students, and Mr. Wright explained how he addressed the issue. In the unit, which sought to integrate measurement in reading, the main character was Jokey, an over-weight beagle. Jokey was ridiculed for his weight by other animal characters in the story. To lose weight, he starved himself (drinking only water), then gorged himself, and again stopped eating. The text glorified his success:

> At the end of two months, you should have seen him. You would never know it was the same dog. He walked on his tiptoes. His belly was very, very small, and his chest stuck out with a row of ribs showing on each side. His legs had big muscles and so did his arms. (student textbook, p. 61)

Mr. Wright could not let this series of lessons go without addressing the serious issues that were presented as a message of the lessons:

> We discussed it as, "This is crazy!" You couldn't lose weight, you'd get sick and go to the hospital. . . . You know, I think it's really important to talk about these issues as they come up. The problem is that it's not scripted in the program and some people teach it without that [discussion]. And I think that that's something that I would hope most people would pick up on, but maybe they don't.

Mr. Wright shared his concern that Reading Mastery did not prepare the students for the FCAT. "Reading Mastery is very basic, limited, you know, 'right-there' questions, and the FCAT is so much beyond that." He struggled with time management issues and had to choose between writing instruction or more developed reading instruction with what little extra time he had during the reading block. The result was a continuously evolving schedule that included Reading Mastery, novel reading, report writing, FCAT writing instruction, FCAT vocabulary instruction, and a constantly changing agenda. Given the fact that Mr. Wright's students were the most needy group of students in the research, this inconsistency may not have benefited them. The unpredictable agenda and the strict behavior management approach Mr. Wright employed created a sense of confusion for the students. The effects of irregularity may have been exacerbated by the fact that many of Mr. Wright's students faced serious problems at home and at school and therefore really needed a consistent, predictable environment. The result was a rather unruly class, which was not helped by Mr. Wright's continuous focus on behavior.

Mrs. Jones: "Is This Going to Help Them?"

Mrs. Jones, the other fourth-grade teacher who volunteered to be in the study, had been teaching for sixteen years and was the only teacher who had no prior experience teaching Reading Mastery. She was the only African American teacher in the research. Mrs. Jones believed that she should do what she was told to do because "that was the right thing to do." On a number of occasions, Mrs. Jones said that she was not in the position to make the decisions and she did not enjoy teaching Reading Mastery, but this was what was decided to be best for her students so she would do the very best she could do and teach the program as asked.

Following the program as prescribed made inclusion of other reading instruction during the reading block impossible. Mrs. Jones had no time to add comprehension strategies not included in the program, nor was there time to infuse literature. All reading the students engaged in outside the textbook was silent independent reading and did not include comprehension instruction. Because Mrs. Jones' reading class was made up of a group of fourth graders, Mrs. Jones also needed to prepare her students for FCAT writing. Before she had to use Reading Mastery, a typical reading period in Mrs. Jones' class included grammar instruction and practice, vocabulary related to the novel the students were reading, reading with comprehension strategies embedded in the lesson, and writing instruction as the final component. With Reading Mastery, she had no time for any additional instruction.

According to Mrs. Jones, *reading* was not part of Reading Mastery. The passages were too short and the questioning was too intensive for the students to experience the kind of reading that was required for them to pass the FCAT reading test. The program focused on fluency, and while Mrs. Jones agreed that fluency is important, she did not see the importance of the weekly rate and accuracy tests:

> I know they need to read fluently, but how is that going to help them on the FCAT, where they have to read long passages? The fluency tests are short passages. They are reading short passages in the reading lessons and the interruptions do not require the students to focus for long periods of time.

These interruptions were the "comprehension tasks" in the scripted lessons. Observational data revealed that the actual number of minutes students read aloud was minimal and supported Mrs. Jones' claim that required reading was minimal. In addition to the number of minutes the students read, the total quantity of text read daily was at times just ten to twelve minutes, with half the time spent questioning, thus supporting Mrs. Jones' assertion that extended reading was not part of Reading Mastery.

According to Mrs. Jones, Reading Mastery did not allow her to meet the needs of individual students. She was not allowed to use her knowledge and expertise regarding literacy instruction and development. Furthermore, the script she was required to follow restricted her instruction and confined student remediation to rereading. Mrs. Jones' discontent manifested itself in uncharacteristically unpleasant interactions between her and her students. These occasional "outbursts" were most often centered around teaching Reading Mastery or preparation exercises for the FCAT testing.

As can be noted from the documented perceptions of their own and their students' learning experiences, all four of the teachers had to compromise their teaching in order to execute the mandate imposed. While their beliefs and understandings of literacy development influenced their response to the mandate, they unilaterally denied that Reading Mastery was a quick-fix solution to the problem of test score achievement. Furthermore, in all four cases, the teachers retained little or no control over their instruction and clearly expressed resentment toward the loss of power over decisions made in their classrooms.

Emotionally Drained Teachers

It is imperative to note the emotional consequences suffered by the teachers, which are a direct result of the mandate that controlled their teaching. As Hargreaves (1998) notes, little research has been aimed at the analysis of reform efforts on teachers' emotional health: "Emotions are virtually absent from the advocacy of and the mainstream literature specifically concerned with educational change and reform" (p. 837). This research, however, specifically inquires how teachers feel about mandated reform and the change required in their pedagogy and therefore does concern itself with emotions. Looking across the cases, we can see a wide range of negative emotions.

Teachers need to be in environments that sustain their emotional energy to teach (Graves, 2001). "What drains energy the most is when your professional options are reduced, or when decisions are made for you, and you can only react to events instead of shaping them" (p. 21). Teachers forced to teach a scripted curriculum are at risk for having their professional energy drained. Teachers in Reading Mastery classrooms do not make decisions. The program prescribes the academic focus for each group of students, predetermines the content and sequence of the lessons, and uses behavior modification techniques to extrinsically control academic and social outcomes.

Revisiting the teachers' words and emphasizing the struggles these teachers endured provide the reader with explicit, powerful emotions. There are a total of thirty-six such statements; Mrs. Phillips contributed fifteen; Mrs. Zeigler shared eleven; Mr. Wright added eight; and Mrs. Jones made two of the statements. Their words, drawn directly from the interview data, do not reflect a healthy teaching environment and reveal the following emotions.

The teachers feel caught and unable to teach:

- You are caught.
- I have not taught writing one-tenth of what I wanted to.
- They are not getting it [comprehension instruction] anywhere.
- A kid will be really stuck on something and you'll want to go to it, knowing that you really can't.

They are frustrated:

- You ought to be able to give everything you've got to those kids.
- It's difficult and it's stressful.
- It's nerve-racking.
- It's very difficult to be torn between doing Reading Mastery and the FCAT. . . . They're not one and the same.
- Fourth grade is very opinionated . . . and we've gotten in a bit of trouble this year.
- This year there was even more stress on timing.
- Researcher asks, "How do you feel about this?" Teacher tears up and responds, "I have a master's degree."
- Everything is chopped up.
- It's really fragmented.
- It's not useful.
- . . . frustrating.
- It's frustrating.
- It's very frustrating.

They feel programmed:

- Autonomy. I don't have any.
- There are people telling us we have to do this and we have to do it this way.
- We were just told this is how it's going to be.
- The script is what is going to get the score up.
- They were keeping track of how many Reading Mastery lessons you do every week.
- I believe they felt we went too slow. Took too many breaks or whatever.
- Time constraints on everything—it's kinda hard.

- You're so constrained to this little box that you know, you just, you just kinda wonder, "Why?"
- I don't think the children see any of it in a real-world realm.
- I feel programmed like a computer.

All these negative emotions lead to a loss of passion for teaching:

- I'm really discouraged. I'm sorry.
- My motivation got less and less; it was a huge problem.
- I'm at the point where, "Oh well."
- You know, it's not easy . . . you have to kinda let yourself go.
- Reading Mastery is not exactly my philosophy of instilling the love of reading in kids.
- You do it anyway because you know you have to.
- It has taken the fun out of teaching.

The teachers' thoughtful participation in this project provided strong evidence that mandated reform has damaging effects on teachers' emotional well-being. This research concurs with Brown's (1993) findings that removing authority for making curricular decisions from teachers leads to a distrusting, problematic environment. When teachers can no longer act upon their professional knowledge, being part of the decision-making process at their schools, they are left with a "perception of powerlessness."

Neither teaching nor learning can occur outside the emotional world of the teachers and learners. We have learned from the business world that "employee morale has become a central priority" and "when workers are disgruntled, distracted, or poorly trained, no brilliant strategy for expanding market shares will compensate for that liability. Why should it be any different for schools?" (Cohen, 2002, p. 533). High-stakes testing and imposing curriculum in classrooms lower the morale of both teachers and students. Comparing schools' standardized test scores and ignoring "the one critical player in the school who makes the biggest difference"—the teacher—do not measure effective teaching.

> For a school to be an intellectual center, for it to have the ethos, the sense of community, and the "spirit" that so many parents and administrators seek, it must celebrate the work of its teachers in a way rarely seen in public schools. It must attend to the needs of teachers, it must accommodate their sensibilities, and it must treat the teachers' contributions with as much genuine concern as it does those of any other constituency—maybe more. (Cohen, 2002, p. 533)

After the Reading Mastery curriculum was imposed on the teachers, the positive sense of community that had previously existed at Shoals disappeared (see the full report). The teachers' professional opinions were once part of the decision-making process in the school; teachers were part of a collaborative team. This empowerment became disempowerment when their curriculum became test driven. According to Buckner (2002), a fourth-grade teacher who struggles with firsthand knowledge that teaching has become more about testing and test scores than about real learning, teachers who make decisions based on a test become powerless. They are powerless to make reasonable instructional decisions and powerless to do what is best for the learners sitting in front of them.

The teachers at Shoals experienced this sense of powerlessness and loss of control over their instruction. The National Reading Panel (NRP) cautions against deskilling teachers and reducing teacher control over the instructional designs implemented:

> The role of the teacher needs to be better understood. Some of the phonics programs showing large effect sizes are scripted in such a way that teacher judgment is largely eliminated. Although scripts may standardize instruction, they may reduce teachers' interest in the teaching process or their motivation. (2002, pp. 2–96)

This research confirms the NRP's speculation that mandated scripted programs do indeed reduce teachers' interest and motivation to teach regardless of their own opinion of and experience with the program mandated. In spite of this insightful concern and expressed recommendation to respect teachers' knowledge, teachers all over the country, much like the teachers in this research, are being mandated to ignore their professional expertise and blindly follow scripts.

References

Bascia, N., & Hargreaves, A. (2000). *The sharp edge of educational change: Teaching, leading and the realities of reform.* New York: RoutledgeFalmer.

Brown, D. F. (1993, April 12–16). The political influence of state testing reform through the eyes of principals and teachers. Paper presented at the annual meeting of the American Educational Research Association, Atlanta, GA.

Buckner, A. (2002). Teaching in a world focused on testing. *Language Arts, 79,* 212–215.

Cohen, M. (2002). Schools our teachers deserve: A proposal for teacher-centered reform. *Phi Delta Kappan, 83,* 532–537.

Datnow, A., & Castellano, M. (2000). Teachers' response to Success for All: How beliefs, experiences, and adaptations shape implementation. *American Educational Research Journal, 3*(3), 775–799.

Elmore, R., & Fuhrman, S. (2001). Holding schools accountable: Is it working? *Phi Delta Kappan, 83,* 67–72.

Engelmann S., & Hanner, S. (1995). *Reading Mastery.* Worthington, OH: SRA Macmillan/McGraw-Hill.

Florida Bill CS/HB 751. (1999). Retrieved September 2, 2004 from *http://election.dos.state.fl.us/pdf/99laws/ch_99-398.pdf*

Florida Department of Education. (2004). List of F schools. Retrieved September 2, 2004, from *http://schoolgrades.fldoe.org/pdf/0304schoollist.pdf*

Garan, E. (2002). *Resisting reading mandates: How to triumph with the truth.* Portsmouth, NH: Heinemann.

Graves, D. (2001). *Energy to teach.* Portsmouth, NH: Heinemann.

Hargreaves, A. (1998). The emotional practice of teaching. *Teaching and Teacher Ed, 14,* pp. 835–854.

Kohn, A. (2000). *The case against standardized testing: Raising the scores, ruining the schools.* Portsmouth, NH: Heinemann.

Merriam, S. (1980). *Case study research in education: A qualitative approach.* San Francisco: Jossey-Bass.

National Reading Panel (2000). Teaching children to read: an evidence-based assessment of scientific research literature on reading and its implications for reading instruction. Washington, DC: National Institute of Child Health and Human Development.

Santman, D. (2002). Teaching to the test? Test preparation in the reading workshop. *Language Arts, 79,* 203–211.

Shelton, N. R. (2003). Mandated literacy programs: How teachers react. Doctoral dissertation, University of Florida, Gainesville.

Weaver, S. W., & Geske, T. G. (1997). Educational policy making in the state legislature as policy expert. *Educational Policy, 11,* 309–329.

15

*"Gracias por la oportunidad, pero voy a buscar otro trabajo . . ."**

A Beginning Teacher Resists High-Stakes Curriculum

NADEEN T. RUIZ

Stanford University

LORENA MORALES-ELLIS

California State University, Sacramento

A focus on high-stakes testing brings with it a focus on *high-stakes curriculum*. By high-stakes curriculum, we mean curriculum materials or programs that are adopted, mandated, and closely monitored by school districts in an intensive effort to improve student achievement. There is an explicit, not implicit, connection made by the school district between the degree of implementation of the mandated curriculum and the promise of raised test scores. An additional characteristic of high-stakes curriculum is the active involvement of institutions beyond the school district itself in overseeing the implementation process and charting the results. These institutions usually include government entities and personalities, such as city councils and state legislatures, and, very importantly, the popular media.

It was in this highly charged, sociopolitical, and educational context that Lorena began her career as an urban elementary school teacher. Nadeen initially served as Lorena's university supervisor when Lorena accepted a paid internship in one of the lowest-performing schools in a large northern California school district. As Lorena's situation became more and more precarious within the school, however, Nadeen became a participant in the struggle between the principal's efforts to make Lorena conform to the district's policy on the implementation of the language and literacy curriculum and Lorena's efforts to advocate for a pedagogy and a curriculum that

---

* "Thanks for the opportunity, but I'll be looking for another job . . ."

199

were better suited to the needs of her students: twenty Spanish-speaking students, grades 1–3, all recent immigrants to the United States.

We employed teacher research methods (Lytle, 2000) to trace the story of Lorena's first year of teaching in order to show the effects of high-stakes curriculum and testing on beginning teachers in urban schools. We locate our story within the growing literature on multicultural social reconstruction-ist teacher education (Cochran-Smith, 2000; Edelsky, 1999; Martin & Van Gunten, 2001). We have noticed that few studies have looked at student or beginning teachers working in districts that have invoked the intensive, high-stakes testing and curriculum policies that are now implemented in many urban school districts. Furthermore, much of this research either stops once credential candidates leave the university and actually enter classrooms as teachers or depends on post hoc questionnaires and interviews.

As teacher researchers in the "middle of the story" that we wanted to tell, we chose narrative inquiry to represent and understand our experience (Clandinin & Connelly, 2000). Clandinin and Connelly explain narrative inquiry as collaboration between researcher and participants in which the inquirers enter the social interaction to live and tell (and relive and retell) the stories unfolding in the context of inquiry. Just as important as the emerging narratives is the illumination of the social context of the narrative inquiry. Consequently, we analyzed our experience as student teacher and field supervisor in terms of nested contexts, beginning with the context of California's policy on language arts instruction and continuing to the focal contexts of our research, the school and the classroom (Dixon, Green, Yeager, Baker, & Fránquiz, 2000). From the very beginning of our work together, we were keenly aware of the pressure exacted upon us and upon Lorena's students by these multilayered contexts.

Key Participants in the Study

At the time of the study, Nadeen was a professor of bilingual and multicul-tural education at a university close to the school district where the study took place. Lorena was in the final phase of a three-semester bilingual teacher-preparation program called the Multicultural Multilingual (M&M) Center at the university where Nadeen worked. The M&M Center focuses on recruiting minority university students to work with culturally and linguis-tically diverse (CLD) students. A prevalent theme running through many of the M&M courses is the need to implement a multicultural education approach across the curriculum, with the ultimate goal of increasing equity for CLD students through social reconstructionism (Campbell, 2000; Sleeter & Grant, 1999).

Lorena entered her first solo teaching experience equipped with what many would consider close to ideal preparation for working with culturally and linguistically diverse urban students. Her teaching credential program had: (1) an explicit mission to develop teachers who are committed to working with poor and minority children; (2) a faculty overwhelmingly of color; (3) a focus on multicultural education as an important way for teachers to work for social justice; and (4) an emphasis on effective language and literacy instruction for second language learners.

The State Context: California's Policies on Literacy Instruction

California's trajectory into its current state of the art of literacy instruction and testing began with the California State Department of Education's Language Arts Framework in the late eighties, which contrary to the prevailing reductionist literacy paradigm, stressed a meaning-based process orientation in reading and writing instruction. Concurrently, a teacher-led movement of whole language instruction, largely based on the sociopsycholinguistic work in reading and writing by scholars such as Ken and Yetta Goodman, gained limited momentum among California teachers, but more so among state department of education personnel and university teacher educators.

From the beginning, the 1987 Language Arts Framework and incipient whole language movement were decried as going against the commonsense notion that reading and writing were overwhelmingly a matter of sound-letter correspondences. Yet the range and depth of this criticism sharply peaked when national reports surfaced regarding California's students' poor testing performance.

A number of scholars have countered with documentation that California's reading and writing scores did *not* dip in the late eighties and early nineties, when a meaning-based process orientation supposedly influenced California language arts instruction (Berliner & Biddle, 1995; Krashen, 2002; McQuillan, 1998). However, a link was forged between California students' poor testing performance and the state department of education's efforts to move literacy paradigms and instruction away from code-based instruction (known to the public as phonics) and toward meaning-based instruction (known to the public as whole language). Since then, No Child Left Behind's Reading First guidelines and a spate of California legislation have mandated a reductionist approach in both staff development and teacher education programs and have guided school districts toward the selection of code-based, reductionist language arts curriculum (Shannon, 2000; Taylor, 1998). Furthermore, the popular media has consistently and emphatically promoted phonics as the antidote to the supposed damage done by whole language.

Raising the Stakes: Cash Rewards for Rising Test Scores

As if the stakes were not high enough already throughout California regarding student test performance, in the spring of 1999 the state unveiled a new program, the Academic Performance Index (API), a few months before Lorena began her internship at Elm Avenue School. Based entirely on standardized test scores—the Stanford Achievement Test (SAT) 9 at that time—the API attempts to provide a school performance index ranging from a low of 200 points to a high of 1,000. The state selected 800 as a target score for all schools. But beyond providing a target, the state tied $677 million to schools showing improved scores. Schools under the target of 800 points had to show 5 percent growth from their 1999 API to their 2000 API; those already above 800 had to show at least one-point growth. In calculating school gains, growth needed to occur among ethnic and low-income groups, not just across the board.

And the state was fairly specific about the rewards it was to distribute in January 2001: a $150 increase in spending per student and an $800 stipend to all staff including office and maintenance personnel. The bonuses for some teachers and principals at the poorest-performing schools where scores improved the most ranged anywhere from $5,000 to $25,000. By tying the API to cash rewards, California made no bones about its bottom line for schools: improve test scores.

The Impact of Sociocultural Factors on State Literacy Policies

Just as important to our study was the analysis of the impact of California's anti-immigration/antiminority policies upon schools with high numbers of CLD students (Gutiérrez, 2001). Gutiérrez cites the voter initiatives that passed in California in the nineties as evidence of *backlash politics*, that is, counterassaults to the perceived loss of power by white Californians, including Proposition 187 (proposing the elimination of health and education services for undocumented immigrants), Proposition 209 (overturning affirmative action in public institutions), and Proposition 227 (eliminating bilingual education except in restricted cases and mandating English instruction for second language learners). The author coined the term *backlash pedagogy* to capture the instructional effects of backlash politics on

California's classrooms. Backlash pedagogy "accepts substantial inequality as a neutral baseline for educational practice and reform, and attempts to enshrine the status quo" (Gutiérrez, 2001, p. 568). In essence, backlash pedagogy conceptualizes linguistic and cultural diversity as a problem to be remedied.

Gutiérrez's sociocultural and historical analysis of the privileged literacy pedagogy in California brings into sharp relief the pressures confronting new teachers working in urban schools with large numbers of CLD students. As if presaging Lorena's experience, the author warns: "Thus, backlash pedagogy is a political intrusion that makes it professionally and, in some cases legally, risky for educators to implement what they know about teaching in an effective and culturally responsive way" (p. 569).

The District Context: High-Stakes Curriculum as a Means to High Test Scores

In 1997 a private foundation purchased the Open Court reading program for Norcal School District and provided a large amount of money for staff development associated with the program. The city council, school board, and district administration were appropriately elated with the gift, especially given the press buzz around the Open Court program. Though Open Court rests on faulty research and false claims (Allington & Woodside-Jiron, 1999; Coles, 2000; Moustafa, 2000; Taylor, 1998), the popular take on the program was that students who were in classrooms where it was implemented outperformed students in control groups and those in "whole language" or "embedded phonics" programs.

Norcal School District threw itself wholeheartedly into the implementation of Open Court. The foundation's gift to the district paid for reading coaches—teachers specially trained in Open Court and released from traditional classroom duties—to work with Norcal teachers. Essentially, Open Court is a whole-class reading program in English that is highly scripted in terms of teachers' actions and discourse and student activities. At the beginning stages of the program there is a very strong emphasis on synthetic phonics and frequent copying of words and sentences in workbooks. Teachers were admonished to follow Open Court exactly and to follow the mandated pacing. Nadeen remembers supervising student teachers during the first year of implementation, when it was typical to see the Open Court program, which began almost at the first morning bell, spilling over to after lunch in teachers' efforts to teach the specific lesson required for that day. In fact, it was at that time that she first heard the label a number of Norcal teachers gave to the reading coaches: the reading police.

Two years after the implementation of Open Court, news from Norcal School District hit the papers again. Throughout California it was reported that Norcal students posted a 12.5 percent gain in students reaching the fiftieth percentile on the SAT 9 in 1999, compared with the statewide average gain of 3.5 percent. This news was picked up by major California newspapers and used as a rationale to widely implement Open Court in California school districts.

The actual facts behind the media splash were different than what the newspapers disseminated. Only two grade levels in the Norcal district posted an average 12.5 percent gain; the other grade levels showed less gain. For example, the 4–6 grade levels posted a 5 percent increase (Lewis, 2000). Furthermore, a recent study of the performance of limited English proficient students in Norcal showed that in 1999 second language learners posted only a 3.3 percent gain (Lewis, 2000). This is .2 percent less than the statewide average of 3.5 percent and certainly not in line with the "dramatic" increases in performance reported in the district newsletter and the city newspaper (López 1999, 2000, cited in Lewis, 2000).

By and large, the teachers in Norcal do not have access to the literature questioning the impact of Open Court on their students' test scores. Instead, they rely on the city newspaper, the district newsletter, and district administrators, all entities that have been relentless in making the case that Open Court and its regimented implementation are both the cause of the district's "dramatic" improvement in student achievement and its hope for future success. In short, the link between high-stakes testing and high-stakes curriculum is pervasive throughout the district.

The School and Classroom Context: A First-Year Teacher's Advocacy and Resistance

Lorena had been offered another bilingual teaching position in a neighboring rural school district but turned it down when she detected that the principal was not a strong supporter of primary language instruction for Spanish-speaking students. In contrast, when the principal at Elm Avenue School, Mónica Barboza, sought her out for a teaching position, Lorena believed that she had found the position of her dreams. Mónica was about to enter her first principalship, but she was a former bilingual teacher and resource teacher in a nearby district. She had graduated from the M&M Center in the early nineties, when there was a strong emphasis on multicultural education though less focus on effective literacy instruction for CLD students. In her subsequent years as an educator in her former district, Mónica had always used Spanish as a medium of instruction and reported to her former M&M professors that she was a strong advocate for bilingual education.

The university coordinators placed M&M students in Mónica's classroom knowing that the students would be able to teach in Spanish in addition to English.

From the outset, much of Lorena's and Mónica's one-to-one interactions occurred in Spanish, signifying their common ethnic and linguistic identities (Trueba, 1999). Lorena and Mónica's shared history as immigrants from Mexico, Chicanas, bilingual teachers, graduates of the M&M program, and persons connected to Lorena's adopted hometown was viewed by Lorena as an indication that she had made the right choice in accepting the position at Elm Avenue School. Nadeen agreed, and when she discovered that the department was assigning supervisors to new interns, she submitted her name to be Lorena's supervisor for fall 1999.

A Description of Elm Avenue School

Elm Avenue School houses preschool through sixth-grade classrooms in a part of the city with widespread poverty. Seventy-one percent of its population was designated English language learners (ELLs). Approximately 75 percent of Elm Avenue's student body were students of color—34 percent Asian, 30 percent Hispanic, 11 percent African American—and the remaining 25 percent were white. Because of these circumstances, the M&M Center considered Elm Avenue School a prime place to send student teachers.

During the year of this study, the majority of the classrooms at Elm Avenue School had students from a mix of language backgrounds and used English as the language of instruction. However, at Elm Avenue School there were four classrooms officially designated as newcomer classrooms. Two of these classrooms historically provided Spanish-English bilingual instruction: the primary classroom (grades 1–3) and the intermediate classroom (grades 4–6). As a bilingual student teacher supervisor since the early eighties, Nadeen had worked in all of the bilingual newcomer classrooms. Lorena was offered the primary position.

It is critical to note that Elm Avenue School's achievement scores were very low. Its 1999 API score of 429 was the lowest in the Norcal district. As an antidote to low reading scores, district newsletters and direct communication from the Norcal superintendent at districtwide staff development days pointed to Open Court.

Such was the context of Lorena's first year of teaching. Elm Avenue School, with an overwhelmingly poor, minority, and limited English proficient population, could only emerge from the bottom of the reading achievement heap with improved SAT 9 scores, and the means to that end were clearly demarcated: Open Court. Through the various ways previously discussed,

Open Court became the high-stakes curriculum Lorena was expected to use with her students.

The Struggle for Primary Language Instruction

Lorena was anticipating the twenty or so Spanish-speaking students, grades 1 through 3, who had traditionally formed the newcomer primary-age bilingual classroom, just as discussed with Mónica during the hiring process. However, Lorena began to receive a number of visits from the Elm Avenue reading coach offering her Open Court materials and talking about how she could assist Lorena in any way that she wanted. Lorena, confused by the coach's offers because of her understanding that she would be providing her students with literacy instruction in Spanish, would nonetheless thank the coach for her support and continue preparing her room and instruction.

Soon after, Lorena began to understand why the coach was offering her assistance with Open Court. Lorena discovered that there was going to be a last-minute change in the composition of her class: instead of twenty newcomer students, Mónica was planning to combine ten of the newcomer students with ten English-speaking, high-performing students. Lorena immediately sought out Mónica to speak about the change. With an assistant superintendent sitting in her office, along with two reading coaches, Mónica assured Lorena that the new idea was a terrific one and that it would become a model for other schools. Feeling somewhat helpless to counter Mónica, Lorena managed to ask her how she would teach the newcomer students to read and write in the combined class. Mónica responded that Lorena would be using sheltered techniques and translation to help the Spanish-speaking students learn through Open Court. Specifically, Mónica offered to have a reading coach present in Lorena's class to "walk [her] through it." At the initial stages, Lorena would be there to translate and support the students' comprehension in Spanish. Mónica gave the example that if the text said "jump," Lorena would physically jump to show her students what the word meant.

Lorena returned to her home the weekend before school dejected, but went back to Elm Avenue School on Monday, a holiday, to ask Mónica to revise her class list back to the original plan. Aiding her in her arguments was the fact that Lorena knew that parents had not given their permission for placement in the combination newcomer/high-performing classroom. Lorena asked whether Mónica was willing to take those parents of the ten high-performing students into her office on the first day of school. Mónica responded that it was up to Lorena to "sell the program." Lorena held firm, however, in saying that she was too unfamiliar with this new configuration to convince the parents to let their children stay in the classroom with ten newcomer students. At that point, Mónica assented to Lorena's request and went out of her office to instruct the secretary to change back the class list to its original form. From that moment on, however, Lorena noted a decrease in the warmth and support Mónica had previously shown her. In fact, at the end of this meeting, Mónica sent Lorena off with the warning that if she did not have more than fifteen students within two weeks of instruction, her class would be eliminated.

In an interview several months after this incident, Nadeen asked Lorena how she was able to take a stand on this issue alone and so early in her teaching. Lorena first responded that she had recalled the many articles and discussions on the efficacy of primary language instruction throughout her credential program and through her work with the Migrant/Optimal Learning Environment (OLE) Project (2000). But Lorena's voice took on an emotional timbre when she added that she vividly remembered how it was to be a Spanish-speaking second grader recently arrived from Mexico and literate in Spanish. Besides not understanding the English-only instruction for many months, Lorena was assigned to do low-level work for years. "I feel cheated," she said. "I was put aside." Lorena further ascribed her being assigned to remedial university courses to that sort of instruction. So using her own negative experiences as an immigrant child submerged in English-only instruction, Lorena stood her ground on providing her incoming students with enriched instruction in their native language in addition to English as second language.

The Primary Language Struggle Continues

On the first day of school, Lorena welcomed into her classroom sixteen Spanish-speaking children recently arrived from Mexico. During the next week, as her student numbers began to increase to twenty, Lorena began a number of assessments to determine the level of her students' reading and writing skills. What she found would be sobering to any teacher, even one from a credential program emphasizing linguistic and cultural diversity. In a group that ranged from ages six to nine, nine students could not write their names (some of those students were chronologically second and third graders), four could not write any letters at all, and around nine could not name more than five letters. Except for four students who had begun their schooling in Mexico, the majority of Lorena's students did not read and, further, were at a very emergent literacy stage. For many, Lorena's classroom was their first formal school experience. Only one student had previously been in a classroom where the language of instruction was English. All other students were designated non–English proficient. All of them were fluent in Spanish.

Lorena took action immediately. In consultation with Nadeen and her former cooperating teacher, she began to implement instructional strategies with a track record in promoting CLD students' literacy development. One such method is roll call variations, which uses meaningful text with second language learners, here, students' names, to teach phonemic awareness and early phonics skills (Espinoza, Ruiz, & Valero, 2002). Another instructional strategy is interactive journals, a method used with readers and writers at all levels, even emergent, to immerse students in listening, speaking, reading, and writing as they interactively write back and forth with a teacher (Flores & García, 1984; Ruiz, García, & Figueroa, 1996). Lorena implemented all these strategies, along with others focusing on teaching CLD students how to read and write, in Spanish.

Nadeen supported Lorena's decision to teach her emergent literate students, who spoke no English, to read and write in Spanish. Despite the popular thinking on the effects of the passage of Proposition 227, the use of primary language instruction in California classrooms was *not* eliminated. Instead, school districts were mandated to use "overwhelmingly English" instruction, not 100 percent English instruction. In the year previous to this study, the bilingual coordinator from Norcal School District had told Nadeen and her university colleagues that Norcal's determination of "overwhelming English" was 60 percent, with the remaining 40 percent of instruction open for primary language instruction.

However, Mónica began to not only question Lorena's use of Spanish language instruction but exert pressure on Lorena to switch to all-English instruction for the language arts. To do otherwise, Mónica repeatedly said, was a "disservice" to the students. Lorena pointed to the district's post-227 policy that, according to Lorena's calculations, would permit her to teach 117 minutes in Spanish. She proposed to do this in the morning for language arts, given both the emergent literacy levels of her students and their non-English-speaking status. Lorena assured Mónica that the rest of her instruction—math, opening calendar activities, English language development, and occasional science and social studies—would be implemented in English. Although displeased, Mónica withdrew her direct pressure for a while but continued to question Lorena's instruction in Spanish. She repeatedly asked for lesson plans and class goals using the Open Court materials, all of which are in English. Lorena finally asked Nadeen to directly speak with Mónica about the issue during one of her supervisory visits.

With the three of them in Mónica's office, Mónica reassured Nadeen and Lorena that she had been one of the principal designers of her former district's bilingual program and that she had supplied the data to support that program. She began to echo a refrain that Lorena was to hear many times that year: "Show me the data." Mónica made the point that she was concerned first with the children. And because the children had only one academic year in Lorena's newcomer class, after which they would have to go into an all-English classroom, Mónica wanted the students to have as much English as possible. Nadeen agreed that Lorena should provide her students with strong English language development. However, she added that if Mónica wanted the students to actually *learn to read* in the short time that they had with Lorena, the best approach was to teach them in their own language, not one that as yet functioned as foreign to them. Mónica ceded the argument but ended the meeting with another admonishment to show her the data. It was clear to both of us that if Lorena could not show Mónica her students' growth in literacy, she would be proceeding on shaky ground with her site administrator, despite Mónica's longtime association with bilingual education.

Monica's continued reference to her role at her previous district in developing the bilingual program showed a favorable stance on bilingual education in a particular context. But Mónica's current context was now very different. Permeating the state, district, and school contexts that she was functioning within was the short-term goal for her school to show increased performance on the SAT 9 in English. Though unspoken, the question in Mónica's mind seemed to us to be: Could Spanish language instruction in reading negatively impact Lorena's students' SAT 9 reading scores and, hence, Elm Avenue's scores? We would have to agree that it could, especially because the early grades' SAT 9 reading tests depend so much on English decoding skills, and Lorena's students were learning those skills in their native language. (However, see Durgunoglu, 1998, which describes how Spanish-speaking students instructed in Spanish were able to read environmental print and spell English words. In addition, strong Spanish literacy development transferred and helped English literacy development; for example, Spanish phonological awareness and letter knowledge accounted for a significant amount of the variance of English spelling.)

The Struggle for Effective Literacy Instruction for CLD Students

The more intense struggle between Lorena and Mónica involved the use of the high-stakes curriculum. Mónica continued to insist that Lorena use the Open Court materials with her newcomer students. Mónica had been successful in ensuring that all other newcomer teachers were indeed implementing Open Court. Among themselves, the newcomer teachers questioned the appropriateness of Open Court for students new to English, and Lorena shared with them that, with Nadeen's support, she had designed a more appropriate instructional plan to teach her students to read, write, and speak

English. Several times during October and November, the other newcomer teachers stopped and thanked Nadeen for supporting Lorena in resisting the implementation of Open Court. They also complained to her that the program did not address the needs of students new to English. However, as Lorena recounted, the other newcomer teachers did not openly confront Mónica about the use of Open Court with ELL students at this time.

The pressure mounted in early November when Mónica executed her first official observation and evaluation of Lorena's teaching. Lorena received what was to her a devastating first evaluation from her principal. Lorena agreed that things had not gone well during the observation. Lorena worried that Mónica would criticize her classroom management. She knew that student discipline was a major thrust of Mónica's reforms at Elm Avenue. For example, when the bell rang at recess, all students had to drop to a crouching position and freeze before the monitors would allow them to move and reenter the classrooms. Under Mónica's direction, students now had to walk silently as a class with their hands clasped behind their backs. Nadeen was not in the classroom during Mónica's observation, but her field notes from supervising Lorena that fall reveal that classroom management and discipline were, as for many beginning teachers, areas that Lorena still needed to work on. What was most clear to Lorena now was that after her first evaluation, she had less of a footing in trying to make the case that the curriculum and pedagogy that she was implementing in her classroom were more effective than the all-English Open Court instruction that Mónica wanted her to move to.

Her fears were confirmed around a week after Mónica's observation. On a Sunday night, Lorena received a phone call at home from Mónica. Mónica informed Lorena that she was not to report to her classroom the following day. Mónica had arranged for a substitute in Lorena's class and Lorena was to go with the school reading coach to observe a newcomer teacher using Open Court with intermediate-grade, mixed-language-background students. The next day Lorena sat through the morning observation in the upper-grade newcomer classroom. She reported to Nadeen that she didn't see the relationship between these students and her own. A number of the newcomer students in this particular classroom were already literate in their first language. As far as Lorena could tell, some of those students were participating well in the Open Court classroom. But she also noted that a number of students were "lost," either mumbling the expected responses a bit behind their peers, sitting disengaged, or appearing to be off task. After the observation, the reading coach directed Lorena to meet with her in order to plan the next week's Open Court lessons, which the coach would now begin observing on a weekly basis.

Covert Resistance

Covert resistance best describes the actions of the other newcomer teachers. None would speak out directly to Mónica or the reading coach, but instead they would clandestinely meet in each other's rooms or the teachers room and criticize the Open Court program in terms of English learners' needs. One longtime newcomer teacher sharing a classroom with another newer teacher made sure that her duties didn't include teaching any of the Open Court curriculum and left that to the teacher with less seniority. The experienced teacher instead implemented a meaningful, interactive classroom tailored to her students' current level of English comprehension that promoted the acquisition of oral and written English. Newcomer teachers continued this covert resistance to the end of the academic year, with one exception, to be discussed subsequently.

Overt Resistance

Nadeen, Lorena, and Mónica held a very tense meeting to explicitly negotiate how Lorena would teach the language arts. Using a side-by-side comparison of Open Court and Lorena's curriculum, Nadeen took Mónica through the first few lessons. She recommended that Lorena follow Open Court lesson components in her English language development period when they contained strategies or materials that were appropriate for use in English (as supported by the research on second language and literacy acquisition). When the lesson components were not supported by second language research, Lorena was to substitute more effective instructional strategies; for example, Nadeen recommended that instead of asking the students to engage in copying exercises, Lorena should use instructional time to do interactive journals with her students, a much more student-active and developmentally rich literacy activity.

   She also recommended that Lorena continue to use writing strategies that are not included or emphasized in Open Court. Nadeen buttressed her arguments for advocating this curriculum not only with the research base in second language and bilingual education that she knew Mónica was familiar with (e.g., the work by Steve Krashen and Jim Cummins) but also by showing Mónica an article she happened to be carrying with her by Allington and Woodside-Jiron (1999), and telling Mónica that the overreliance on phonemic awareness activities resulting in the exclusion of meaning-based instruction was a "straw house about to fall." At the end of the meeting Mónica agreed that Lorena could continue her language arts instruction as outlined by Nadeen. Lorena and Nadeen felt they had won not only the battle but also perhaps the war against inappropriate instruction for her emergent literate

CLD students. Lorena could go on to teach reading and writing to her CLD students as she had learned to do through the M&M program.

Lorena, however, continued to raise her voice in other public contexts to advocate for CLD students. In April, Mónica approached Lorena with an invitation to return to the school the following year but on the condition that Lorena fully implement Open Court (three and a half hours per morning) in English. Up to that moment, Lorena had hoped that she could stay on at Elm Avenue School and continue working with the type of students in her current classroom. However, Lorena responded with an expanded version of the words used in our title: "Gracias por la oportunidad, pero a la vez voy a buscar otro trabajo ..." ("Thank you for the opportunity, but at the same time I'll be looking for another job ..."). Despite Nadeen's and Lorena's best efforts to implement a pedagogy and curriculum that met the needs of Lorena's Spanish-speaking students, Lorena now did not have a teaching position at Elm Avenue School for the following year.

Conclusion

Through our narrative we attempted to depict the effects of high-stakes curriculum on a beginning teacher, Lorena, and her strategies to resist curriculum that she felt was not consistent with the needs of her Spanish-speaking, recent immigrant students.

Regarding the question of the impact of high-stakes curriculum on a beginning teacher, it is clear that one effect was the need to call for assistance. Lorena knew that she wanted to advocate for more appropriate pedagogy for her students, but with the pressures of first-year teaching and, most importantly, with the uneven power relations between her and the principal, Lorena asked for help from her university supervisor. This was possible because as an intern, Lorena was still part of a credential program and consequently had access to a supervisor who could try to equalize the power distribution between Lorena and the principal. Though this strategy was initially successful, the principal made it clear at the end of Lorena's first year that it was she who had the final say over the curriculum at her school.

Another effect of high-stakes curriculum not explicitly mentioned in our narrative was less tangible but certainly present in our study: high stress. At the beginning of the year when the struggle was most intense between Lorena and the principal, Lorena rapidly lost weight and had emotional responses with family and friends when discussing the situation, among other stress indicators. For the only teacher willing to speak out for more appropriate instruction for CLD students—the teacher with the most tenuous status—tension was an everyday occurrence.

Perhaps the most dramatic effect of Lorena's resistance was the professional risk that she incurred (Gutiérrez, Baquedano-López, & Asato, 2000). After only one year of teaching, Lorena felt that she had to leave the school. Some would say that Lorena could have chosen to stay; the principal did, in fact, invite her to return. But the principal did not offer Lorena the option of effective instruction for CLD students. Without the direct protection or assistance from a university supervisor, and without overt, sustained assistance from her teacher colleagues at the school, Lorena felt that she could not continue the resistance effort alone in the coming year, and she chose to leave.

In an attempt to resist high-stakes curriculum and advocate for appropriate CLD pedagogy, Lorena employed several strategies. She participated in the covert resistance practiced by most of the newcomer teachers by listening to and joining in teachers' complaints. However, Lorena also overtly resisted by openly discussing with Mónica what she was resisting and why. She also engaged the help of her university supervisor. Working together, Lorena and Nadeen used research on effective language arts instruction with CLD students in oral and written communications with the principal as their primary means to advocate for curriculum change. Though successful in the short run, we were unable to counteract the pressures that the principal felt to implement the expected high-stakes curriculum.

As a beginning teacher and university supervisor we feel that our story raises several issues for consideration in the literature on multicultural social reconstructionist teacher education. One issue concerns the preparation of new teachers to defend their instructional beliefs and practices. Lorena, while familiar with the research on CLD instruction, did not expect to have to cite that research in defense of her beliefs and practices within the first weeks of her internship. Fortunately, as an intern, she could enlist the help of her university supervisor, but beginning teachers who have finished the credential program do not have ready access to their former university instructors. Teacher education programs that stress social justice, then, must now consider specifically how to prepare candidates to speak out well, and with substance, if they are to advocate for appropriate instruction for historically marginalized students.

Being the lone voice of resistance at this school did not prove effective in countering high-stakes curriculum; given the pressure of the state and district to implement high-stakes curriculum, change would have required a chorus. Perhaps multicultural social reconstructionist teacher education programs now need to offer beginning teachers organizing strategies for resistance so that their voices, often those with the lowest status in the school, can be heard and eventually counted.

In closing, we do not feel that we were successful in our efforts at Elm Avenue School. Lorena had planned on staying several years at the school, working as a bilingual teacher among the students and families who most needed her. Nadeen felt that she could bring the principal around to see that CLD students need, at the very least, modifications of high-stakes curriculum to successfully acquire literacy skills in English. We were both disappointed in the results of our collaboration. These feelings, however, are the very ones that have spurred us to write this chapter. It brings us a measure of hope that readers may use our experience as a springboard for both discussion and action—action that eventually brings about equitable literacy instruction for CLD students.

References

Allington, R. L., & Woodside-Jiron, H. (1999). The politics of literacy teaching: How "research" shaped educational policy. *Educational Researcher, 28*(8), 4–13.

Berliner, D., & Biddle, B. (1995). *The manufactured crisis: Myth, fraud, and the attack on America's public schools.* Reading, MA: Addison-Wesley.

Campbell, D. (2000). *Choosing democracy.* Upper Saddle River, NJ: Prentice Hall.

Clandinin, D. J., & Connelly, F. M. (2000). *Narrative inquiry.* San Francisco: Jossey-Bass.

Cochran-Smith, M. (2000). Blind vision: Unlearning racism in teacher education. *Harvard Educational Review, 70*(2), 157–190.

Coles, G. (2000). *Misreading reading: The bad science that hurts children.* Portsmouth, NH: Heinemann.

Dixon, C., Green, J., Yeager, B., Baker, D., & Fránquiz, M. (2000). "I used to know that": What happens when reform gets through the classroom door. *Bilingual Research Journal, 24*(1 & 2), 1–6.

Durgunoglu, A. Y. (1998). Acquiring literacy in English and Spanish in the United States. In A. Y. Durgunoglu & V. Verhoevan (Eds.), *Literacy development in a multilingual context* (pp. 135–145). Mahwah, NJ: Lawrence Erlbaum.

Edelsky, C. (1999). *Making justice our project.* Urbana, IL: National Council of Teachers of English.

Espinoza, P., Ruiz, N. T., & Valero, A. (2002). Optimal learning environments for bilingual preschool children. Unpublished manuscript. Sacramento: California State University, Sacramento.

Flores, B., & García, E. (1984). A collaborative learning and teaching experience using journal writing. *Journal of the National Association of Bilingual Education, 8,* 67–83.

Gutiérrez, K. D. (2001). What's new in the English language arts: Challenging policies and practices, y qué? *Language Arts 78*(6), 564–569.

Gutiérrez, K. D., Baquedano-López, P., & Asato, J. (2000, winter–spring). "English for the children": The new literacy of the old world order: Language policy and reform. *Bilingual Research Journal (1 & 2)*, 87–112.

Krashen, S. (2002). Whole language and the great plummet of 1987–92: An urban legend from California. *Phi Delta Kappan*, pp. 748–753.

Lewis, S. C. (2000). The performance of English language learners in a highly-scripted, synthetic phonics curriculum: Deconstructing an "effective" reading program. Master's thesis, California State University, Sacramento.

Lytle, S. (2000). Teacher research in the contact zone. In M. L. Kamil, P. B. Mosenthal, P. D. Pearson, & R. Barr (Eds.), *Handbook of reading research, volume III* (pp. 691–718). Mahwah, NJ: Lawrence Erlbaum.

Martin, R. J., & Van Gunten, D. M. (2001). Reflected identities: Applying positionality and multicultural social reconstructionism in teacher education. *Journal of Teacher Education, 53*(1), 44–54.

McQuillan, J. (1998). *The literacy crisis*. Portsmouth, NH: Heinemann.

Migrant/OLE Project. (2000). *The Migrant/OLE Project* [web page]. Available: *www.educ.csus.edu/projects/ole*

Moustafa, M. (2000, June). *The research base of Open Court and its translation into instructional policy in California.* Available: *http://instructall.calsatela.edu/mmousta*

Ruiz, N. T., García, E., & Fiqueroa, R. A. (1996). *The OLE Curriculum Guide.* Sacramento, CA: California Bureau of Publications.

Shannon, P. (2000). If you ain't got the ABCs. *Reading Teacher, 54*(1), 64–66.

Sleeter, C. E., & Grant, C. A. (1999). *Making choices for multicultural education.* Upper Saddle River, NJ: Merrill.

Taylor, D. (1998). *Beginning to read and the spin doctors of science.* Urbana, IL: National Council of Teachers of English.

Trueba, E. T. (1999). *Latinos unidos: From cultural diversity to the politics of solidarity.* Lanham, MD: Rowman & Littlefield.

16

Proven Programs, Profits, and Practice

Ten Unprofitable but Scientific Strategies
for Improving Reading Achievement

RICHARD L. ALLINGTON

University of Tennessee

The passage of the most recent reauthorization of the Elementary and Secondary Education Act of 1966 (ESEA)—the No Child Left Behind Act of 2001 (NCLB)—has introduced a new twist in federal educational policy. While NCLB has several unique features, it largely represents an intensification of a forty-year-old federal policy of top-down management and centralized decision making.

Since its origination, ESEA legislation has provided funding with strings attached. It is, for instance, the ESEA that has been identified as the primary cause of the expansion of standardized testing in U.S. schools (Timar, 1994), since accepting federal dollars has long meant collecting achievement data in an attempt to document that the added funding enhanced student achievement, particularly in reading (Allington, 2002). Federal funds have always come with limits on how those funds could be spent. But recent federal legislation has added a new layer of centralization: the mandated use of research to justify the expenditure of federal funds.

Unfortunately, much of the research available seems to be largely neglected in federal policy making. In this chapter I explore both the shifts in federal policy and the selective focus on specific research findings while neglecting other research findings. I will suggest that federal policy making, and thereby educational practice, has been shaped by the profit potential inherent in some research findings that is not a characteristic of the neglected research findings.

A Short Recent History of Federal Policy Making Concerning Reading Education

Only recently have federal policy makers begun to include "research-based" concerns in educational programs legislation. It seems that the Comprehensive School Reform and Development (CSRD) legislation of 1997, an extension of the earlier Goals 2000 legislation crafted during the administration of the first President Bush and continued during the Clinton administration, was the first federal policy that specifically required research-based designs to qualify for federal funds. The CSRD provided funding for school districts that adopted one of several whole-school reform designs. The available options were those "research-based" programs that had survived the New American Schools (NAS) competition established in the early 1990s to find "systemic" reform efforts that reliably improved student achievement. Thus, school districts could apply for the CSRD funding to implement reform models such as Success for All, Comer School Development, Accelerated Schools, and so on. The ten-year evaluation of these federal efforts to improve achievement, primarily in high-poverty schools, found that "the original hypothesis, that by adopting a whole-school design a school could improve its performance, was largely unproved" (Berends, Bodilly, & Kirby, 2002, p. 173). In other words, the evidence, after a decade, indicated that none of the reform models reliably enhanced reading achievement across all sites although each model had some successes.

Perhaps buoyed by early reports from the entrepreneurs (e.g., Siegfried Engelmann, Robert Slavin, Ethna Reid, James Comer, McGraw-Hill, Great Books Foundation), many that had developed one of the ten CSRD models, the Reading Excellence Act of 1998 (REA) was passed during the Clinton administration. The REA specified a continued emphasis on the use of "innovative strategies and proven methods . . . based on reliable research . . . replicated successfully in schools." Thus, state applications for federal funds had to specify a research base for their plans to spend federal moneys and school districts had to likewise specify a research base for their plans. The American Federation of Teachers (1998) chimed in with a listing of seven "proven programs" for fostering reading achievement. Then came the NCLB, with a tighter focus on funding only those plans that "employ proven strategies and proven methods . . . based on scientifically-based research . . . replicated successfully in schools." Thus over the course of a decade or so, federal policy makers adopted a model for reform that increasingly limited the options available for spending federal dollars to those efforts that could be justified from the available research evidence. And the notion that there were proven programs emerged in federal policy.

Today, *evidence-based instruction* is the hot new buzz phrase out of Washington. As a researcher I suppose I should be pleased. But I'm skeptical instead. I'm skeptical because as a researcher I'm well aware of the limitations of research in providing clear answers about what works. Four problems plague any attempt to translate research findings into guidelines for educational practice.

The Limitations of Research

The first problem is that of the contingent nature of research evidence. Scientific evidence most often indicates that *it depends*. Will reducing class size improve achievement? Usually, yes, but you see, it depends. It depends on whether teachers work in an organizational system that allows them to take advantage of smaller classes. One-size-fits-all textbook adoptions, for instance, work against the success of smaller classes because it means that teachers still must teach against an organizational grain if they are to provide lessons that a range of kids will successfully experience. It depends not just on whether the teacher has the autonomy to create tailored lessons but whether the teacher has the expertise and initiative to do so. The generally favorable impact of class size reduction reported in the literature indicates that many teachers have the autonomy, expertise, and initiative to design and deliver appropriately tailored instruction. But that same literature shows that achievement does not necessarily improve in *all* classrooms when smaller classes are provided. It depends.

A second problem is that statistical differences in average achievement outcomes between control and treatment groups might be so small as to be of little practical significance. Venezky (1998) noted that Success for All raised achievement significantly but very modestly such that the majority of students were two or more years below grade level at fifth grade. The smallish differences were magnified by the six-year treatment costs associated with implementing the model.

That leads to a third concern. The most popular methodologies in the federally defined scientific research make use of mean statistic comparisons to indicate which instructional plans work better. In other words, the scientific research mandated in federal law for evidence-based instruction typically tells us which instructional approach or plan worked better, *on average*. On average, for instance, reducing class size does improve achievement, but it does not improve the achievement in all classrooms nor for all students.

There are many ways to impact average achievement, and a rise in average achievement does not mean that the benefits observed benefited all subjects equally. For instance, we might develop an intervention that raises the achievement of only the top 20 percent of students. That would raise average achievement. Or maybe our approach raises the achievement of only the lowest-achieving 20 percent. That too would raise average achievement. Or we might raise the best students' scores by ten points while also lowering the worst students scores by five points. Still, average achievement would rise.

The point is that raising average achievement in a research study might benefit some subgroups (or penalize them) without having a generalized positive effect on achievement. A statistically significant rise in achievement does not necessarily raise all ships. It might raise only the yachts. Current research methodologies too rarely report on whether the effects benefited only some subgroups (Torgeson, 2000). In far too many of the intervention studies with struggling readers, for instance, a quarter or more of the students benefited hardly at all.

The final problem is that most research fragments the curriculum and the act of teaching. That is, we have many more studies of the impact of adding a specific routine to a lesson than we have studies of complete reading programs. We have more research on adding a brief demonstration of a decoding or vocabulary development or comprehension strategy to a reading plan than we have demonstrations of the impact of a full reading curriculum. And even when we have an analysis of a full reading program, we have virtually no studies that systematically manipulated the several components of any program to attempt to identify those components most useful in developing reading proficiency (Pressley & Allington, 1999).

So we have lots of studies, mostly short-term, that suggest that adding a bit of this or that improves some students' learning of this or that. This sort of research can be useful but it can also be misleading because we are always adding a bit of this or that to some larger set of reading instructional and practice activities that are rarely well documented. And we never really know whether there might be other things that we could add, or variations on what we added, that would prove even more useful.

Evidence and Entrepreneurship

There is yet another issue that is troubling and that seems to introduce a bias into the equation whenever reforms—evidence based or not—are initiated. This issue is one that might be described as the power of profit potential. Both for-profit corporations and individual entrepreneurs figure into this.

Large corporations exist to generate a profit for shareholders. This point was driven home at a conference on the reading wars sponsored by the Brookings Institution and held at Harvard University in the fall of 1999 (Loveless, 2001). I presented data illustrating the various and numerous links between researchers, one large corporation, and educational reform initiatives in California and Texas. I suggested that policy making in these two states seemed to have been heavily influenced by entrepreneurial researchers who worked for the corporation to the benefit of that corporation. I suggested that only some research was highlighted and that corporate entrepreneurs were situated to shape these states' policies on reading instruction through multiple statewide conferences and by developing policy statements for the state education agencies. That seemed an important phenomenon to me.

When I was finished, the first question I was asked was, "So what's your point?" I reiterated what I thought was the primary point, corporate influence on state educational policy making, and the questioner responded, "Yes, I heard that, but what's the problem?" He then went on to argue that a corporate head had a fiduciary responsibility to shareholders to attempt to maximize corporate profits and that successfully influencing state educational policy to benefit the corporation would indicate that he accomplished, in fact, just what was expected of him. I paused.

I guess he was correct. I also knew that this was a line of thinking that had never occurred to me. In other words, it was but a variation on the old "What's good for General Motors is good for America" theme. But I was worried more about what was good for students and teachers than about what was good for shareholders. It wasn't even that this corporation produced a terrible product because, truth be told, it produces an array of reading curriculum products that represent a wide range of orientations. What bothered me was the notion that corporate profits were the bottom line.

I've thought about this exchange for a while now and I'm still convinced that what's good for corporate America is not always, or maybe even typically, what's good for students and their teachers. I've also begun to wonder how an emphasis on profit potential might shape the sorts of evidence that get used in decisions about the design of reading instruction. I've concluded that evidence that can be translated into a profit center seems more likely to be highlighted than evidence for which there seems to be little profit potential.

I know of no way of proving this hypothesis, so here I resort to providing evidence on ten instructional practices that have garnered sufficient research to suggest the practices can be considered research based. I suggest that one of the reasons there seem to be few proponents of these ten evidence-based practices is their lack of profit potential.

Ten Research-Based, Low-Profit Potential Practices

Writing, Sound Stretching, and Phonemic Awareness

Much has been made of the importance of the development of full phonemic segmentation as an early literacy proficiency. The now infamous "phonological core deficits" have been tapped as the major source of difficulty in early reading failure (Lyon, 1996). Perhaps. But why has the scientific evidence on what may be the most powerful instructional activity for fostering phonemic segmentation been largely ignored? Two recent empirical studies (McGill-Franzen, Allington, Yokoi, & Brooks, 1999; Scanlon & Vellutino, 1997) have demonstrated that when kindergarten teachers promote early writing activity, encouraging invented spelling, growth in phonemic segmentation—the ability to isolate individual phonemes, or sounds, in words—is reliably and readily developed. This is especially true when teachers demonstrate sound stretching as they write the morning message and interactive chart stories and whenever they compose in front of their students.

In the McGill-Franzen et al. (1999) study, kindergarten teachers were randomly assigned to training (or not) on how to use early writing both to foster early literacy development and agency and to track student development as part of a larger kindergarten reform effort. Students from the classrooms of the teachers who were exposed to this training significantly outperformed children from the other classrooms on virtually every literacy measure and specifically in their ability to identify individual phonemes in spoken words. In the Scanlon and Vellutino study (1997), kindergartners identified as at risk of early literacy failure who were enrolled in classrooms where teachers promoted early writing with sound stretching obtained significantly higher phoneme awareness scores at the end of the year while the amount of phonics instruction had no observed effect. The researchers also noted,

> of all the varied foci of language arts instruction in kindergarten, only the proportion of time devoted to focusing on the internal structure of words reliably distinguishes between groups of at-risk children who differed on reading achievement at the end of first grade. . . . It should also be noted that none of the teachers were employing any of the experimental or published programs currently available for training in phoneme awareness. Rather, phoneme awareness activities generally occurred in the context of writing, typically as sound analysis in the service of "figuring out" the spellings of words used in more meaning-based writing activity. (p. 204)

It is hard to make a profit from encouraging teachers to promote early writing activity even with demonstrations of sound stretching.

Word Walls

Word walls are teacher constructed and present high-frequency words, primarily, that children will encounter often as they read and write. Making a word wall requires only that the teacher have access to card stock (on which the words are written), some tape, and a marker or two. But word walls provide scaffolding for early readers and writers, a tool that allows them to self-monitor both reading and spelling, and works to develop the instant recognition of those high-frequency words that are not decodable but appear in nearly every sentence we read or write. Cunningham (2004) summarizes the research on this inexpensive classroom instructional tool. She notes that word walls (1) develop sensitivity to orthographic structure, to the internal structure of words, (2) foster instant word recognition, and (3) promote self-regulation in both reading and writing. Each of these proficiencies is an important component of early literacy development.

Just Plain Writing

Somehow the National Reading Panel (2000) failed to examine the research on the role writing can play in reading development (Pressley, Dolezal, Raphael, Mohan, Roehrig, & Bogner, 2003). It seems that since the NRP didn't report the rich research on reading-writing reciprocal relationships (Tierney & Shanahan, 1991), it vanished from view. Nonetheless, there is a substantial body of scientific research supporting promoting writing across the grades to foster growth not just in phonemic awareness but in a variety of orthographic and comprehension skills (Hefflin & Hartman, 2003).

Stotsky (1984) synthesized the research on writing-reading relationships. She found better writers read more than poorer writers, better writers tended to be better readers, and better readers produced more syntactically mature compositions than did poorer readers. Tierney and Pearson (1984) also reviewed the writing-reading research and noted that both reading and writing involve similar cognitive processes. To be successful, both activities require the use of background knowledge—both general world knowledge and knowledge of text structures and conventions. Both require memory strategies in organizing, tapping, and remembering information. And so on.

Writing activity, composing actually, according to the research of Langer and Applebee (1987) helps students clarify and consolidate what has been learned from reading, thereby enhancing understanding. In addition, composing after reading often illuminates misunderstandings or incomplete understandings that must be resolved and may work to foster reformulation or extension of what was read.

Finally, writing can make text structure more explicit to students. Recognizing how an author has structured a text is an important aspect of comprehension. To make clear the structure of a simple narrative, we might use the story mapping strategy. To assist middle school readers, we might engage them in using the various text structures found in informational texts, including textbooks. For instance, we might explore the problem-solution structure by demonstrating just how authors develop this line of argumentation. Then students would compose their own problem-solution arguments.

Providing students with opportunities to explore various text structures enhances their reading comprehension of texts using those structures.

Extended Independent Reading

Even though the NRP noted that little experimental evidence supported independent reading, it also noted that the hundreds of correlational and cross-sectional studies indicated extensive independent reading was important to reading development. But it added a caveat. To wit:

> Although correlational findings may be useful, they also can be deceptive because correlations tell nothing about the direction or sequence of a relationship. That good readers read more could be because reading practice contributes to reading attainment, but it could also be simply that better readers choose to read more because they are good at it. If this is true, then it is reading achievement that stimulates reading practice, not the reverse. Although there is an extensive amount of correlational data linking amount of reading and reading achievement, such studies do not permit a clear delineation of what is antecedent and what is consequent. (NRP, 2000, p. 3–10)

But it is hard to imagine that reading is unlike every other human proficiency in that practice doesn't matter. I have summarized the research available on extended reading elsewhere (Allington, 2001) as have others (Krashen, 2004; Stanovich, West, Cunningham, Cipielewski, & Siddiqui, 1996). And the NRP noted that the lack of true experiments on this issue cannot be used to argue that extensive reading is *not* an important aspect of reading development.

What the NRP did say, though, was that the scientific evidence did not support the use of various incentive programs for expanding independent reading. In other words, arranging for free pizzas, stickers, or bonus points for reading volume did not seem to increase the amount of independent reading children did. The NRP warned that investments of money and time on such schemes could not be supported by any scientific evidence.

Discussion After Reading

The evidence is in that having students discuss what they read—as opposed to interrogating them about what was read—promotes growth in understanding

(Applebee, Langer, Nystrand, & Gamoran, 2003; Fall, Webb, & Chudowsky, 2000; Taylor, Pearson, Peterson, & Rodriguez, 2003). It's odd that outside of school no one really interrogates, or quizzes, people about what they've read. Imagine your surprise if a friend who saw you reading *The Lovely Bones* (Seebold, 2002) began by quizzing you. "What was the detective's name? The young girl's who was murdered? The murderer's? Her father's?" Even worse, imagine if you did not answer correctly (most cannot) and you were told to go back and read the book again. Developing children's ability to engage in literate conversation is a powerful, but again unprofitable, way to foster reading development.

Reading Aloud to Children

While reading aloud to children is not a substitute for children actually reading themselves, there is an extensive scientific research base illustrating the many positive outcomes of reading to children (Brabham & Lynch-Brown, 2002: Stahl, Richek, & Vandevier, 1991). The most common finding is one of vocabulary growth as a result of reading to children. But reading aloud also enhances reading motivation, develops genre knowledge, and even develops core curricular knowledge. All this is enhanced when teachers regularly model the sorts of thinking readers do while they read. "I'm wondering why anyone would allow ten-year-old boys to march at the front of an infantry attack," for instance, raised while reading *The Boys' War* (Murphy, 1995) aloud to a group of fourth graders.

Appropriate Texts, Readers Theatre, and Other Fluency-Enhancing Devices

Fluency is another one of those aspects of reading that has been highlighted recently, after a long period of dormancy (Allington, 1983). Suffice it to say that too many children struggle through texts word by word with little or no fluency. It is hard to imagine that such reading performances generate much motivation for further reading activity. But the first step toward fluent reading involves making sure that kids have books they can actually read accurately and with comprehension. Almost any reader can exhibit dysfluency when given material on an unfamiliar topic with many unknown words. Too many children sit all day with books far harder than they can manage, such as that fourth grader who reads comfortably at a middle second-grade level but who has a desk full of fourth-grade-level texts. Providing these children with books they can actually read improves their reading performance, not surprisingly (O'Connor, Bell, Harty, Larkin, Sackor, & Zigmond, 2002).

Only the best readers in many classrooms have a desk full of books they can read accurately, fluently, and with comprehension. A case of the rich getting richer, by design. But just-right books won't automatically make a dysfluent reader fluent, especially after years of interruptive reading lessons in too-hard books. However, repeated rereadings and extensive independent reading seem well-documented methods for developing reading fluency (Kuhn & Stahl, 2003). Readers theatre activities (Worthy, Broaddus, & Ivey, 2001) have also been shown to foster fluency and to enhance understanding of materials being read. None of these fluency-development activities costs anything.

Choice Words

Everyone knows that expert teachers seem to have a way of knowing just what to say just when. Johnston (2004) provides a very readable review of the research documenting the impacts of some of the "choice words" the most effective teachers use to foster identity and agency as well as reading and writing development that might be measured on a standardized test. He notes that when a teacher asks, "Did anyone notice . . . ?" or says, "What are you thinking about? Stop and talk to your neighbor about it," or "Who else would like that book?" she is communicating a number of important things that impact children's notions about reading and writing and about readers and writers. Such talk also impacts their reading and writing behaviors. But such talk is necessarily highly personalized and cannot be scripted. Hard to develop ad copy for marketing teacher talk.

Motivation

How is it that after a federally funded research center spent a recent decade (1990s) studying children's motivations for reading that almost none of the talk about scientific reading instruction includes any mention of the huge amount of empirical evidence on how to foster (or undermine) children's reading motivation (Pressley et al., 2003)? The scientific evidence identifies factors such as choice of reading materials and writing topics and access to interesting texts as important to fostering engagement and continued motivation (Guthrie & Humenick, 2004). Similarly, positive classroom interactions, high-success activities, and peer interaction are also identified as critical variables of classroom literacy instruction (Guthrie & Knowledge, 2001; Taylor et al., 2003). These are no-cost, no-profit scientific findings. But any discussion of these factors has been, at best, subdued recently.

Teacher Expertise

While discussion of teacher expertise (or lack thereof) has appeared, darn little effort is being exerted to promote developing expertise in teaching reading. Yes, there are those "y'all come" sessions where hundreds of teachers get talked to about what the research says, but the scientific research on developing teacher expertise documents that venue as patently ineffective. We have good evidence that we can create reading teacher–preparation programs that produce more expert teachers. These teachers promote greater literacy development than others prepared in less engaging and less effective teacher-preparation programs (International Reading Association, 2003). And we have evidence that extended professional development with a focus on reflecting on one's teaching also promotes expertise and concomitantly student reading growth (Birman, Desimone, Porter, & Garet, 2000; Richardson, 2003; Strickland & Kamil, 2004). But few states or school districts seem to invest heavily in improving teacher preparation or funding professional development programs that reflect what the research says. A few for-profit companies (Sopris West, Canter, Voyageur, Skylight) are marketing professional development products, but these products reflect little of the research about effective teacher learning (Birman et al., 2000).

Summary

So there you have it. Ten largely ignored research-based practices that have been documented to improve children's literacy proficiencies, even those narrow proficiencies measured on standardized achievement tests. I'll continue to argue that the inattention to these research-based practices lies more in the profit problem than in any insufficient evidence base.

Research-based ideas that can generate a profit have many proponents. First are the publishing companies who buy ad copy in professional journals, who do direct-mail advertising, who send sales representatives into schools and district offices, who purchase large blocks of space for displays at professional conferences, who have wine-and-dine budgets. Second come the entrepreneurs who stand to earn a royalty when the product is sold. Entrepreneurs who may also be federally funded researchers, professors, school district consultants, and so on. Almost all entrepreneurs regularly engage a variety of audiences and customers.

But who promotes a research-based practice that seems an unlikely profit center? Almost no one.

When entrepreneurship and profit potential are mixed with powerful political agendas, much of what we know gets ignored or contradicted. Such seems the case at the moment. Instead of developing teacher expertise in early writing as a way to enhance phonemic awareness, we get loud and frequent promotions of expensive planned curricular packages, some delivered via a computer, promoted by powerful corporations and author-entrepreneurs.

And the evidence for these packages is far less consistent than that for early writing (Patterson, Henry, O'Quin, Ceprano, & Blue, 2003; Pokorni, Worthington, & Jamison, 2004).

Instead of engaging children in independent reading activity, the press is on to place them in planned one-size-fits-all curricular packages that provide lots of consumable, low-level seatwork activities (McGill-Franzen, Love, Zmach, & Solic, in press). This, even though the NRP acknowledged that independent reading seemed to work at least as well as typical seatwork in promoting test score improvements. Instead of support for engaging, motivating classroom reading environments, we get standardized reading programs in which every child is marched, in lockstep, through the same controlled and contrived texts and activities. As Darling-Hammond (1997) notes, "Standardized practice is malpractice when viewed from a perspective of professional accountability. Professional teachers should be allowed to focus on doing the right things rather than on doing things right" (p. 66).

Instead of programs that engage children in rich and varied composing activities, we see commercial five-step formulaic writing packages and commercial reading test-prep materials. Instead of readers theatre or read-alouds we see pseudoword speeded recognition practice and expensive systems where a computer delivers packaged but barren vocabulary drill and practice. So it goes. Profitable programs continue to trump scientific evidence. And federal educational policy sustains the profits.

References

Allington, R. L. (1983). Fluency: The neglected goal. *Reading Teacher, 36,* 556–561.

Allington, R. L. (2001). *What really matters for struggling readers: Designing research-based programs.* Boston: Allyn & Bacon.

Allington, R. L. (2002). *Big brother and the national reading curriculum: How ideology trumped evidence.* Portsmouth, NH: Heinemann.

American Federation of Teachers. (1998). *Building on the best, learning from what works: Seven promising reading and English language arts programs.* Washington, DC: Author.

Applebee, A. N., Langer, J. A., Nystrand, M., & Gamoran, A. (2003). Discussion-based approaches to developing understanding: Classroom instruction and student performance in middle and high school English. *American Educational Research Journal, 40,* 685–730.

Berends, M., Bodilly, S., & Kirby, S. N. (2002). Looking back over a decade of whole-school reform: The experience of New American Schools. *Phi Delta Kappan, 84,* 168–175.

Birman, B. F., Desimone, L., Porter, A. C., & Garet, M. (2000). Designing professional development that works. *Educational Leadership, 57*(8), 28–32.

Brabham, E. G., & Lynch-Brown, C. (2002). Effects of teachers' reading-aloud styles on vocabulary acquisition and comprehension of students in the early elementary grades. *Journal of Educational Psychology, 94,* 465–473.

Cunningham, P. M. (2004). *Phonics they use: Words for reading and writing.* New York: AllynBacon.

Darling-Hammond, L. (1997). *The right to learn: A blueprint for creating schools that work.* San Francisco: Jossey-Bass.

Fall, R., Webb, N. M., & Chudowsky, N. (2000). Group discussion and large-scale language arts assessment: Effects on students' comprehension. *American Educational Research Journal, 37,* 911–941.

Guthrie, J. T. & Humenick, N. M. (2004). Motivating students to read: Evidence for classroom practices that increase motivation and achievement. In P. McCardle & V. Chhabra (Eds.), *The voice of evidence in reading research* (pp. 329–354). Baltimore: Paul Brookes.

Guthrie, J. T., & Knowledge, K. T. (2001). Promoting reading motivation. In L. Verhoeven and C. Snow (Eds.), *Literacy and motivation: Reading engagement in individuals and groups* (pp. 159–176). Mahwah, NJ: Lawrence Erlbaum.

Hefflin, B. R. & Hartman, D. K. (2003). Using writing to improve comprehension: A review of the writing to reading research. In C. C. Block, L. Gambrell & M. Pressley (Eds.), *Improving comprehension instruction: Rethinking research, theory, and classroom practice* (pp. 199–228). New York: Guilford.

Hoffman, J., & Pearson, P. D. (2000). Reading teacher education in the next millennium: What your grandmother's teacher didn't know that your granddaughter's should. *Reading Research Quarterly, 35,* 28–44.

International Reading Association. (2003). *Prepared to make a difference.* Newark, DE: Author.

Johnston, P. A. (2004). *Choice words: How our language affects children's learning.* Portland, ME: Stenhouse.

Krashen, S. (2004). False claims about literacy development. *Educational Leadership, 61*(6), 18–21.

Kuhn, M. R., & Stahl, S. A. (2003). Fluency: A review of developmental and remedial practices. *Journal of Educational Psychology, 95,* 3–21.

Langer, J. A., & Applebee, A. N. (1987). *How writing shapes thinking: A study of teaching and learning.* Urbana, IL: National Council of Teachers of English.

Loveless, T. (2001). *The Great Curriculum Debate.* Washington, DC: Brookings Institution.

Lyon, G. R. (1996). The state of research. In S. Carr & W. Ellis (Eds.), *Learning disabilities: Lifelong issues* (pp. 3–61). Baltimore: Paul Brookes.

McGill-Franzen, A., Allington, R. L., Yokoi, L., & Brooks, G. (1999). Putting books in the room seems necessary but not sufficient. *Journal of Educational Research, 93,* 67–74.

McGill-Franzen, A., Love, J., Zmach, C., & Solic, K. (in press). The confluence of two policy mandates: Core reading programs and 3rd grade retention. *Elementary School Journal.*

Murphy, J. (1995). *The boys' war.* New York: Clarion.

National Reading Panel. (2000). *Teaching children to read: An evidence-based assessment of the scientific research literature on reading and its implications for reading instruction.* Available: *www.nationalreadingpanel.org*

O' Connor, R. E., Bell, K. M., Harty, K. R., Larkin, L. K., Sackor, S. M., & Zigmond, N. (2002). Teaching reading to poor readers in the intermediate grades: A comparison of text difficulty. *Journal of Educational Psychology, 94,* 474–485.

Patterson, W. A., Henry, J. J., O'Quin, K., Ceprano, M. A., & Blue, E. V. (2003). Investigating the effectiveness of an integrated learning system on early emergent readers. *Reading Research Quarterly, 38,* 172–207.

Pokorni, J. L., Worthington, C. K., & Jamison, P. J. (2004). Phonological awareness intervention: Comparison of Fast ForWord, Earobics, and LiPS. *Journal of Educational Research, 97*(3), 147–157.

Pressley, M., & Allington, R. L. (1999). What should educational research be the research of? *Issues in Education: Contributions from Educational Psychology, 5,* 1–35.

Pressley, M., Dolezal, S. E., Raphael, L. M., Mohan, L., Roehrig, A. D., & Bogner, K. (2003). *Motivating primary grade students.* New York: Guilford.

Richardson, V. (2003). The dilemmas of professional development. *Phi Delta Kappan, 84*(5), 401–406.

Scanlon, D. M., & Vellutino, F. R. (1997). A comparison of the instructional backgrounds and cognitive profiles of poor, average, and good readers who were initially identified as at risk for reading failure. *Scientific Studies of Reading, 1,* 191–216.

Stahl, S. A., Richek, M. A., & Vandevier, R. J. (1991). Learning meaning vocabulary through listening: A sixth-grade replication. In J. Zutell and S. McCormick (Eds.), *Learner factors/Teacher factors: Issues in literacy research and instruction* (40th Yearbook, pp. 185–209). Chicago: National Reading Conference.

Stanovich, K. E., West, R. F., Cunningham, A. E., Cipielewski, J., & Siddiqui, S. (1996). The role of inadequate print exposure as a determinate of reading comprehension problems. In C. Cornoldi & J. Oakhill (Eds.),

Reading comprehension difficulties: Processes and intervention (pp. 15–32). Mahwah, NJ: Lawrence Erlbaum.

Stotsky, S. (1984). Research on reading/writing relationships. In J. Jensen (Ed.), *Composing and comprehending* (pp. 7–22). Urbana, IL: ERIC Clearinghouse on Reading and Communication Skills and the National Conference of Research on English.

Strickland, D. S., & Kamil, M. L. (Eds.). (2004). *Improving reading achievement through professional development.* Norwood, MA: Christopher-Gordon.

Taylor, B. M., Pearson, P. D., Peterson, D. S., & Rodriguez, M. C. (2003). Reading growth in high-poverty classrooms: The influences of teacher practices that encourage cognitive engagement in literacy learning. *Elementary School Journal, 104,* 4–28.

Tierney, R., & Pearson, P. D. (1984). Toward a composing model of reading. In J. Jensen (Ed.), *Composing and comprehending* (pp. 33–45). Urbana, IL: ERIC Clearinghouse on Reading and Communication Skills and the National Conference of Research on English.

Tierney, R. J., & Shanahan, T. (1991). Research on reading-writing relationships: Interactions, transactions and outcomes. In R. Barr, M. Kamil, P. Mosenthal, & P. D. Pearson (Eds.), *Handbook of reading research* (Vol. 2) (pp. 246–280). New York: Longman.

Timar, T. (1994). Federal education policy and practice: Building organizational capacity through Chapter 1. *Educational Evaluation and Policy Analysis, 16,* 51–66.

Torgeson, J. K. (2000). Individual differences in response to early interventions in reading: The lingering problem of treatment resisters. *Learning Disabilities Research and Practice, 15,* 55–64.

Venezky, R. L. (1998). An alternate perspective on Success for All. In K. K. Wong (Ed.), *Advances in educational policy* (Vol. 4) (pp. 145–165). Greenwich, CT: JAI.

Worthy, J., Broaddus, K., & Ivey, G. (2001). *Pathways to independence: Reading, writing, and learning in grades 3–8.* New York: Guilford.

17

Honor Thy Teachers

JOANNE YATVIN

Most of us in education believe that motivation is at the heart of learning. When our students are unmotivated, we teachers are just spinning our wheels. The creators of the commercial programs described in previous chapters pay lip service to the concept of motivation by trying to make lessons fun or interesting. Too often, this is a hopeless task because the rules and repetitions they rely on are the antithesis of children's ideas of fun and interest. Even when these programs hit upon an appealing story or an engaging activity, they fail because they are grounded in a tradition of authoritarianism that asserts, "We know what you should learn and when and how. Just do it."

Those who understand best the fallacy in such an approach to learning are the good teachers in ordinary classrooms. They know that even when children's eyes are fixed on a lesson and their mouths are spouting correct answers, there is no assurance that anything related is happening in their heads. In a few days, when students come to the next carefully sequenced lesson, today's "learnings" may have vanished like smoke. Good teachers have far better ways to help children learn. They don't have to stand on their heads to make dull stuff interesting. They know how to find the intersections between a child's world and the school curriculum and how to pull from material that is inherently interesting to children the skills and knowledge society believes they should master.

In this chapter I will describe the work of two teachers who are not bound to commercial programs, not constrained by scripts, and not terrorized by tests. The core of their teaching is still the pursuit of a personal mastery of teaching as art, not subservience to anyone else's version of science. Moreover, there is nothing scientific about my examination of their practice. I chose teachers I know well, whose work I admire, and I did so without consulting anyone else or checking to see if their students' test scores were high. One, whom I will call Jeanne, is an old hand, having taught for thirty years in several schools and at various grade levels. Now she teaches two half-day blocks of sixth-grade language arts and social studies in a small middle school. The other, whom I will call Mary, has just completed three years of teaching, all of them in first grade. Yet she is close to Jeanne in age, having raised her own five children before embarking on a teaching career. Both teachers have master's degrees in education. Both teach in medium-size cities that have the look of suburbia. Jeanne's school is in Wisconsin; Mary's is in Oregon. Both have classrooms that are large, clean, and well equipped. This year the majority of their students are middle-class and white, but in the past each has had experience working with larger proportions of poor children and children of color. In addition, both have special needs students in their classrooms full-time.

Literacy Immersion in a First-Grade Classroom

Mary calls her literacy program balanced, by which she means that part of what she does is direct, explicit teaching of skills, and part is a whole language focus on text meaning and structure. Although I agree that her program is indeed balanced, I don't see balance as its key feature. I would be more inclined to call it literacy immersion by design. In Mary's first-grade classroom, carefully planned and executed literacy activities dominate a two-and-a-half-hour daily block and also permeate the rest of the day, even recreational breaks. For example, when Mary plays Simon Says with her students, she does not use the terminology we are all familiar with from childhood, but instead asks children to put their hands on their clavicles or mandibular joints. There is no busywork in this classroom, only focused instruction and engaged student involvement. I never saw Mary or her students wasting time.

In order to have so many worthwhile activities going on all at once, Mary has created an elaborate and stable classroom structure and made it visible to her students. Students know the daily order of class activities and what their individual roles are in each. They know the processes for doing different types of tasks and the acceptable ways of securing, handling, and replacing materials. Students have a daily reading ticket at their desks on which to check off the tasks they complete on their own during the literacy block, such as independent reading. Their inherent motivation to read is enhanced by homemade plastic telephones they use to read into and hear their own voices. Mary calls this whisper reading. In matters of behavior, Mary makes extensive use of visual and oral signals so that she doesn't have to repeat common admonitions or explanations. She may tell the class to "make good choices," ask them to do things "Q and Q" (quick and quiet), or say, "Glue your bottoms to the rug." Reminders to individual children who are not following classroom procedures are specific and encouraging: "I'd love to call on you, Jeremy, but I've got to wait until you raise your hand." And they are always followed by "Thank you very much."

For the content of literacy instruction, Mary has assembled a wealth of materials from many different sources. The school district has provided a commercial reading program for all its teachers but allows them to use their professional judgment about when, how, and how much of it to use. In addition, Mary has many publishers' supplementary collections and stand-alone books she has bought or borrowed. A significant number of books on hand are nonfiction.

The books Mary uses for instruction are clustered around the themes she has chosen for the year, such as friendship and safety. One day I saw activities on the science theme of plants. With the whole class grouped before her, Mary reviewed the story "The Little Red Hen," which she had read aloud previously. In fact, she had read three different versions of the story and expected children to be able to compare and contrast them. Today, however, the emphasis was on how wheat is grown and made into flour. Later, in small groups, children read nonfiction books about various plants and prepared to draw sequences of pictures depicting stages of plant growth and write captions for them. A few days later, after listening to a story about a clever bear who tricked a hare into giving him all the produce from a plot of land, children set up categories of root vegetables, stalk vegetables, and flower vegetables. In a whole-class activity, children read a paragraph chorally from a chart about agriculture in which some of the words were new and technical. On the second reading, Mary elicited synonyms by asking, "What word could we use instead of *crops*? [*Plants.*] What word could we use instead of *irrigation*? [*Watering.*]" Because the context of the paragraph suggested the word meanings, this was not hard for the children to do.

Mary has divided her class into six reading groups. When I questioned whether six groups were too many for any teacher to handle, she insisted that that was the number necessary to keep her groups productive because there were marked differences in the reading competencies of her students. I saw her meet with three groups during the reading block time while two other groups met with two fifth-grade student tutors[1] for about fifteen minutes. Mary would work with those groups the following day. Whether or not a group meets with the teacher on a particular day, it is obvious that the students get substantial reading practice every day.

---

[1] Mary prepares lesson plans for her tutors, which consist mostly of an outline for having children read familiar material aloud. Student tutors do not instruct.

At any given time, all children have with them a plastic bag of three to five books in which they are at different stages of reading. One or two books may be personal choices for independent reading; the other books have been thoroughly read and discussed in small groups or are being worked on currently. When a reading group meets, children might reread a story mastered previously, with Mary as narrator and children taking the parts of characters; search for information in a nonfiction book they read the day before; or take a picture walk through a new text and draw inferences about the plot. At any stage of reading, Mary's questions are as much about the structure of a book and reading strategies as about content. In addition to focusing on plot, she might ask: "How can we tell who the main character is?" "What do good readers do when they don't know the meaning of a word?" or "Do you think this book is fiction or nonfiction?" In Mary's view of reading, content, structure, and strategies are all needed to construct the meaning of a text.

Practice is a major factor in Mary's literacy program, enabling all children to master the books they read, but it is not a let's-all-do-the-same-thing-again type of practice. Children go over books and other materials in many different ways. For example, every day they are expected to read to themselves, a partner, upper-grade tutors, classroom volunteers, and parents at home. As Mary reads a book aloud, she often repeats sections or asks children to read in chorus along with her. Such repetitions are purposeful, allowing children to enjoy a wonderful bit of language they may have missed or to clarify a plot event they are fuzzy about. When children read aloud to classroom volunteers, they bring books they have already mastered so that reading is an experience of pleasure and pride. On one occasion I saw a grandfather of one of the students spend most of the morning listening to children read. By my count, twelve children read to him, and more were clamoring to do so when literacy time ended. Reading vocabulary is also reinforced through oral practice of songs, poems, and games. Children do handwriting exercises every day that are more than just practice in forming letters. As far as possible, Mary uses them to reinforce knowledge, vocabulary, phonics, appropriate behavior, and self-esteem. For example, one day's text to be copied was, "When you smell smoke, be smart and crawl down low."

Getting smart is a constant theme in Mary's classroom. The belief she communicates to her students is that they all can get smart by using their minds and working hard. To guide them, she models smart strategies and describes her internal thought processes aloud. She prepares children to listen carefully to a story and think about it by putting on her own real thinking cap and having the children put on their imaginary ones, "so [they] can get smart." She is also very good at catching children getting smart and pointing out publicly and specifically how they are doing it: "Now you're making connections between this book and the one we read last week. That's smart."

Mary says that she teaches phonics systematically, but by the time I got into her classroom, two-thirds of the way through the year, all phonics instruction— and there was a lot of it—was embedded in other types of activities. When I asked her about this, she told me that for three months at the beginning of the school year she uses a section of a commercial reading program to teach all the letter-sound correspondences. From then on, she reinforces and extends phonics knowledge through the use of a word wall, charts, handwriting exercises like the one noted earlier, as-needed group instruction, and individual guidance in self-correcting misread or misspelled words. When Mary composes an informational chart with her class, she expects children to help her spell most of the words. When they are reading together, she may pull out hard words for analysis or ask children to find words that rhyme. In a reading group, if a child gets stuck on an unfamiliar word, Mary may ask her to make an analogy to another word she knows or to chunk it into familiar parts. When children write independently, they are expected to get spelling help from the many print sources available in the classroom and their own knowledge of word structure. For example, there is a word wall organized around onsets and rimes and high-frequency sight words. If a needed word is not there, children are expected to look for a rhyming word. Any word listed on the word wall is considered a "no excuse" word that must be spelled correctly in children's writing. Informational charts composed by the class highlight key vocabulary words from recent themes that children often wish to write about. Children also make personal dictionaries for frequently used words and words they and Mary have discussed in writing conferences. In addition, children may go back to books they've read in the past or to the classroom dictionary.

Although several types of writing activities have already been mentioned, I haven't emphasized Mary's commitment to authentic writing. She wants children to understand that adults write for real purposes in their lives and gives them frequent opportunities to do the same. They write messages to their parents informing them about school events, letters to the principal expressing their views, and reminders to themselves and their teacher. Often, when a child makes a request or asks a question Mary can't deal with on the spot, she will ask him to write it down so she can respond later. "That's why we're learning to write," she tells students, "to help us remember important things." A daily class news bulletin, composed together, lets everyone know what to expect and when and gives them the chance to prepare accordingly. When children misbehave, they have to explain to their parents in writing why they made a "bad choice" and say which "good choice" they will make the next time.

To complete my description of Mary's teaching, I want to recount an incident not directly related to literacy. Before my first visit to her classroom, Mary talked to me about her class, noting that she had one little girl who was very difficult to manage because of hyperactivity and accompanying misbehavior. Once in the classroom, I soon spotted the child, although she was not doing anything outrageous. She spotted me, too, and came up to talk and show me her work. After a bit of conversation, she leaned over conspiratorially and whispered in my ear, "My teacher is really fun." I could have written an evaluation of Mary's teaching right then. When the most challenging student in the class expresses that sort of opinion, you can bet her teacher is doing a great job.

Developing Middle School Students' Full Potential

Jeanne, the middle school teacher, puts no label on her literacy program, seeing it as a distillation of all she has learned about children and teaching over the years. But in talking about it, she does emphasize the primacy of helping each child develop his or her full potential as a language user. She is very aware of the physical and emotional changes middle school students are going through and their desire to be considered grown-up. Consequently, her literacy program is built on students' needs, interests, and dreams as they traverse the rocky territory from childhood to adulthood. As I see it, the program is a student journey of internal and external exploration with the teacher as the guide. That journey is intellectual, social, emotional, and cultural, and although it passes through the state's standards and the school's curriculum, its destination is the development of personal competence and character.

At the beginning of the school year Jeanne asks students to write a letter telling her what they are looking forward to in middle school and what they are concerned about. Jeanne does not grade this assignment. Primarily, she uses this means to find out who each student is beneath the preadolescent facade. Typical student responses include pleasurable anticipation of making new friends and exploring new topics and trepidation about too much homework and bullying by older students. But there are more individual concerns expressed, too: worry about being made fun of because of a physical feature, shyness about speaking out in class discussion, fear of stumbling while reading aloud in front of the class, and determination to work harder and get better grades. Secondarily, Jeanne finds out who her students are as writers. She notes their levels of fluency, attention to conventions, and ability to organize their thoughts. One or two students will surprise her with a metaphor or the easy use of sophisticated sentence construction. The letters as a whole are kept private, but Jeanne does ask students to each share one sentence with the rest of the class so they can see that they all have goals and concerns in common. This is one of the ways that Jeanne begins to build a community of learners in her classroom.

At the same time that students write, Jeanne writes a letter to the whole class, sharing her goals for the year. I am going to quote these in full because I think they characterize her style of teaching.

I want to
- help each individual move toward his or her potential, challenging him-or herself to the greatest extent possible

- build a sense of community within my classroom, where everyone feels safe to learn, where mistakes are opportunities and diverse ideas are embraced

- promote a sense of curiosity and a joy of learning where students take responsibility for their own learning

- take action to improve the world by caring for others and the environment

What I saw in Jeanne's classroom was a strong dual emphasis on developing community and nurturing individual creativity and independence. Not only were most of the learning activities designed for students to work together in different-size groups and in varying combinations of people, but there were also frequent individual conferences and written communications between students and their teacher. There was much less formal instruction and much less prestructuring of activities than one would find in a typical middle school classroom. In the best sense of the word, Jeanne is a hands-off teacher, allowing students to find their own way through increasingly difficult tasks but always there with guidance when needed.

Jeanne's two-hour teaching block is divided into three major components: thinking and discussion, research, and literature study. The academic content of the class is the study of ancient cultures from Mesopotamia to the Middle Ages, as prescribed by the district's sixth-grade social studies curriculum. Much of the literature students read is connected to that content, but other books have been selected for relevance to contemporary social issues, such as poverty, immigration, and the environment, and preadolescent interests, such as peer relationships and family interactions. All the books offered to students have been nationally recognized as high-quality literature.

In the study of any theme, students usually have a choice of several pieces of literature to read along with a variety of informational books. Since Jeanne does not use textbooks for teaching the curriculum, she rotates large sets of theme-related materials through her classroom. Her personal collection of books and magazines is so voluminous that she must box parts of it up and move them into cabinets when students are not using them. She relies on the school library and public libraries for both literature and informational books, using the county library system when necessary to gather enough multiple copies and audiotaped versions for students' needs. She also uses some commercial materials, such as simulation units, resource materials from professional organizations, and programs developed by other teachers.

A typical morning in Jeanne's classroom begins with daily oral thinking, an exercise involving the analysis and synthesis of language. Early in the year she uses analogies with missing components on an overhead projector and asks students to complete them. After a few minutes of thinking and writing, students debate answers, explaining or defending their choices. Jeanne tells her students that there can be several right answers and that even a wrong answer may have lots of good thinking behind it. When I visited, several students volunteered answers and explanations and several more challenged those answers. One student who gave an answer spoke again a few minutes later to say, "I disagree with myself." So, although there is an air of competitiveness in these discussions because students do want to be the one with the best answer, there is also a sense of freedom to be wrong and pride in the depth of one's thinking. Discussions may also lead into new topics. Rejecting the word *right*, suggested as an equivalent to the word *legal*, one student declared, "Slavery was legal, but it wasn't right." As the year goes on, Jeanne uses other kinds of verbal puzzles, taken from books or newspapers, to generate thinking, clear oral expression, and discussion.

Research projects begin early in the year also. Deliberately, Jeanne starts students off with an abstract category, such as *new*. She wants to set students' thinking free, not constrain it. Students brainstorm all the "new things they can think of, from rock groups to New Zealand to medical technology," and sharpen their focus through discussion and some preliminary identification of possible information sources. Then each student lists five specific topics related to the idea of new, and Jeanne makes the final selection based on what she thinks is manageable for that student to research and write about. The research process for early projects is for students to find twenty-five facts from at least one information source and write them in their notebooks in their own words, sort those facts into two categories (one focused, the other miscellaneous), and construct a trifold brochure consisting of two paragraphs, one illustration, and two new vocabulary words and their definitions. As the year goes on, Jeanne moves students from topics based on their own interests to topics directly related to social studies units. She also increases the number of facts, source materials, and categories. But in Jeanne's view, more is not necessarily better. She wants students to have repeated opportunities to do the same type of assignment, becoming more confident, resourceful, and independent as they progress.

Presentations of research information are not traditional reports in Jeanne's classroom. Students are encouraged to make them original and exciting, perhaps a short play, a class game, or a book aimed at younger children. I saw students working on a version of *The Magic School Bus* that could be used to introduce first graders to the topics the sixth graders had researched. In this way, Jeanne subtly brings different literary and informational forms into the social studies curriculum and teaches students how to use them.

Literature study is grounded in the operation of small groups. Jeanne selects four or five books, related to the current social studies unit or a contemporary issue, introduces the books to the whole class, and then allows students to state their preferences. Since three or four literature circles of similar size need to be formed, each one composed of individuals whose skill levels and work habits are compatible, Jeanne cannot always honor students' preferences. Although she does mix students of different abilities in these groups, she feels it is very important to have combinations of people who will bring out the best in each other. On the rare occasion when Jeanne cannot give a student any of his top book choices, she meets with that student to work out a compromise and guarantees a first choice on the next round of books. Then, she publicly recognizes the student's maturity and flexibility in being willing to accept a book he did not choose.

Literature circles meet only once a week, but then for an extended period of time. Each student is responsible for a predetermined role in a circle meeting, such as discussion director, vocabulary person, plot summarizer, or quotation finder. Circle meetings are neither question-answer sessions nor outpourings of emotion. Jeanne expects students to be prepared to discuss substantive issues, supporting assertions with concrete examples, but she does not test their memory of details or demand formal analysis of literary structure. Informally, students may summarize parts of the plot or note literary techniques. While supporting students in their roles, Jeanne may also guide the discussion at times or highlight interesting features students have missed. Thus, she tries to walk a narrow line between teacher and peer in these literature circle meetings.

After a book has been read and discussed, the reading circle creates a plan for sharing it with the rest of the class. The students' aim is both to celebrate the book experience they've just shared and to generate enough interest so that others will want to read it, too. Some typical sharing plans are reenactments of scenes, video commercials, drawings of scenes from the story, constructions of settings, and silent tableaux in costume. These sharing times are also opportunities for students to learn new skills, such as video production or the use of computer software. Jeanne advises groups when asked but does not attempt to influence their choice of presentation. At this point, they have earned the right to an independent course of action.

The concept of accepting errors as a necessary part of the learning process is a strong thread in Jeanne's philosophy of teaching, and she explicitly communicates this concept to her students. Early in the year the class reads a book titled *Mistakes That Worked;* throughout the year they take time to discuss mistakes they've made and how they fixed them. As she works with groups and individuals on their projects, Jeanne allows them to follow their own decisions, biting her tongue even when she knows they are off track or headed for insurmountable obstacles. Jeanne says that students often self-correct and avoid disaster, persuading her that they are wiser and more mature than she thought. But even when completed projects are seriously flawed, she and they see them as learning experiences upon which to build. As she goes over a project with a student or group, she notes its strengths but also zeros in on its weaknesses and pushes students to think about how they might avoid similar mistakes in future projects. One comment that is almost her mantra goes something like this: "I'm not worried about this problem now because we have the rest of the year to work on it. But if you haven't overcome it by June, I'll be worried."

There is one more element in Jeanne's program that does not appear in a description of her curriculum or her schedule. That is the improvement of students' organizational skills: meeting deadlines, accurate and sufficient note taking, planning time use, keeping one's learning materials in order and accessible, and checking, checking, checking. Jeanne insists that each student have a planning calendar and use it. She shows them how to note events and other time-related information briefly and understandably and sets aside time daily for students to bring their calendars up to date and check for approaching events. She reminds them to check that they have their homework (and lunch) before they leave home in the morning and to check that they have everything they need when they leave school in the afternoon.

Almost all students—even ones much older than Jeanne's—have trouble with long-term assignments, letting things go for too long and then doing a hurry-up job at the end, which may result in a mediocre performance. Understanding this very human tendency and knowing how it can adversely affect school achievement, Jeanne works hard at explaining to her students why they should pace their work and at showing them how to do that. She also monitors progress, offering practical advice to those who have let themselves get behind. Jeanne's emphasis on organization is related to her knowledge of adolescent behavior and her awareness of the increasing demands academic work puts on them as they proceed through high school and beyond. She also lets her students know that good organizational skills will buy them greater independence from their parents and teachers. Adults notice how middle schoolers manage their responsibilities and are likely to offer more freedom to those who do it well than to those who don't.

Although none of Jeanne's students came forth to testify about the fun in her classroom, I saw many signs that indicated they were absorbed in their work and proud of their accomplishments. Students were eager to speak in discussion and did so knowledgeably; there were no "I dunno's." While Jeanne was occupied with a group or an individual, other students continued to work, their voices low and their movement minimal. No one seemed uncertain about what to do or how to do it. I saw only a few incidents of fooling around or social conversation. They passed quickly and students went back to work without teacher intervention. Although no project presentations were held while I was in the classroom, I was able to look at several examples of completed projects and found them lovingly done with attention to details, artistic flair, and humor.

Two Professionals, Two Programs

Some of the sources of differences between Mary's and Jeanne's programs are obvious: they teach different grades in different schools and have different amounts of teaching experience. But others are not apparent until you know more about their teaching situations. In Jeanne's middle school of 250 students, teachers are organized into teams, and there is a high degree of philosophical agreement and collegiality among the entire staff. In Mary's larger, less unified elementary school, she has to rely on an informal network of like-minded teachers, her own reading, and districtwide inservice training for support. Jeanne's school district is not especially concerned about test scores because it has a long history of high student achievement that enables it to ride out any yearly fluctuations. Although her state has published a set of standards, neither the department of education nor the legislature has pushed them aggressively on school districts. Mary's district and state, on the other hand, are more caught up in the politics of the standards movement and have exerted pressure on schools to raise test scores. In addition, the district is a growing one, with rapidly increasing numbers of nonnative English-speaking students. Jeanne, as a thirty-year veteran in the same school district and a frequent leader in professional development activities, has established a reputation for excellence among parents and the district administration. As a result, she has more autonomy, greater access to resources, and less need to prove herself than Mary, who, though respected by those who know her, is still a novice.

Beyond the program variations caused by external forces, however, there are more subtle differences that come from within the teachers themselves. Mary has structured her program to give her students maximum support as they work toward independence. Jeanne has structured hers to give students maximum freedom as they work toward the same goal. Although both teachers are familiar with educational research and the professional literature, they are independent thinkers, choosing those techniques and materials that seem best suited to their students and their own personalities. And change is part of their repertoires, not only because new ideas continually emerge in their field but also because they feel each group of students is different from previous groups and the classroom program must be tailored to each group's needs.

Out of the many good teachers I know, I chose to describe Mary and Jeanne because they exemplify what smart, skilled, and sensitive teachers can do when allowed to create their own literacy programs. Although not every teacher has the talent or energy to become a Mary or a Jeanne, if set free from scripted programs, one-size-fits-all methodologies, and external decision making, and given opportunities to learn, sufficient materials of their own choosing, and administrative support, the vast majority would become the competent literacy teachers we want—and so desperately need—in all our schools.

AUTHOR'S NOTE: The teachers whose programs are described in this chapter are Pam Perrin (Mary), Jacob Wismer Elementary School, Beaverton, Oregon, and Nan Youngerman (Jeanne), Spring Harbor Middle School, Madison, Wisconsin. Pam was enrolled for a year and a half in the Oregon Continuing License program I teach at Portland State University. I visited her classroom several times while she was my student and afterward. Nan was a member of my teaching staff when I was an elementary principal and three years ago was my granddaughter's sixth-grade teacher.

I thank both these master teachers for giving me access to their classrooms, allowing me to interview them, providing me with documents, and critiquing drafts of this chapter for accuracy. In many respects, this chapter is their work, not mine.

18

The Power of Literature Discussion

KAREN K. BROWN

Montgomery County Public Schools

Literature has a way of inviting us to respond with our hearts as well as with our minds. It seems to be an inevitable occurrence for readers, as they become engaged in a story, to interweave it with their own life stories. Even in very traditional classrooms with three reading groups, students naturally respond to and personalize stories whenever possible, relating them to their own life experiences. Throughout my teaching career I have noticed that the most intimate and honest discussions that occur with my students seem to happen as a result of sharing a piece of literature.

As a teacher, I believe it is so important to celebrate each child's gifts, strengths, culture, and background. It is paramount that we share the best literature with children in order to encourage them to love reading and writing. I want my students to find themselves in the stories we read together and feel free to share their responses. But I also hope that I can make a difference in children's lives and effect change for the better in our society. I want to help influence students to become critical and responsible citizens of our world. I believe that if I examine social and ethical values with my students, we can help make the world a better place.

I began using literature study groups in my third-grade classroom as part of my transition from traditional reading instruction to more holistic literacy teaching. I was privileged to work in a very challenging school with a principal who had a vision for change. She believed that by building self-esteem and providing meaningful literacy instruction, we could help our students, who live in poverty and have difficult home and neighborhood situations, achieve great things. She asked me to create a program that would promote best literacy practices throughout our whole school. She trusted me

243

to create and fashion my program and gave me a large budget to purchase books that were culturally relevant to our changing and ever more diverse population. I was therefore able to purchase award-winning multicultural books in multiple copies for literature groups.

I taught students from every grade level in the school library several times a week, taking flexible small groups of students who were struggling to read, as well as academically talented students. Joyful literacy experiences were planned and celebrated as my students learned together. However, as the program progressed, I found myself wanting to provide opportunities for my students to look more critically at and think more deeply about what they read. Beyond simply enjoying reading, I wanted them to discover how books related to the world in which they lived. Although there were many things in the world that I felt powerless to change, I hoped that by examining injustices and inequities in the world through the books they were reading, my students would develop the capacity to critique and act upon them, even if on a smaller scale within the world of our classroom.

Creating a Climate That Encourages Critical Reflection

As I worked with students in the literature groups and heard them speak about serious social problems that impacted their lives, I realized how deeply they think and care about our world. They are remarkably capable of communicating when literature discussions take place within democratic classrooms where everyone can share his opinions and every member has a voice. By creating an equality of power within the classroom, I was able to shake off the authoritarian voice that permeates the traditional classroom (see also Brown and Fu, 1995; Short and Pierce, 1990). As my students perceived that I respected them as individuals and would listen to their responses to literature and life stories, they began to trust me.

Sharing the Personal as a Teacher-Reader

I have often taken risks in discussion groups, sharing very personal feelings and responses to our reading. I can recall a time when we were discussing *Nadia the Willful,* by Sue Alexander (1983), a story about a Bedouin girl who is mourning the death of her brother. As we discussed our personal experiences of grief over the death of our pets or family members, I took a risk in sharing feelings and responses to deaths in my own family. My students responded in kind.

Girl 1: I feel like Nadia because when my uncle died, my mother and father didn't want me to talk about him.

Boy 1: It's good to cry and it gets stuff out. Sometimes it makes you feel better.

Mrs. B.: It takes a long time to get over the death of someone you love. My dad passed away some years ago and often I will think of him and miss him. I might say something to my husband and that makes me feel better. The night after my dad died, my husband stayed up with me all night, listening to stories about my dad and me. We sat up and looked at photos by flashlight and I talked and talked. It meant so much to me that my husband listened to my stories. It helped me deal with my grief.

Girl 1: That's what I try to do with my uncle. I try to let it out, but I still feel sad. I feel like Nadia in the story. You can't get over it until you talk about it. I wish it was like in *Missing May* [Rylant, 1992], the book. They were trying to bring back May's spirit. I wish someone could bring back my uncle. It would be neat if we were cats and we had nine lives. Like when one person in a family dies a baby is born.

I shared my own stories, authentically modeling my own responses to the book and revealing myself as a person and a reader. It felt very strange at first to share such intimate feelings with my students. But by sharing my personal responses to the literature, I participated in the group discussion as a member of the literate community, instead of as an authority over meaning (see also Brown and Fu, 1995). As Karen Smith states, "As teachers, we need to continuously share our lived-through experiences using reflective, critical response. We need to listen to students' responses as they begin to be more insightful so that we can illuminate their richness for other's consideration" (1990, p. 28). Only when we accept diversity of expression and interpretation by valuing our students' responses and sharing our own can real critical readers and thinkers blossom in our classrooms.

Books for Reading the World

There were two ways that I encouraged discussion of social issues with literature. These were in the choice of books that we read and in allowing our group to find new roles, as I balanced my role of teacher while becoming a member of the learning community. In choosing books to share with my students, I considered their interests and looked for books that could potentially evoke emotional and thoughtful responses. But I also tried to pick books that addressed themes such as racism and prejudice, equality, treatment of others, and other issues that are ever more crucial in today's world.

I was also careful to include books that portrayed culturally diverse characters. I especially like Patricia Polacco's books because of the beautiful way that she weaves loving relationships between people of various cultures. I feel that her books are extremely important to use with my students because they provide a model for good relationships for all people. Books like *Chicken Sunday* (1992) and *Mrs. Katz and Tush* (1993) also beautifully depict people of color and those of other ethnic heritages in familial relationships of trust and love. This is a wonderful model for our children of how people of different races can enrich each other's lives by sharing their cultures and lives with each other.

By selecting books that would open our discussion to viewing the world's inequities, I was giving the children an arena to talk about the issues that they cared deeply about in their world. I generally presented several such books to each group, and the group members chose the ones they wished to read. I never imposed the topics of discussion, but because I offered literature that addressed social, ethical, and emotional issues, students tended to focus on these issues in their discussions. Over the years, as I have worked with students in literature groups, we have discussed such topics as crime and gun control, war and military retaliation, the suicide of a loved one, the dangers of dating through the personal ads, prejudice and racial issues, acceptance of differences, Ku Klux Klan activity in the neighborhood, familial disharmony, alcoholism, and spousal and child abuse. Many of these discussions were intense, sensitive, and thoughtful.

Dilemmas for Teachers in Critical Literature Discussions

Reflecting back, I see that I would often stop our discussion short of exploring issues as deeply as needed in order to make students think more critically. There were times when I needed to take more of a leading role. Sometimes I would hold back from asking questions that made us explore a topic more fully or from offering a personal reflection that might have helped direct the discussion to a deeper level. Part of this was naïveté and the other part was fear. In a diverse public school community, there exists a wide range of cultural and ethical values. It may therefore be risky to look at hard questions and controversial issues about the world with our students. It raised many doubts for me. Was it appropriate and wise for me as a teacher to discuss personal and social issues with my diverse student population? As a novice teacher I was often cautioned against speaking too directly about personal issues or opinions. I was afraid that I would be perceived as too radical. Sometimes I also would sense my ethnic difference and doubt my ability to speak knowingly about equity issues. Since I was the white teacher, what did I know about the struggles of people of color? I had been so careful about developing positive relationships, respecting my students as thinkers and learners, and celebrating their cultures and traditions. I could see that they were also trying to show respect to me. Occasionally one of my students would slip and say something negative about white people. Then I'd realize that even my youngest students had to deal with the issues of racism and prejudice. I was trying to undo the effects of racism and prejudice in our world, yet I am a member of the majority race that continues to dominate and hurt the minority culture.

I worried about criticism from administrators, teachers, or parents for letting kids talk about hard issues. Sometimes students would share strong emotional responses to books. What would happen if I didn't know how to respond to a student's comments? Are educators allowed to let students talk about the evils of racism and inequality, war and retaliation, or the political situations that we are hearing about on the news? Is the classroom the arena where critical dialogue should occur? What if we all don't have the same perceptions, experiences, background, or perspective? Will it get us involved in too heated a debate? What might occur if students were allowed to talk about issues too critically? These questions sometimes hindered me from pushing the discussion to the critical level I desired in my classroom.

My advice to teachers is to just do it, but to use extreme sensitivity and professional judgment. Guide carefully discussions that touch on highly emotional, provocative, or age-inappropriate issues. Students are aware of the news about crime, terrorism, and war. They need to process these things, but if issues are too sensitive for public interchange, we must seek other outlets for expression, such as private discussions or even counseling services. But, it is crucial that whenever possible, we provide opportunities for students to use books as a vehicle to understand themselves and the world around them (see also Peterson and Eeds, 1995; Short and Pierce, 1990; Pierce and Gilles, 1993). Avoiding the realities of our students' present and future is not the answer!

Looking in on Critical Literature Discussions

Reflections on Students' Lives and Neighborhoods

I learned a great deal about my students and their neighborhoods, lives, and fears as we discussed literature. I grew up and still live in the area where I am teaching, but I was unaware of some of the events the students described. Sue Alexander's book *Nadia the Willful* (1983) brought forth a discussion of instances of crime and gun use in the neighborhood.

Boy 1: Yesterday in my neighborhood this man shot his wife and then killed himself. It's the green house by the 7-Eleven; I knew them too. They had all these German shepherds.

Mrs. B.: I know where that is. Doesn't it seem scary when things like that happen in your neighborhood!

Boy 2: Ever since the murder in the parking lot at Value City, my mom won't let me play in the alley because my house is right near where it happened.

Boy 1: My mom won't go to that mall anymore . . . and she won't let me go to the arcade there.

Boy 2: I was in the arcade in the mall and this guy left this package and there was a gun in it.

Girl 1: My mother wants to get a gun but she's afraid my baby sister might find it and there might be an accident.

Girl 2: My father has a gun but he only has it in case someone comes into our house to hurt us.

Girl 1: My mother wants to move out to the country where we'd be safer. I wish we could move to some other country like England where we'd have peace . . .

The murder we were discussing touched our whole community. The victim was someone the students all knew. The students shared their anxiety and fear of living in a violent society where they often feel unsafe. I feel that children need to be able to discuss these issues in a supportive atmosphere where they can try to make sense of the world they live in.

Looking at Contemporary Issues in Our World

Children have a vested interest in the world and are concerned about social issues more than adults might expect. Students bring their experiences and perceptions of the world to their reading of a text. They continually raise contemporary issues and concerns as they discuss books in literature circles. I have been astounded as some of my struggling readers, usually silent in traditional reading groups, achieve a depth of understanding and reflection through literature discussion (see also Urzua, 1992).

In sharing their ideas about the text during the literature study group on Mary Downing Hahn's *Doll in the Garden* (1989), the students focused on one of the secondary characters, Mrs. Cooper, who as a child was mistreated by a strict father. They spoke about the effects of neglect and abuse on the life of this character and the resulting bitterness and behavior toward others in the story. When one of my most reluctant readers shared the reason he thought Miss Cooper was so mean, I realized that he had perceptions that reached far beyond the text. Such a deep interpretation of the character might have been left unspoken if he had been in his homogeneous reading group working on skills in a workbook.

Girl 3: Mrs. Cooper's father abused her by locking her in the basement.

Mrs. B.: Are some forms of discipline OK and others not OK?

Girl 3(and all others): Yes!

Girl 1: But her father was probably abused when he was a child. It goes through families, her father's father hit him all the time and he didn't do anything to deserve it. So when he grew up, he locked Carrie in the cold basement as a punishment.

Boy 1: She never had a doll because her father wouldn't let her . . . and when her dad punished her, he made her sit in the cold damp basement. That's child abuse!

Fifth-grade girls reflect on women's roles and relationships as they share their ideas about answering personal ads in the newspaper during their discussion of mail-order brides in Patricia MacLachlan's *Sarah, Plain and Tall* (1985):

Girl 1: Sarah and Pa's letters remind me of those personal ads where people try to meet dates through the newspaper. I don't think it's a good idea. You meet a man and you don't know what he's up to . . . you don't know anything about him.

Girl 2: I saw these commercials on television . . . you dial one or two if you like this person or the other one.

Girl 1: You don't know where these guys have been.

Girl 3: He might have another wife somewhere that he doesn't tell you about or he might shoot you.

Girl 4: You have to be careful or you might get into trouble like I did. [*She covered her mouth after her statement, as if she hoped no one heard.*]

During this discussion, one student who was having some behavioral problems in my class opened up and helped me understand her better by her self-disclosure. I was more compassionate and patient with her after hearing her story. We may chuckle at this discussion but we also gain an appreciation for the world our students live in and some of the dangers and fears they face as they are entering puberty.

In the school where I first started using literature circles, the demographic makeup of the school was 60 percent African American and 35 percent Caucasian with 5 percent other minorities. The students had been attending school together since kindergarten and got along well. Classmates had a genuine affection for each other. In discussions of literature such as Jerry Spinelli's *Maniac McGee* (1990) and Theodore Taylor's *Cay* (1987), students politely skirted issues of injustice and equality and focused instead on secondary themes such as family disharmony and friendship. The students willingly shared serious family issues but avoided the central issues of interracial relations and segregation that are at the core of both books. During one of the conversations, one student shared the most disturbing family stories of domestic violence and alcohol abuse. Another student took exception to his sharing such stories so openly. After the meeting, I had a talk with the student who expressed his discomfort and then realized that he too had issues that were causing him pain. Through this experience I was able to seek help for him from the guidance counselor for a problem that would have remained invisible. I also, however, became more acutely aware of the boundaries that must be drawn for sharing such personal and private family situations in the classroom (see also Brown et al., 1996). We, as teachers, must seek the help of trained professionals who can best assist students in dealing with their painful personal lives.

Honest Dialogue About Racism and Segregation

A few years later, I moved to another school, as a reading specialist. I again met with small groups in literature circles. Although hesitant at first, perhaps because I was the new white teacher in a school that was 99.5 percent African American, I found that these students comfortably entered into discussions about racial issues. I encouraged my students to speak freely and not to worry about offending me. Although these students were more reserved about sharing their personal lives in relation to the text than the more diverse students I had taught previously, I discovered that they were eager to talk about social issues. The trust they had in each other as they shared thoughts, feelings, and concerns about their lives and society gave me renewed hope for our future world (see also Brown and Fu, 1995).

Students in both second and fourth grades reacted to issues of prejudice and segregation in Peter Golenbock's *Teammates* (1990), a story about the friendship between Jackie Robinson and Pee Wee Reese. The part in the book that talks about the Ku Klux Klan evoked an immediate, strong reaction. One student said that there was a creek behind the middle school where the Klan hung out and kids wouldn't play there because they were scared. Another boy told of threats the Klan made to his family. These stories surfaced in two separate literature groups at different times in response to the same part of the book. Although I grew up and still live in a neighborhood not far from where my students live, I had never heard of these Klan activities. This alerted me to the fact that although I feel that I have a close relationship with my students, I don't really know about all the things they are facing in their lives.

A fourth-grade group was enraged by the bigotry exhibited in Jackie Robinson's story, and one student who had seen the film *Schindler's List* with his family made the connection between prejudice and the destruction of Jewish people in World War II. In the fourth-grade discussion group, students drew comparisons between the Holocaust and Hitler's annihilation of the

Jews and the Klan activity and the persecution endured by black people in the South. I was continually impressed with the ability of my ten- and eleven-year-old students to analyze contemporary and historical social issues.

In another group, Mildred Taylor's short stories "The Friendship" and "The Gold Cadillac" (1987) provided a framework for discussion of the highly emotional issues of injustice, segregation, and racial distrust.

Girl 1: In "The Friendship," I thought "The Friendship" was sad because he treated the boys . . . the two little boys, he treated them different because they were black. It started out when the children went to Mr. John's store and the youngest brother had touched the glass and . . .

Girl 2: He said he had filthy hands . . .

Girl 1: And his skin was as black as dirt.

Girl 2: It made me feel sad and I thought if it was in real life that it would make his family feel really sad.

Boy 1: Even if I was John Wallace and I had made a promise a real long time ago, I would have kept it even though I was around other white people and it was against the law for a black person to be called mister. I would have still kept my promise because he made a commitment and he should have kept it.

Mrs. B.: Their friendship should have gone beyond that, don't you think?

Students related to the negative treatment of African Americans in another emotionally charged short story in the same volume, "The Gold Cadillac," which was discussed in concert with Taylor's "The Friendship."

Mrs. B.: Mildred Taylor chose to put two of her stories together into one book. Think about some of the similarities and differences.

Girl 5: I think that in both stories there is segregation.

Girl 1: John killed Mr. Tom because he was black, and in "The Gold Cadillac," the whites, they locked the husband up because they thought he had stolen the car but he really didn't and he should have explained it to them . . .

Girl 4: [*Reads from book*] "But as they traveled deeper into the rural South, there are no more admiring glances for their wonderful car. Only suspicion and anger for the black man behind the wheel. For the first time in their lives, Lois and her sister find out what it's like to be scared because of the color of their skin."

Using History as a Catalyst for Critical Discussion

I used books that had historical settings and themes to allow students to examine the social and political issues of the Civil War and World War II.

Interesting critical questions emerged. What right does one group have to kill another group just because of its race, religion, or political position? What right does one country have to bomb another?

Patricia Polacco's beautiful picture book *Pink and Say* (1995) provided students with an opportunity to explore and discuss issues of equality and equity, war, slavery, and freedom in relation to bonds of friendship, reflected in Pink and Say's caring relationship.

Boy 1: I think I can kind of apply that to me. I think that Pink would be a good person because he was saving someone that was a different color skin from his and basically it sounds like to me he didn't care if someone was white, Chinese, black, or all those other types of people; he just cared, he just cared that Say was hurt.

Boy 2: I wouldn't want to be killed just because I was black; it's not fair.

Girl 4: I like the part where they try to hold their hands to try to struggle to stay together. And I think that if you saw this page right here of both hands just holding each other, you can tell that they were friends.

Boy 1: Pink got murdered, because after he died they had hanged him up, they had thrown him in the lime pit.

Mrs. B.: So it was a very brutal death, wasn't it?

Boy 2: Hey, guess what, they didn't even have no funeral for Momo Bay or him, that's terrible.

Girl 4: I think that in other parts of America there are some people that are still in slavery. I think the author is trying to say that it doesn't matter about what your skin color is but it's your attitude and the way you act. She was trying to say that you really don't have to worry about what other people think about, you just have to think about how you feel about yourself.

Girl 4: Pink and Say also teaches respect for other people even if they are different from you.

Children spoke wisdom beyond their years about a horrible event during World War II. We looked at the moral issues involved in the use of the atomic bomb in Japan as we read and discussed *Sadako and the Thousand Paper Cranes*, by Eleanor Coerr (1977). The students were very moved by the story of the young girl, Sadako, a victim of leukemia caused by radiation from the atomic bomb dropped on Hiroshima, Japan, by the Americans before Sadako was even born. Students were very actively engaged in discussion about the innocent people who suffered as a result of the bombing. They also actively debated the policy of retaliation in war as well as other wartime injustices. As students read an engaging story of the sad effects of war on the lives of children, they were reminded of so many senseless acts of violence that they had heard about on the news.

Girl 1: I think that the U.S. shouldn't have dropped the bomb on Japan just to get even with them for bombing the base in Hawaii, Pearl Harbor. The U.S., they were trying to get back at the Japanese so they bombed Hiroshima.

Girl 2: If they keep dropping a bomb on each other the people would get really scared and lots of people would die.

Boy 1: They shouldn't keep trying to get revenge because revenge causes more deaths and more and more people keep dying.

Girl 2: If they kept dropping bombs, they are acting like two little kids fighting over something on the back porch.

Girl 1: If there was another bombing, I'd feel really scared and sad because hundreds of people would die each day.

Girl 2: I think there is war going on right here in Baltimore City because there are kids fighting and kids killing other kids.

Boy 2: People are fighting right here in this country and people sometimes don't mean to but they end up hurting an innocent bystander. That's the same thing as the bombings; they killed people that they weren't trying to kill too.

What mature insights from my ten-year-old students! They understood the effects of the bomb as well as the violence in their own city today. Our students live in a world with difficult and dangerous situations. They watch the news just as we do. They experienced terrorist acts as they watched the victims of September 11 on their TV screens. They also hear of or experience murder and violent crimes that happen in their world. They fear the same things that adults do, and like adults they are looking for answers.

In this literature circle, Lee, a Vietnamese boy, was always quiet and never entered in any class discussion. He seemed uninterested during class most of the time. During this lively and sensitive discussion, Lee said: "I learned that you have to be careful how you treat your family, because you never know what might happen to them. You don't know how long they'll live and so you have to watch what you say and how you treat them." I was impressed not only by what he said but also by the fact that he had finally spoken in the group. I was amazed by my student's sensitivity and mature perspective on life. I learned that Lee was a thoughtful, deep thinker who read far beyond the text into his own life and experience.

Imagining Positive Cross-Cultural Relationships

Literature such as Patricia Polacco's books often provides young students with their first glimpse of positive and loving cross-cultural relations. When my students looked at the cover of Patricia Polacco's *Chicken Sunday* (1992), which depicts two African American boys and a Ukrainian girl embracing an

African American grandmother, they asked if she was white and wondered how the characters were related. I commented that they seemed to be a loving family, regardless of the difference in their cultural backgrounds.

I think about a first-grade group of students who were reading *When I Am Old with You,* by Angela Johnson (1990). When we came to the page where the girl and her grandfather meet a white family while they are hiking and extend greetings, one little girl said, "*Oooohhh*, white people, why are they talking to them?" With this surprising question, it saddened me that even as a six-year-old, my student was sharing her struggle with racial harmony in her world.

Sometimes teachers are the first role models for racial understanding in children's lives. In one literature group a young boy said, "Mrs. Brown, if all white people were like you then we wouldn't have any problems at all. You are different from them." Though complimented by his statement, I was extremely sad that he had so little experience with positive racial relations. When I read *Uncle Jed's Barbershop,* by Margaree King Mitchell (1994), with a group of second graders, another student echoed the same thought when she said, "You are different, Mrs. Brown. You respect us." This affirmed for me the importance in critiquing systems of domination in my practice.

Final Thoughts

As I have engaged in critical literature circles over the years, I have been impressed by students' abilities to discuss social issues and engage in sophisticated, thoughtful discussion. Our children are keenly, socially aware and conscious of the issues that surround our turbulent society. As we learned to trust each other, I saw time and time again that they are often wise beyond their years and can even offer creative and thoughtful solutions to real problems.

Through the literature circles, I learned to know my students and gained a real appreciation for their hopes and fears in the face of racial prejudice and other contemporary societal problems. The journey can be enlightening, gratifying, and enriching. It also can be frightening and intimidating, as teachers enter into discussions with students on topics traditionally considered taboo or off limits. This very situation indicates how the systems of domination that control society have impacted our practice. We are pressured as teachers to teach in ways that maintain the status quo rather than effect change.

I feel myself fortunate to have been in schools where I was able to teach reading in the way that I believe helps students become critical readers, writers, and thinkers. I was able to choose the methods and materials that I felt would encourage students to love to read. Students could find their culture and life within the pages and chapters of wonderful children's literature that touched our hearts and allowed us to reflect together on the world we live in. Had I been teaching in a school system that mandated the use of a commercial program or phonics series, I would not have been able to engage my students in the rich reader response that is possible in literature circles (see also Eeds and Peterson, 1995; and Brown et al., 1996). I would not have learned as much about my students' abilities to be such deep thinkers and reflective readers.

I cherish the intellectual and professional freedoms that I, remarkably, still have in my work as a reading specialist in diverse schools. My heart is full of hope for our future world as I see my students prepare to become thoughtful, contributing members of society. They will, I trust, bring about a society in which all people have freedom and voice.

References

Brown, K., Blasi, M., Fu, D., & Altwerger, B. (1996). Forging new roles and relationships in literature study groups. *The New Advocate, 9*(3), 209–225.

Brown, K., & Fu, D. (1995). Authentic dialogue in literature study groups. *Literacy: Issues and Practices 12*, 53–61.

Eeds, M., & Peterson, R. (1995). What teachers need to know about the literary craft. In N. L. Roser & M. G. Martinez (Eds.), *Book talk and beyond: Children and teachers respond to literature* (pp. 10–23). Newark, DE: International Reading Association.

Newkirk, T. (1992). *Listening in.* Portsmouth, NH: Heinemann.

Peterson, R., & Eeds, M. (1990). *Grand conversations: Literature groups in action.* New York: Scholastic.

Pierce, K., & Gilles, C. (Eds.), in consultation with D. Barnes. (1993). *Cycles of meaning: Exploring the potential of talk in learning communities.* Portsmouth, NH: Heinemann.

Short, K., & Pierce, K. (1990). *Talking about books: Creating literate communities.* Portsmouth, NH: Heinemann.

Smith, K. (1990). Entertaining a text: A reciprocal process. In K. Short & K. Pierce, *Talking about books: Creating literate communities.* Portsmouth, NH: Heinemann.

Urzua, C. (1992). Faith in learners through literature studies. *Language Arts, 69*, 492–501.

Children's Books Cited

Alexander, S. (1983). *Nadia the willful.* New York: Dragonfly.

Coerr, E. (1977). *Sadako and the thousand paper cranes.* New York: Dell.

Golenbock, P. (1990). *Teammates.* New York: Harcourt Brace.

Hahn, M. D. (1989). *The doll in the garden.* New York: Avon.

Johnson, A. (1990). *When I am old with you.* New York: Scholastic.

King Mitchell, M. (1994). *Uncle Jed's barbershop.* New York: Scholastic.

MacLachlan, P. (1985). *Sarah, plain and tall.* New York: Harper & Row.

Polacco, P. (1992). *Chicken Sunday.* New York: Scholastic.

Polacco, P. (1993). *Mrs. Katz and Tush.* New York: Scholastic.

Polacco, P. (1995). *Pink and Say.* New York: Scholastic.

Rylant, C. (1992). *Missing May.* New York: Dell.

Spinelli, J. (1990). *Maniac McGee.* New York: Harper Collins.

Taylor, M. (1987). *"The friendship" and "The gold Cadillac."* New York: Dial Books for Young Readers.

Taylor, T. (1969). *Cay.* New York: Dell Yearling Books.

A Call to Action

BESS ALTWERGER

After reading the chapters in this book, you may find yourself in yet a new state of shock and awe: shock from the realization that political and economic forces, rather than sound educational analysis, lie behind the transformation we see in schools and reading programs; awe at how effectively a policy of fear and intimidation has managed to muffle voices of opposition and resistance, even in light of the documented dangers of mandated for-profit commercial programs and other NCLB-related impositions on classrooms.

If, like me, you recognize the potential of education and literacy for creating critical and enlightened future citizens, you feel a sense of outrage that our schools have become the new marketplace for ensuring corporate profit and that our students have been sentenced to instructional regimes that will turn them into docile and compliant workers. I don't remember voting for a national referendum on whether we should turn our schools into training camps for corporate employment! When did we as a nation decide that we want our next generation of citizens to be dulled into passivity and obedience, unable to use literacy effectively as a vehicle for critical and creative thought? When did we decide to define literacy as a mere technical skill rather than a source of personal and social communication, enrichment, and empowerment? When did we decide that teachers are no longer to be professionals entrusted with the future of our children, but rather cheap labor for training corporate America's "twenty-first-century workforce"?

As a community, we owe it to the children in our care to provide a meaningful, challenging, and intellectually stimulating literacy education, crafted for them by professional educators who are responsive to their strengths and needs. Instructional mandates, scripted teachers manuals, and hours of dulling, sedentary drill and practice have no place in literacy education for a democratic society. Teachers must have the freedom to use their professional judgment and knowledge of their students to select appropriate instructional and assessment strategies. If, as some critics might argue, there aren't enough of these teachers to fill our nation's classrooms, then deprofessionalizing teaching and imposing scripted programs will certainly not create them.

Quality teacher education and professional development will. To provide this we need but a fraction of the billions of dollars in contracts that current literacy policies have won for McGraw-Hill, Houghton-Mifflin, and other commercial reading program publishers. With sufficient resources, perhaps we can begin to envision an expert twenty-first-century teacher force!

We have come to a fork in the road, and it is time to make a decisive and determined turn. We simply cannot afford to relinquish our democratic rights as parents, teachers, teacher educators, and concerned citizens to shape the future of our schools and our society. The economic and political forces we face are formidable, but our voices will be strengthened by the power of our knowledge as well as the power of our numbers. We must keep present in our minds that every right we have today has been hard won by ordinary people who envisioned a more just and equitable society. The struggle that began at our lunch counters and in school buses continues today, albeit in a less palpable form. Today, the oppression experienced in our nation's public schools, especially in poor communities, presents itself in the squandering of resources for the goal of corporate profit, instructional straitjacketing in pursuit of standardization and accountability, threatening of schools with state takeovers and privatization, and worst of all, dulling of minds for the sake of uniformity of skill performance.

We cannot rely solely on electoral politics to fight this struggle for us; the road to our current situation has transcended political parties, with NCLB receiving bipartisan support in Congress. Exerting pressure on our elected officials is certainly important, but it will be effective only if we continue to build and expand the independent movement of fellow teachers, parents, and community activists around our nation who are speaking out. (See *www.fairtest.org* for a listing of many of these organizations.) This book contributes to the movement by providing new information that can be translated into action. We now have the political and economic analyses, the scientific research data, the real-life stories of the consequences of today's policies, and visions of the future that are needed to win this "battle for the classroom."

As in all grassroots rights movements, however, we need a carefully articulated set of goals that can galvanize potential activists. I believe that our educational rights have been so eroded by current corporate and governmental policies that we now need a teacher, parent, and student bill of educational rights. Whether this evolves into legislation, or becomes a stamp of approval for any school district that adopts it as policy (thereby attracting teachers and parents), it will nevertheless provide the movement with a concrete set of principles with which we can all agree, regardless of theoretical or pedagogical orientation toward literacy curriculum, political affiliation, or school district resources. I now propose a draft of such an educational bill of rights with a proposed set of principles for your consideration.

The Teacher, Parent, and Student Bill of Rights

Teachers, parents and students shall have the right to

- full and equitable allocation of public funds for every public school system, including resources for classroom, school, and neighborhood libraries
- education free of mandated programs and high-stakes testing resulting in punitive consequences for students, teachers, and parents
- curriculum decisions determined by and reflective of the unique goals and needs of local school communities
- instructional decisions based upon individual needs of students as identified by classroom professionals through ongoing assessment
- availability of the full range of instructional approaches and materials for selection and use by classroom professionals
- fully funded professional development opportunities designed and selected by local school communities to improve and maintain quality of instruction
- freedom from corporate intrusions or legislative policies that infringe upon the above rights of teachers, parents, and students

These principles can become the focus of debate within communities and online across the nation through websites of various organizations and coalitions such as Fair Test, the Assessment Reform Network, Rethinking Schools, Move-On, Classroom Struggles, local PTAs, and professional organizations. They can be circulated and presented at meetings and events by any stakeholder in public education, sent to various media outlets for broader exposure, and used as the impetus for public rallies and demonstrations.

Even these strategies will not be enough, however, to accomplish our goals. We need to engage in wide-ranging acts of opposition and resistance, from very subtle to very bold. Although in many European countries teachers have a history of political activism, we do not generally share that history. All citizens need to become active in their own way and in their own time. I offer a few suggestions:

- Augment the mandated program with a rich literacy curriculum tailored to the needs of your students. Communicate this to parents.

- Wear a colored armband or a political button on test day and encourage parents and students to do the same.
- Run and/or support candidates for local school boards who oppose mandated programs, high-stakes testing, and NCLB.
- Exert pressure on your local and national teachers unions or organizations to represent your concerns at meetings, in newsletters, and during contract negotiations.
- Hold grade-level or schoolwide forums for parents to present information and concerns about the deleterious effects of current policies on their children and school.
- Join existing or form new coalitions of teachers, teacher educators, parents, and community organizations concerned with current education policy to plan public meetings, rallies, peaceful demonstrations, and other actions.
- Use local media outlets whenever possible, including radio, but be prepared to produce your own alternative form of communication: newsletters, websites, email discussion lists, and so on.
- Stay informed about new research findings, investigative reports, and national news regarding the impact of and opposition to mandated reading programs and federal education policies.

When a black box is found and analyzed following an air crash, the information it yields leads to appropriate action for preventing future disasters. Through this volume and numerous others, a solid body of information resulting from research, analysis, and firsthand experience is available to all of us. Let's determine to use it thoughtfully and purposefully to reclaim reading, our classrooms, and our schools. Information is indeed power, if it is used to guide the future.